Project Management
for Supplier Organizations

Reviews for

Project Management for Supplier Organizations: Harmonising the Project Owner to Supplier Relationship

Adrian has produced a guide that deals with the realities of project management. He addresses the key issues that cannot be controlled by rules and procedures, including the interaction between people, the relevance of organisational structures and the importance of stakeholders. He uses practical experience to guide us through the management of the full project lifecycle from a supplier and owner organisations view. This helps the reader understand the challenges of their counterpart. This is a wide-ranging and practical guide.

Steve Pears, Managing Director, telent Technology Services Limited

Much has been written about project management over the last ten to twenty years. Around the world well developed project management Bodies of Knowledge (and methodologies) have developed. One area that is ignored by Bodies of Knowledge is the conflict between the owner organisation and the contracting organisation. These two parties have much in common. They both want a successful project but they measure success in different ways. One wants to maximise profit, while the other wants to maximise the benefit derived from the output. This creates conflict and tension in the project. This book is about how to manage the tension to generate creative solutions for the benefits so both parties get what they want.

Paul Naybour, Parallel Project Training, UK

Although private supplier organizations have always existed, they haven't always been as keen to share their secrets and hidden ways, as their publicly funded customers. This book really opens up the differences in approach between supplier organizations and owner organizations and serves as a solid foundation for both areas. Dealing with the uncertainty of facts and circumstances is a common theme throughout and we are shown some important ways of addressing our own over-confidence and assumptions. What is great about this book is that the author has an entertaining and light-hearted approach of simplifying some complex concepts. He shares important methods and models as well as his own secrets.

Neil Murdy, ABB Global Process Template Owner – Projects

This is a precious addition to the project management literature. The beauty of this book is that it encompasses a theoretical framework of project management with its profession and practice. This contribution also embraces and covers in good depth the APM body of knowledge. Adrian's book is essential reading for academics, practitioners and project-based businesses.

Taha Elhag, University College London, UK

Project Management for Supplier Organizations

Harmonising the Project Owner to Supplier Relationship

ADRIAN TAGGART

Routledge
Taylor & Francis Group

LONDON AND NEW YORK

First published in paperback 2024

First published 2015 by Gowar Publishing

Published 2016 by Routledge
4 Park Square, Milton Park, Abingdon, Oxon OX14 4RN

and by Routledge
605 Third Avenue, New York, NY 10158

Routledge is an imprint of the Taylor & Francis Group, an informa business

Publisher's Note
The publisher has gone to great lengths to ensure the quality of this reprint but points out that some imperfections in the original copies may be apparent.

British Library Cataloguing in Publication Data
A catalogue record for this book is available from the British Library

Library of Congress Cataloging-in-Publication Data
Taggart, Adrian.
 Project management for supplier organizations : harmonising the project owner to supplier relationship / by Adrian Taggart.
 pages cm
 Includes bibliographical references and index.
 ISBN 978-1-4724-1109-9 (hbk) -- ISBN 978-1-4724-1110-5 (ebook) -- ISBN 978-1-4724-1111-2 (epub) 1. Project management. I. Title.
 HD69.P75T34 2015
 658.4'04--dc23

2014033761

ISBN: 978-1-4724-1109-9 (hbk)
ISBN: 978-1-03-283697-3 (pbk)
ISBN: 978-1-315-60239-4 (ebk)

DOI: 10.4324/9781315602394

Contents

List of Figures

List of Tables

List of Abbreviations

APM	Association for Project Management
APMP	Association for Project Management Professional
B2B	Business to Business
B2C	Business to Consumer
BOOT	Build Own Operate Transfer
BOT	Build Operate Transfer
CMS	Configuration Management System
CPFF	Cost Plus Fixed Fee
CPIF	Cost Plus Incentive Fee
CPPF	Cost Plus Percentage Fee
ITB	Invitation to Bid
ITT	Invitation to Tender
KPI	Key Performance Indicator
NEC	New Engineering Contract
OBS	Organizational Breakdown Structure
OJEU	Official Journal of the European Union
OO	Owner Organization
PBS	Product Breakdown Structure
PERT	Programme Evaluation & Review Techniques
PFI	Private Finance Initiative
PMI	Project Management Institute
PM	Project Manager
PMP	Project Management Plan
PMP®	Project Management Professional
PPP	Public Private Partnership
RACI	Responsibility Assignment Matrix
RFQ	Request for Quotation
SO	Supplier Organization
W5H	Who, What, Where, Why, When, How
WBS	Work Breakdown Structure

To Mum, to Dad and to Cath – the best things that ever happened to me.

Preface

To this day I remember the frustration.

I wanted (I really, really wanted) my business card to have the title 'Project Manager' under my name, but to my perpetual irritation, the company insisted upon 'Contract Manager'.

'Contracts' weren't the reason I did the job I did. 'Contracts' were routine, boring, administrative, bureaucratic. They didn't need a 'manager' they just needed a supervisor; some patsy who would simply tick the various boxes, fill in the necessary forms and do all the other steps that the process required.

No, this wasn't what I wanted. I wanted to command, to direct, to decide, to be in charge, to be the focal point, the driving force of some creative and exciting adventure that was delivering the future. I wanted to be a 'Project Manager'.

'What's the difference?' I would plead. 'Customers think less of me', I would argue. 'It just confuses people', I would cry.

Looking back now, with the perspective offered by age, I see that my frustration was largely explained by an ambitious young man's vanity and desire for recognition, but there is another element that intrigued me then, and still does now – the technical element – is 'Project Management' the same as 'Contract Management'?

Retrospection also shows the irony of my predicament because it was as that 'Contract Manager' that I was to enjoy many of the happiest moments of my career. Although, subsequently, I did get to enjoy the title I coveted (and in more than that one organization), and the thrill and excitement of being that focal point was just as satisfying as I had hoped for, it was no more or less demanding and exciting than my time as a 'Contract Manager'.

My enjoyment of both of these roles had a very great impact on me, so much so that the path of my subsequent career has been devoted to helping others realize the same experience. As a university lecturer, a business consultant and a trainer I have helped people with the management of their projects such that they too can enjoy the rewards that this wonderful role has to offer, and to avoid the dangers that are the flip side of such positions of influence.

Whereas the nuances of a particular title no longer consume me, the technical aspect of the question posed above still does. Further, in my opinion, this question remains largely unanswered by the published literature and the various bodies of knowledge posed by the project management intuitions (such as the Association for Project Management (APM) in the UK and the Project Management Institute (PMI) in the United States). This has been a growing source of frustration to me, especially when preparing delegates for the various qualifications offered by those institutions such as the APMP or PMP®. It is this frustration that has moved me to write this book and can be summarized as follows.

The role of a 'Project Manager' is different depending upon the commercial relationship of their organization to the project.

The classic situation for a project manager is when the organization for whom they work initiates a project that will create an asset that they will own and operate. A bakery, for instance, may introduce a new custom-made high capacity oven. The reason they do this is to benefit from the operation of the new asset (e.g. bread baked cheaper and faster). The project is a speculative investment and will be deemed successful if the benefits of ownership exceed the additional costs. Most of the books on the subject of 'Project Management' are written predominantly from this perspective, one of an 'Owner Organization' (OO).

The difficulty is that, in the experience of the author, this is not the situation that most 'Project Managers' find themselves in.

A far more common scenario involves the project manager working for an organization that creates a bespoke asset which will be the deliverable, or part thereof, of a project. To continue the example above, this new asset will be the same custom-made oven, but it will be sold to the 'Owner Organization'. The reason the organization embarks upon it is not to benefit from the operation of the oven; it is to profit from its sale. The oven is the 'goods and services' exchanged within a business deal and the right to this monetary reward is established in the contract agreed with the 'Owner Organization'(OO). It is this document that becomes the principal project document for this 'Supplier Organization' (SO) and so it could be said that it is managing a 'contract' rather than a project.

I do not advocate the strict adoption of the term 'Contract Manager' as opposed to 'Project Manager' – this would only serve to complicate issues further – but I do advocate the promotion of a deeper appreciation of how 'Project Management' must be tailored, depending upon the commercial relationship of one's organization to the project. Currently, regardless of whether the manager in question is a member of an 'Owner' or 'Supplier' organization we describe them as a 'Project Manager', and, by implication, expect them both to undertake identical 'Project Management'. However, close inspection reveals that 'Owner' and 'Supplier' organizations have some perspectives on the 'project' that are very different and, in turn, this has an impact on the management approach they choose to adopt. Project lifecycle models, attitude to changes, risk and resource management are topics where such differences are acute and the interests of a project manager within the SO is poorly served by the literature which predominantly takes the view of the OO.

This book seeks to address that deficiency and interprets the lexicon of project management primarily from the perspective of the Supplier Organization (SO).

This, however, does not render it irrelevant to those practitioners within the OO. All but the smallest of projects involve the OO engaging the SO who collectively form the overall project team. For this team to operate successfully, the interests of each party must be understood and aligned. Consequently it is as important for the Supplier Organization (SO) to recognize the Owner Organization's (OO) predicament as it is for the OO to understand that of the SO.

The book is structured to assist an organization, primarily a SO, as it moves to embrace project management because, for example, it chooses to move away from the manufacture of standard products, to the creation of bespoke products. It explains the nature of the new challenges projects will present, the changes this will demand of its structures, culture and practices, and the management competences it must master.

To this end, it is divided into four sections.

'Project Management' is appropriate only when addressing projects and, outside of this, its adoption will result in expensive failure. Accordingly, Part 1 clarifies the defining characteristics of projects, the challenges they pose, and hence the rationale for the various project management techniques that have evolved. It also considers the implications that these have for the organizations involved both in terms of the structures adopted and the culture that evolves, and how these contrast with those organizations that are not involved in projects.

Part 2 examines the perspective of the Supplier Organization (SO) upon the project with which it is engaged, both in terms of its role within the overall project team and the activities with which it engages. The latter is explored by reference to a lifecycle model specific to the SO. In doing so it contrasts the interests of the SO with those of the Owner Organization (OO) and identifies where they are aligned and where they diverge.

For a successful relationship, the terms of engagement between the Owner Organization (OO) and the Supplier Organization (SO) require careful consideration such that the interests and abilities of each party are fully recognized. Building upon the analysis established earlier, Part 3 explores the myriad of options for contracts and procurement structures and how and where each is appropriate. It also contains a whole chapter dedicated to the management of changes; a critical aspect of the relationship between OO and SO.

Part 4 contains a number of separate chapters and each is dedicated to an individual management topic and its practice within a project environment. The topics are selected, firstly, because they are key competences required by a Supplier Organization (SO) involved in projects, but secondly because they are not competences strongly evident within organizations not engaged in projects. Consequently, as a SO moves from the non-project to the project environment, these are the areas where a shortfall in management exercise will be most evident.

PART I

The Challenge of Projects

Chapter 1
What is a Project and Why Project Management?

'What is a project?'

The question is so simple but the answer is not.

Given the title of this book, it is imperative that we are able to provide an answer to the question, and indeed much of this chapter is devoted to such an answer, but before we embark on that it is helpful to remind ourselves of why the question is so important.

Projects and Non-Projects and Why We Need to Differentiate

Imagine if we cannot answer the question.

If we cannot differentiate between projects and other endeavours then how can we object to every creative process being called a project? Further, if every creative process is a project how does project management differ from any other type of management?

If everything becomes a project then the term fails to have any significance and if this is the case what is the point of having a 'Project Management' training course, book or qualification? In such circumstances the word 'Project' becomes meaningless and can be struck out; 'Project Management' becomes just generic management and the skills of a 'Project Manager' would be as appropriate to launching a space rocket as they would be, say, to running a bakery.

For the concept of 'Project Management' to have any relevance at all to an organization, it must satisfy itself that it is actually engaged in project work and to do this it needs to be able to define what a project is and understand how it differs from its other endeavours.

Defining a 'Project'

Consider the following two scenarios. The first involves the construction of a main Olympic stadium. Inevitably such buildings offer a radical and cutting-edge design since they become the iconic symbol of each Olympic Games.

Would you consider this endeavour to be a project?

Secondly, consider a factory making consumer goods. Along the length of the factory is a production line that manufactures 250 washing machines each day. Let us imagine it is midday and the 125th machine of the day is about to be started. Imagine escorting it down the line and overseeing its construction.

Would you consider this endeavour to be a project?

Most readers would be happy to describe the first scenario as a project, but would be reluctant to describe the second scenario in the same way. Why is this the case?

The question is trickier if we consider the similarities between the two scenarios.

Both have a financial budget and both will have a finite timescale. Both create something new (a product), both use resources and both are technically challenging. They are similar, but we are happy to describe only one of them as a project. Why?

It is appropriate, here, to take advantage of the work of others.

ESTABLISHED DEFINITIONS OF A PROJECT

Project management is a mature discipline and there are many professional organizations around the world whose mission is to refine and promote the subject. Two of the most popular organizations are the Project Management Institute (PMI) based in Pennsylvania in the United States, and the Association for Project Management (APM) based in Buckinghamshire in the UK. They offer the following definitions of a project:

> *A unique transient endeavour undertaken to achieve a desired outcome.*
> *(APM, 2006)*

A temporary endeavour undertaken to create a unique product, service or result. (PMI, 2013)

These excellent definitions warrant further examination. The first point to note is that, unsurprisingly, there is a significant similarity between the two definitions. The key adjective the two definitions have in common is the word 'unique'.

Two other adjectives are similar. Reach for your dictionary if you like but even then you will find it difficult to differentiate between the two words 'transient' and 'temporary', with the expression 'not permanent' seemingly applying to both.

Both definitions consider a project as an endeavour leading to some kind of output, however, the difference in quite how this output is described is noticeable with one favouring a 'desired outcome', the other a 'product service or result'. The difficulty in finding the precise words reveals that the outcome of a project is complex.

Thus, we can assume that a project is characterized by these four features:

- Unique.

- Temporary.

- Transient.

- Complex outcome.

They provide the key for a deeper understanding of what a project is, the challenges it poses and ultimately the rationale for project management as a discrete and separate branch of management.

We investigate them and their consequences, as follows.

The Consequences of Projects Being Unique

The obvious point to make about our Olympic stadium, above, is that to be iconic, it has to be different. Certainly, there are other sports stadia around the world but none look and operate quite like this one. It is designed and built specifically for this individual application, i.e. it is a bespoke product. When completed it will be the only one of its type. It will be unique.[1]

In the second scenario the word unique simply does not apply. The 125th washing machine of today will be identical to the others made today and the tens of thousands made in the proceeding weeks and months. It is a standard product.

THE HIGH DEGREE OF UNCERTAINTY

The significance of this difference becomes clearer if, just as we are to start each of these two endeavours, we ask ourselves the following questions:

- How much will it cost?

- How long will it take?

- What will it look like when it is finished?

- What precise sequence of actions do we need to follow to complete the assignment?

In the case of our washing machines all of these can be answered at the very outset with precise estimates.

In the case of our stadium, no such luxury exists. Here, especially at the commencement of the endeavour and especially if the stadium is of a truly radical design, the answers are little better than educated guesses and come with a level of imprecision to match.

This high degree of uncertainty at the outset, even about fundamental aspects, is a key characteristic of the project environment and one of the main reasons why projects are so difficult to manage successfully. Very many of the project management techniques are direct responses to the need to reduce this uncertainty as much as possible, as quickly as possible. It will only be eliminated by the end of the project, too late for the management team, who, during the

---

1   Usually, the product is the unique element of a project but this is not always the case. For instance a project may be initiated to create a standard product but to do so using a different manufacturing technique, or by using alternative equipment, or in a different location. In each of these cases the challenge is to do something which has not been attempted before and as such the word 'unique' is applicable and hence the use of the word 'project' justified.

project, will be faced with the unenviable obligation of making decisions in the absence of full knowledge.

It is very important to acknowledge here that this uncertainty is there not because of any failure on behalf of the team managing the project. It is there because it is a feature of projects. Project managers will deploy expertise and specialist techniques to try and deal with the challenge but, fundamentally, the presence of uncertainty is not due to their failings.

Such high levels of uncertainty present many practical difficulties. Consider the following.

HIGH RISK OF OVERALL FAILURE

When faced with making decisions in the face of high uncertainty, there is every chance that the wrong decisions will be made, with dire consequences.

The probability of our 125th washing machine not performing as expected is negligible but this stands in stark contrast to our new sports stadium. The record shows that such projects frequently flirt with disaster.[2]

The reality is that all projects face a high risk of failure and whilst the project management team will seek to mitigate this risk, they will not be able to eliminate it.

The lack of precedents for unique endeavours does not only create uncertainty about money and time. It also has consequences for the management of the technical aspects of the project product.

For our washing machine there are opportunities for the partially completed product to be assessed continuously throughout its manufacture. Within the organization it is known precisely what an acceptable washing machine looks like at the various points. This knowledge exists because the manufacture of the machines is a routine operation which has been completed very many times and it can be expressed in a set of procedures and rules that can exert a very effective control over the creative process. Simple adherence to these rules will result in a successful outcome.

---

2   The troubled facility created for the 1976 Olympic Games in Montreal, the chaotic preparation of the stadia for the FIFA World Cup in Brazil in 2014 and the reconstruction of Wembley Stadium in 2007 are notable examples in this respect.

This is very different to the situation within a project environment, posed by the creation of a bespoke product.

If the product is unique then, by definition, there are no identical precedents and so no one knows for sure what it should look like at the various points of its construction. Procedures, rules and suchlike to control the creative process are far less prevalent and there is far more reliance upon those undertaking the work to attest to whether 'it feels right'.

The very different perspectives on rules that are a consequence of these two differing scenarios have profound implications for the methods of governance appropriate in each.

A non-project environment, characterized by near total knowledge and a repeated process, can achieve good governance simply by using extensive rules that are strictly enforced.

The bespoke, uncertain and often haphazard nature of the project environment does not support this approach and considerable latitude and scope for judgement must be granted to those managing the work. In these circumstances a strict and inflexible rule-based governance approach will simply not work.

This is a lesson that many project organizations have learnt only at great cost.

The Consequences of Projects Being Temporary

'You do realise we are building pharaoh's tomb?', was the expression a colleague of the author once used.

We were having a torrid time working on a difficult and unpopular project and this remark, although somewhat cynical, was conveying a very significant point. My friend had started his career as an apprentice in the shipyards of Glasgow and this had made him shrewd. He thought more than he talked and did not miss much of significance.

His remark alluded to the pyramids in Egypt that served as tombs to the pharaohs. The commonly held narrative explains that the pharaoh's wealth and possessions were accommodated alongside his mortal remains. The ancient

Egyptian belief system was such that these possessions would be required to ensure a very comfortable afterlife for the recently deceased ruler. Accordingly, grave robbers were a very real concern since they and their criminal enterprises could easily deprive an unlucky pharaoh of the very experience the pyramids were designed to provide. Therefore the pyramids were furnished with many devices such as secret passageways and secret doors to confound these would-be thieves. However, by necessity, the slaves who built these pyramids were familiar with these security arrangements and as such they constituted a major impediment to the pharaohs' post mortem comfort, should they ever be tempted off the 'straight and narrow'. A convenient solution to this was found whereby, upon completion of the building project, the slaves were murdered and their remains simply tossed into the basement of the pyramids.

Modern-day Egyptologists would be likely to violently disagree with the veracity of this version of events, but the story is sufficiently well known for it to offer an insight into a fundamental problem with projects, namely, they do not offer their practitioners any long-term job security.

My friend was making the simple point that, torrid as our current situation was, only unemployment lay beyond it.

The temporary nature of projects is most obvious in the context of the teams that deliver them. They are a temporary arrangement that only exist as long as the project. Project teams are therefore unusual in the world of work since they work diligently to do away with the only reason for their existence.[3]

By contrast, teams engaged in non-projects (often referred to as 'Routine Operations') are designed to survive beyond just one cycle. When one washing machine is complete, they simply start the next. So, if this team worked faster and better then the machines would be cheaper, sales would increase and hence their job security would be enhanced.

This represents one of the major reasons why the soft skills are so important to project managers. An understanding of the human condition

---

3   Many readers will be employed by organizations that deliver successive projects and the completion of one project does not lead to termination of employment. These types of organizations are referred to as 'matrix' organizations and have special characteristics, some of which they share with organizations engaged in non-project work. They will be addressed in some detail in Chapter 2 but for the purposes of this chapter it is appropriate to consider what may be referred to as a 'pure project', like our stadium project, a characteristic of which is its temporary management structures.

is very valuable when trying to motivate someone to work themselves out of a job.[4]

The Consequences of Projects Being Transient

As acknowledged above, the words 'transient' and 'temporary' have very similar definitions that describe a state that is not permanent. For our purpose we need to stretch the boundaries of good grammar to emphasize a slight difference that exists between the two definitions; a difference that is perhaps more familiar to physicists and engineers.

The difference is this.

Consider using the light in your room. You can turn the light on and then, after some time, you turn the light off. The illumination is temporary but whilst the light is energized the level of emitted light is constant.

Contrast this with turning on a radio and then, after some time, turning it off. Again the radio is on for only a temporary period but, critically, whilst it is on the volume of sound is not constant, it is in a state of flux, it is changing all the time; it is transient.

Projects are both temporary, in that they are not permanent, but they are also transient in that whilst they do exist they are constantly undergoing change.

This has huge relevance for those who seek to manage projects because many of these changes are not random; they are predictable.

We, as people, undergo change during our lives. Our physical size, emotional security, energy levels, priorities, all change over time. These changes are not random, they are known about, they apply to everyone and hence they are predictable. Knowledge of this makes managing our lives, and that of others, a much easier prospect, as anyone with an adolescent child will readily confirm.

It is the same for projects.

---

4   In practice, the involvement of individual project team members is even more volatile than the life of the overall project team. Most likely, an individual will be a member of a sub-team which will only exist until the fragment of the project for which the sub-team is responsible, is complete. For this reason the make-up of the overall project team is always changing.

Many of the changes are known about, they apply to all projects, and hence they are predictable. Knowledge of them, and how they lead to generic models of project lifecycles, is an enormous boon to anyone trying to understand and manage projects and the teams that deliver them. Chapter 4 addresses this topic in detail.

The Consequences of Projects Having Complex Outcomes

Projects are deceptively complex entities and nowhere is this more relevant than in the consideration of what they actually achieve. Consider the following.

CHANGE

If the world is the same at the end of the project as it was at the beginning, then the project manager will have failed. At the most fundamental level, projects deliver change!

To illuminate this, consider the management of the production line creating our washing machines. The management team seek to keep the line in operation. Much effort is spent in sustaining the supply of raw materials, ensuring work rosters are full and the pace of work is upheld. The emphasis is on maintaining the status quo, on avoiding disruption, on avoiding change. This is most prevalent within the maintenance division where even its very name reveals its ethos: maintain.

Compare this to our project. Projects usually create something new, but often they involve destruction, demolition or removal. What each has in common is that they are delivering some kind of change.

This is the root of so many project difficulties because it can be safely asserted that people have a natural resistance to change. Admittedly, some of us are more resistant than others but if it is a change that: 1) affects us; 2) is something upon which we have not been consulted; and 3) is in any way vague as to its purpose or content, then our default position is to resist it.

Of course much change is positive and if we stand to benefit then we will be more positively disposed towards it, but as a general point our attitude to change is not neutral and our bias is towards the negative. No one has articulated this particular facet of human nature better than Machiavelli and his conclusion stands repetition here:

> *There is nothing more difficult to take in hand, more perilous to conduct, or more uncertain in its success, than to take the lead in the introduction of a new order of things. For the reformer has enemies in all those who profit by the old order, and only lukewarm defenders in all those who would profit by the new order, this lukewarmness arising partly from fear of their adversaries ... and partly from the incredulity of mankind, who do not truly believe in anything new until they have had actual experience of it. (Machiavelli, 1513)*

Projects are affected by, and in turn affect, a great many people. Anyone fitting into this classification is known as a 'stakeholder'. It is a very loose brief and as a consequence an average project can include a very large number of stakeholders.

Within this classification are all the groups and individuals who possess the skills, knowledge, resources, contacts, influence, facilities, apparatus and general wherewithal to ensure that the project is a success. It will also include those who will ultimately judge whether or not the project is a success.

For these reasons alone 'stakeholder management' is an important (possibly the most important) element of project management. Unfortunately, very often it is the hardest facet of the project to influence.

The reason for this is, of course, the fact that not everyone will be in favour of the project. Take any project and typically there will be about 10 per cent of the stakeholders who view the project as an excellent idea and will freely give of their time, resources and expertise to support it. By the same token about 10 per cent will think the project a disastrous idea and will give freely of their time and expertise only to confound, disrupt and, in extremis, sabotage the project team's efforts. The other 80 per cent, frankly, will not be bothered, and wish the project would just simply go away.

If we consider that, in some instances the 10 per cent who are vehemently opposed to the project are those with the skills and resources very necessary for success, then we can begin to understand just how demanding 'stakeholder management' can be of both time and energy.

Clearly, non-project endeavours also affect people, but in the absence of such fundamental change, the attendant issues are not as prevalent in the non-project environment. There is an order of magnitude in the difference between the two environments in respect of the demand for 'stakeholder management'.

However, there is an upside for the project environment. There is something inherently appealing about working to deliver such change since it is through these that human progress occurs. At the end of each difficult day, a project manager can comfort themselves with the knowledge that they are indeed 'delivering the future'.

PRODUCTS AND BENEFITS

The author once heard a story (most likely apocryphal) about a factory built to manufacture cassette tapes.[5]

The factory was completed on time, under budget and the commissioning trials demonstrated that it was capable of producing cassette tapes in a quantity and quality that exceeded the dreams of all those involved.

Was the project a success?

At the point of commissioning of the factory, we are compelled to answer in the affirmative since the project manager has delivered the factory (the product) within the criteria laid down for it.

There are no prizes for guessing what happened next. A competitor created something called a Compact Disc (CD).

Demand for cassette tapes quickly collapsed and the financial return hoped for (the benefit) never materialized, indeed the backers incurred a considerable loss.

Was the project a success?

This is an example of a project successfully delivering an excellent product but failing to realize benefit.

There are a number of important observations to make here.

Firstly, the ultimate measure of project success is whether it delivers sufficient benefit. The timely and economical delivery of a technically sufficient

---

5 This may stretch the historical knowledge of some of our younger readers but suffice to say that after vinyl records, the favoured medium for storing music was a spool of magnetic tape contained within a plastic case; the cassette tape.

product is but an aid to the realization of this benefit and not the end in itself. There are very many projects for which delivery of the product was late, horrendously over budget and/or technically compromised, but still delivered considerable benefit when the product was eventually operated. Concorde, the Panama Canal, are these projects failures?

Secondly, there is more to realizing benefit than having a great project product. Having staff trained and wanting to operate the product (the factory in this example) is indispensable, as is a demand for the goods ultimately produced. Too many would-be entrepreneurs have learned too late that if you haven't got a market then you haven't got a business, and that this simple truth holds regardless of how good the product is and how prodigious their talents.

Thirdly, the final verdict of success cannot be delivered until very late in the day. Benefit is only realized during the operation of the product and the necessary calculus, often, can only occur long after the delivery team have left the stage. Indeed the definitive comparison of benefits and costs can only be made once the project product has been finally safely disposed of. (The first fleet of commercial nuclear power stations were built in the UK and are now being decommissioned at astronomical cost. How does this affect the verdict on the success or otherwise of the project that created them?)

These difficulties in assessing project success only serve to underline how complex project outcomes are.[6]

Real Projects and Their Management

The above text seeks to describe a project, and the environment it gives rise to, so as to compare it to a non-project. The polemic approach is appropriate to emphasize the points to be made, but it is largely an artificial concept since no real creative endeavour neatly drops into the 'wholly unique' or 'wholly repetitive' box.

A CONTINUUM OF CREATIVE ENDEAVOURS: FROM 'PROJECT' TO 'ROUTINE OPERATIONS'

In practice, each and every creative endeavour has some aspects which are unique and some which are repetitive, even though the relative balance

---

6   The various levels of project success and the interplay between products and benefits is addressed in detail in Chapter 16.

between the amounts may vary enormously. The balance between the two can be acknowledged by reference to their position on a continuum defined by a pure project at one end and a pure non-project at the other.

The degree to which of the 'pure' classifications an endeavour will tend towards can be assessed by reference to the following criteria based upon those characteristics of a project described above, irrespective of size of the endeavour (see Table 1.1).

Table 1.1   Project assessment criteria

Criterion	Examples
Degree of uniqueness	Although this is most readily applied to the product, it can relate to any aspect of the project or its environment. The parameter must be considered from the perspective of the team carrying out the work and their particular experience and expertise.
Stability of the team (this encompasses the temporary and transient aspects and their implications for team dynamics and motivation)	This category includes: 1. The relationships between the members and sub-teams both from a contractual and historical perspective. For instance are they all employees of the one corporation or are they a group of contracting companies brought together just for the purposes of the project? 2. Do the participants know each other already? Some groupings are formed through temporary contracts but include individuals who have worked together many times before and who have very mature and long-standing relationships. 3. The intentions of the sponsors post-project also have relevance here. Is it truly a case of 'deliver and disband' or is the project simply the beginning of a permanent relationship or engagement?
Complexity of outcome	This encompasses such aspects as: 1. The magnitude of change being delivered by the project. 2. Contextual issues such as the degree to which the change is supported or resisted by stakeholders. 3. The number of factors in the project environment, beyond the product, that are required for the project benefit to be realized.

Figure 1.1 offers such a continuum and is populated with some examples of typical endeavours and where they would be expected to lie. It should be noted that the assessment is wholly subjective and qualitative.

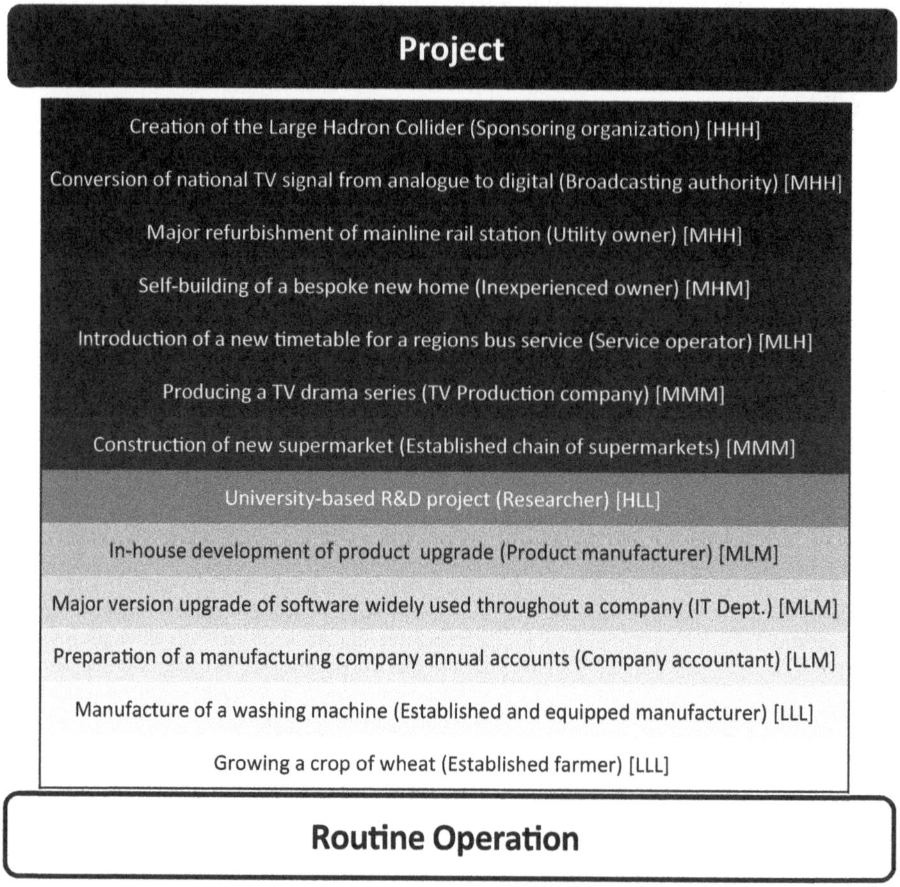

Project

Creation of the Large Hadron Collider (Sponsoring organization) [HHH]

Conversion of national TV signal from analogue to digital (Broadcasting authority) [MHH]

Major refurbishment of mainline rail station (Utility owner) [MHH]

Self-building of a bespoke new home (Inexperienced owner) [MHM]

Introduction of a new timetable for a regions bus service (Service operator) [MLH]

Producing a TV drama series (TV Production company) [MMM]

Construction of new supermarket (Established chain of supermarkets) [MMM]

University-based R&D project (Researcher) [HLL]

In-house development of product upgrade (Product manufacturer) [MLM]

Major version upgrade of software widely used throughout a company (IT Dept.) [MLM]

Preparation of a manufacturing company annual accounts (Company accountant) [LLM]

Manufacture of a washing machine (Established and equipped manufacturer) [LLL]

Growing a crop of wheat (Established farmer) [LLL]

Routine Operation

Figure 1.1   Continuum of Creative Endeavours

Notes: 1. Assessment is from the perspective of the party stated within the brackets.
2. Characters in square brackets indicate assessment of the endeavour against criteria of:

   Degree of uniqueness
   Degree of temporariness and transience
   Complexity of outcome

   Assessment made as:

   H – High
   M – Medium
   L – Low

APPROPRIATE MANAGERIAL RESPONSES

When faced with having to manage the various endeavours discussed, organizations must make decisions about the most appropriate organizational techniques and cultures.

At either end of the continuum this is a relatively simple decision. The creation of washing machines invites 'Operations Management' and its attendant structures and cultures, whereas those endeavours at the other extreme warrant 'Project Management' and its attendant structures and cultures. The real difficulty comes when addressing those endeavours that sit in-between.

Organizations faced with this prospect will realize that there is some merit in either approach, and the creation of a management response that combines the best of both is a very difficult proposition, especially since the two managerial approaches can be diametrically opposed. Further, such organizations may find little assistance from the literature since most books discuss each approach from the idealized positions associated with the extremes of the continuum.

Many organizations have a background associated with one of these extremes and, through a change of circumstances, need to embrace change. For instance an organization manufacturing identical products may find that the market increasingly demands bespoke models, thus requiring them to manage an increase in 'uniqueness' of their output. Another may need to reduce overheads by 'outsourcing' many of their key processes and thereby increase the transience and temporariness of their organizational structures. Another may choose to supply 'solutions' rather than selling standard products, which will involve them choosing the appropriate product model and thus increase the complexity of their involvement.

In each of these instances the organization's endeavours will migrate from the bottom to the top of the continuum, requiring them increasingly to embrace aspects of project management.[7]

The following chapters in Part 1 further explore the differences in structure and culture associated with the organizations that address these different types of endeavours, located at the extremes of the continuum. As such it indicates

---

7   There are instances where organizations may choose to move in the opposite direction, and for good reason, but this book does seek to address their concerns.

the manner of challenges faced by any organization attempting a migration along the continuum.

Part 4 of this book addresses, directly, selected aspects of project management which are deemed particularly relevant when such a migration is undertaken.

References

Association for Project Management, 2006. *APM Body of Knowledge*, 5th edn. High Wycombe: APMKnowledge.

Machiavelli, N., 1513. *The Prince*.

Project Management Institute, 2013. *A Guide to the Project Management Body of Knowledge (PMBOK® Guide)*, 5th edn. Pennsylvania: Project Management Institute Inc.

Chapter 2
Structure of Project Delivery Organizations

What empowers one individual to exert influence (to have authority over) another? Consider society prior to the Industrial Revolution when most of us would have been peasants, working the land to eke out sufficient for ourselves and our families. The most influential people then were the feudal lords and the source of their power was largely derived from who they were since entitlement to such positions was a birthright.

Others did exert influence. Hollywood would have us believe that characters like Robin Hood exerted at least as much influence as the local feudal lord, but unlike them, Mr Hood derived his ability to influence fellow peasants from his own talents and, in particular, his charisma.

Both of these sources of authority were recognized by Max Weber (1947). This famous German sociologist and philosopher was interested in power and authority within groups and in addition to these two he recognized a third type – legal authority.

By this, one is able to exert influence over others simply by dint of one's office, or position. A rational and legal system of regulations specifies positions with defined powers of authority attributed to them. Individuals are then appointed to these positions and can assume the authority over specified others, that is vested in that position. It is this that underpins the concept of 'bureaucracy' and hence the iconic hierarchical structures that so many of us recognize in our 'Organizational Charts', 'Organizational Breakdown Structures' or 'Organigrams'.

It is this source of power, and the structures it leads to, that provides the primary means by which the companies and public bodies that constitute the modern industrial society (or indeed post-industrial) can operate.

Communication Flows in Hierarchical Organizational Structures

Let us consider such a hierarchical structure (see Figure 2.1).

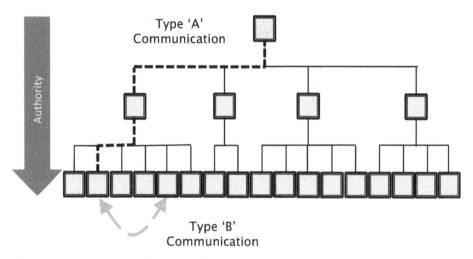

Figure 2.1   Communication within a bureaucracy

The diagram consists of solid lines and boxes, but what do these boxes represent and what flows up and down the lines?

We tend to think of the boxes (the 'nodes') as people, but a more accurate description would be a role, or position. Such a description is in keeping with Weber's analysis that differentiates between the individual and the office that they hold. We commonly use these diagrams to determine who the manager is and who their subordinates are. Tracing the line upwards from any node will identify the incumbent's manager, tracing it downwards identifies their subordinates. Formal or 'legal' authority can be said to flow downwards, through the organization, along the lines.

The fact that each role has only one manager is in accordance with what is sometimes referred to as the 'unitary chain of command'. Such a simple scenario removes any ambiguity and is consistent with one of Weber's characteristics of a bureaucracy whereby there must be a clear chain of command.

The lines also represent a major route of communication. We spend a considerable amount of time communicating with either our Manager or our subordinates and so significant amounts of information flow up and down the lines. It is, however, a special communication type since, consistent with the authority flow described above, one party always has 'legal' authority over the other. Let us label this as communication Type A.

However not all communication involves mangers and subordinates. Much of it is between peers and this does not run along the chart's lines; it runs across them. Let us consider such communication, where neither party has formal authority over the other, as Type B communication.

The significance of these different types is best addressed in an example. Let us consider the following situation.

Imagine you occupy role 'X' within the accounts department of our factory making washing machines described in Chapter 1. Your role involves processing 'Goods Received Notes' that are generated within the warehouse, which come under the jurisdiction of the Operations Director. Imagine that, while attempting to process a note generated by one of the forklift truck operators, you realize the form is missing some vital information that is preventing you from completing the task. The forklift truck driver needs to complete the form with the missing information. How is the driver to be communicated with, Type A or Type B? Figure 2.2 relates.

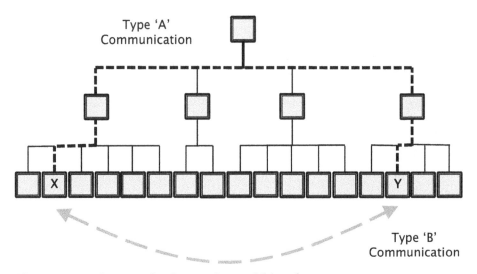

Figure 2.2   Communication options within a bureaucracy

Let us imagine it is a nice sunny day and a walk over to the warehouse appeals so you elect to challenge the driver directly and opt for Type B.

On arrival at the warehouse you quickly locate the driver in question and point out his omission.

'Please accept my unreserved apology. The fault is wholly mine and I shall rectify it immediately' is their reply.

The swift resolution points to the many advantages associated with Type B communication.

It involved only the two people directly affected and so there was no delay by relaying the message; there was no opportunity for corruption of the message through a chain of intermediaries; it did not become conflated with other extraneous issues; and the errant party was not embarrassed by others being made aware of their error. The communication was effective and efficient.

However, let us consider the situation when our challenge led to the following very different reply from our driver: 'You're damn right it's not filled in and I'm sick of you lot moaning about it from a comfortable office. It's easier for you to get the information yourselves so why don't you just go and do that now and get out of my way before I run you down'.

Faced with such intransigence you will revert to Type A communication. In its purest form, this will involve you pushing the issue up to your manager. In turn they may have to push it even further up the organization since it must reach a role that has authority over both the accounts and operations departments, and able to issue the relevant instruction.

The disadvantages to this are numerous and mostly derive from the ample opportunity for corruption of the message, delay in its transmission, drawing in other issues, and suchlike.

It does however have one significant advantage since when the message does arrive with the final recipient it will do so as an instruction from someone who has 'legal' authority. The argument will be over.

The point to be made is that although the organizational structure is ostensibly designed around Type A communication, there are many advantages of Type B communication. However, these advantages are only open to those who are prepared to collaborate with their colleagues and not insist on formal instruction from above. In doing so they are accepting influence derived from charisma and persuasion rather than just formal power derived from one's position.

THE 'SILO EFFECT'

There is often a reluctance to embrace Type B communication, especially when it involves communicating with others who we perceive as being outside of our immediate peer group.

In an organizational context, the identity of our peer groups is most readily defined by the particular branch of the hierarchy in which we reside. The effect is to divide the organization structure into vertical slices and this phenomenon is well known as the 'Silo Effect'. Within each peer group (or vertical slice or 'silo') there is much collaborative Type B communication but between the different peer groups there is little or none (see Figure 2.3).

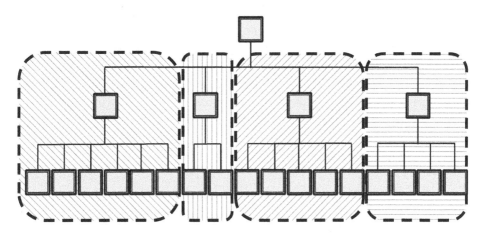

Figure 2.3   The 'Silo Effect'

Division of any aggregation of people into peer groups has a potent effect on the interpersonal dynamics within. Put very simply, it provokes a 'them and us' mentality whereby, although cohesiveness exists amongst members within the same peer group, there is often conflict between the groups. In the event of any such inter-group conflict, individuals often feel the need to 'take sides' which can further reinforce the division between different groups, which in turn can lead to further alienation and opportunity for conflict. The outcome can be extreme with each rotation reinforcing commitment to one's own group and hostility to others. (Consider the hostility between opposing groups of sports fans, between different nationalities, different religious groups and the like.)

In an organizational context, inter-group rivalry can be very destructive. At your place of work is the relationship between personnel from different departments or locations always harmonious and mutually respectful? Alternatively, does a degree of envy, disrespect and even naked competition creep into proceedings?

Knowledge of this dynamic, however, can be used to our advantage when designing our organizational structures. We can choose the basis upon which the organization is decomposed into peer groups, and by doing so anticipate where cohesiveness will exist, and where it will not.

One of two approaches is generally taken, giving rise to the two structures described below.

Functional Organizations

Consider the organization making the washing machines described in Chapter 1. Below the head of the organization (the Managing Director) we would expect to see the other directors with titles such as:

- Operations Director.

- Procurement Director.

- Sales Director.

- Research & Development Director.

Each of these titles contains a verb that relates to the function that is carried out in the group so formed. This is the feature that all members of this group have in common and even though it is highly likely that different members of the same group are working on different tasks (products), they all perform the same function. For this reason it is known as a Functional Organization.

The superior, collaborative, Type B communication will take place amongst those with a common interest in just one specialism. It is for this reason that this type of group is renowned for its ability to promote excellence in that specialism. In particular, it provides an ideal learning environment where apprentices of the specialism in question can access many role models and tutors.

In this arrangement the restrictions of the 'Silo Effect' prevents incumbents 'seeing the big picture', beyond the needs of their own function. As such it seriously inhibits co-operation and integration between different functions. This problem is not too serious if the same overall operation is being repeated constantly as, say, within a factory mass-producing the same identical product, where the needs of each function are well understood and, over time, incorporated into the established ways of working. Indeed, in these circumstances a Functional Organization is capable of remarkable performance, especially in terms of the efficiency of its use of resources. However, when the required products are not identical and changes to established ways of working are required, the Functional Organization will struggle.

Other pros and cons of the Functional Organization are summarized in the following table.

Table 2.1   Pros and cons of Functional Organizations

	Pros	Cons
Functional Organization (Note: pros of Functional Organizations tend to be cons of Projectized, and vice versa)	• Excellent environment for promoting functional excellence. • In concert with above, very good opportunities for training and learning. • Obvious career path. • Excellent communication within team (manager usually did subordinates' job at some point in career). • Capable of very efficient use of resources. • Strong team identity. • Excellent for retaining corporate knowledge and experience.	• Encourages 'silo mentality' (dedicated to own team and tendency to conflict with other functional teams). • (Hence) Very poor for cross-functional integration. • Poor for development of broad perspective and hence general management skills. • Very resistant to change. • Very little focus on, and service of, individual customer. • Very poor at dealing with unusual circumstances. • Poor for developing general management skills (cross-functional perspective).

Task Force Organizations

Consider the organization creating the Olympic stadium, also described in Chapter 1. Below the head of the organization we would expect to see roles with titles such as:

- Power Supply Manager.

- Structures Manager.

- Seating and Customer Accommodation Manager.

- Track & Sport Facilities Manager.

Each of these titles contains a noun that relates to the element of the overall product that is being created by the group so formed.

The feature that all members of this group have in common is that they all work to complete the same task and this task is defined as the completion of a specific product, or fragment thereof. Each group will contain sufficient designers, manufacturers and installers to achieve this task and for this reason the organization is referred to variously as a Task Force, a Projectized Organization or a Project Team.

Because each of the different functions is represented within each group the superior, collaborative, Type B communication will take place across functions. It is for this reason that this type of organizations excel at complex and innovative endeavours that require close liaison between different functions.

It is this enhanced cross-functional integration and the motivational benefits of focusing a team around a specific output, that are the primary reasons why this type of structure is favoured by organizations delivering high profile projects.

In this arrangement the restrictions of the 'Silo Effect' inhibit those aspects which require integration between groups delivering different tasks. These can be associated with integration, for instance when two groups are making sub-products which must ultimately interface with each other, but more usually they are associated with inefficiency and an absence of 'economies of scale'. This is because different groups are often performing tasks with similar functional elements and this can lead to duplication of effort.

Another very attractive feature of these types of organization to project work is that once a task has been completed, the group responsible can be dispensed with. Helpfully, this avoids the need, (and hence costs) of maintaining expensive resources beyond when necessary, but, unhelpfully, it also means that knowledge and expertise is being continually lost. It also means that the overall structure is always changing as tasks are completed and new ones started. In this respect we can see how this is consistent with the 'temporary' and 'transient' aspects of projects that were discussed earlier in Chapter 1. It can be said that the overall organization has a 'revolving door' with groups (and individuals) constantly entering and leaving.

Other pros and cons of the Task Force Organization are summarized in Table 2.2.

Table 2.2   Pros and cons of Task Force Organizations

	Pros	Cons
Task Force (or Projectized Organization) (Note: pros of Projectized Organization tend to be cons of Functional, and vice versa)	• Very strong dedication to project purpose. • Flexible. • Effective at dealing with various challenges. • Strong team identity. • Develops broad perspective and good management skills. • Excellent for cross-functional integration. • Facilitates 'revolving door' aspect.	• Poor at retaining expert skills and experience. • Poor at retaining historical knowledge. • Inefficient use of resources. • Little opportunity for the long term and hence long-term commitment of members. • Constant state of flux.

Organizational Continuum

Although Functional and Task Force organizations share the overall hierarchical pattern of Weber's bureaucracy, they represent very different organizations in terms of their ways of working, and hence their attractions and detractions. These render each suitable for a particular type of work – Functional Organizations for routine operations, and Task Force Organizations for projects.

They are best thought of as idealized models that help an understanding of what happens within an organization but it is relatively rare to come across pure examples of either because, in an attempt to foster the pros and minimize the cons of both, most real organizations are hybrids; a combination of the two idealized structures. Any such hybrid is described as a Matrix Organization.

As with any hybrid, the relative quantities of the ingredients can be varied to create different outcomes and so it is with Matrix Organizations.

This is best considered by reference to an Organizational Continuum (see Figure 2.4). Within this, the extremes are defined by the two idealized models. Along the continuum in-between, is an infinite range of possibilities for unique blends of the two, and hence an infinite variety of Matrix Organizations. However, only three are generally considered a Balanced, a Weak and a Strong Matrix, as discussed below.

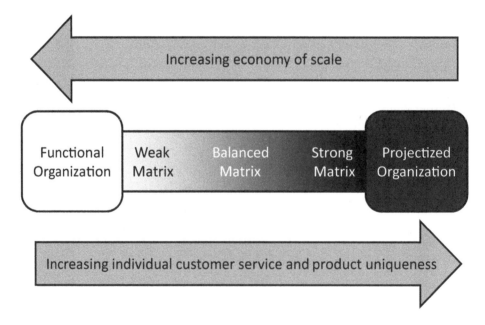

Figure 2.4   The Organizational Continuum

The Matrix Organization

DESCRIPTION

The matrix seeks to simultaneously secure the advantages of both function and task orientated organizations. It does this by combining two authority structures in one organization and having some managers responsible for the function and others the output (the task). When combined they form a matrix. This is represented visually within Figure 2.5, though it is difficult to highlight the two integrated authority structures within one diagram.

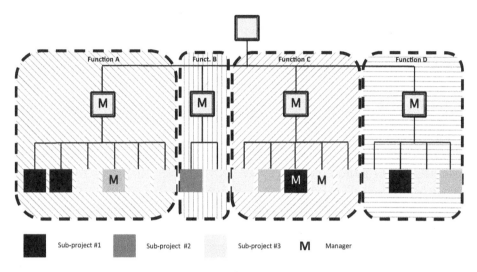

Figure 2.5   The Matrix Organization structure

As can be seen, the defining characteristic of a Matrix Organization is that those workers in the middle come under the authority of two managers; one responsible for the function, the other the task. Ostensibly this does away with the need for Type B communication since authority can flow along functional and task lines, however as we shall discuss below, the effect can be the exact opposite.

WEAK, BALANCED AND STRONG MATRICES: TRAVERSING THE ORGANIZATIONAL CONTINUUM

As suggested, Functional Organizations are most appropriate for delivering repetitive, routine operations whereas Task Force Organizations are more appropriate for project work.

There is therefore a correlation between the ideal type of organization and the type of work at hand. In simple terms, we would expect a consistency between the location of a particular organization on the Organizational Continuum (Figure 2.4), and the location of its work on the Continuum of Creative Endeavours (Figure 1.1). It is therefore helpful to consider the need to traverse the Organizational Continuum from Functional to Task Force, not least because this is the migration that can be expected of an organization that starts to embrace project work.

Imagine a company making assemblies of kitchen units for domestic dwellings using a predominantly manual process. Since each of the packs contains identical kitchen units a Functional Organization is adopted. However, imagine at some point a lucrative deal is struck to supply a house builder with kitchens. The design is almost identical to the standard (some small dimensional changes) but the customer insists on a single person contact with whom they can liaise for progress, delivery and technical queries. The MD sees no difficulties with this and chooses a young graduate, fresh from college and full of enthusiasm to be the project co-ordinator and to liaise with both the customer and the in-house functions.

Appointing someone with responsibility for one overall deliverable and a pan-function interest means it is no longer a purely Functional Organization; it is a Matrix. In this instance when the person with responsibility for the product has very little authority (associated with a project expediter or co-ordinator role) it is referred to as 'Weak Matrix'.

Many readers will have occupied the role of 'Project Co-ordinator' early in their career and probably remember it as one of their most fraught experiences. The established functional managers will, most likely, see them as an unwelcome interference; some youngster telling them how to do a job they have spent years perfecting. The co-ordinator and the changes they attempt to instigate will, most likely, be ignored. It is highly likely that the organization will fail to satisfy the customer, and highly likely that blame will be laid at the foot of the co-ordinator's door. In this instance the co-ordinator will be held accountable for something they do not have sufficient authority to control.

Imagine, however, that although this contract failed, the MD is attracted by the potential profits in bespoke kitchens and pursues further work of this type. Mindful of the failures of last time he recognizes that the co-ordinator did not have sufficient authority to influence the functional mangers, so next time a similar contract is attempted a 'Project Manager' is assigned to the work.

Having both functional and project managers at the same level of authority is known as a 'Balanced Matrix'. Its failures come into sharp focus if we consider what will happen if they hold opposing views. In practice it is usually necessary for one to have the slightly higher authority. If it is deemed that the functional manager has the higher authority then the organization reverts to a 'Weak Matrix', however if the project manager is deemed to have the upper hand then the organization becomes a 'Strong Matrix'.

The latter situation will involve a dilution of the role of the functional manager. Rather than instructing their workforce on the work at hand they would become more associated with a personnel manager type role. Their departments would become 'resource pools' that simply provide individuals to be seconded to the various project teams, as and when required, who would then come under the instruction of the 'Project Manager'. The need to manage and develop 'Project Managers' would become highlighted in such an organization and in all likelihood a 'Manager of Project Managers' position would emerge.

In the example offered it is likely that a structure such as this would only be embraced if the organization had started to deliver fewer, higher value kitchens that were very bespoke to individual customers.

From a 'Strong Matrix' it is a relatively straightforward step to a 'Task Force' structure by, for instance, outsourcing some of the various functions. The effect would be that a temporary team can be assembled for each contract, which will disband once the work is completed.

THE PROS AND CONS OF THE MATRIX

The first point to make about a Matrix Organization is that it is not a coherent hierarchical structure. A fundamental characteristic of a bureaucracy as defined by Weber is a clarity of authority. Matrix structures fail to satisfy this fundamental requirement since there is a duality of authority. The concept of unitary chain of command is corrupted and abandoned.

As indicated above, this problem is brought into sharp focus if we consider those scenarios when a function and task manager have opposing views on what is to be done. How does a worker respond when their two bosses are offering conflicting instructions?

It is not surprising therefore that the biggest drawback of a Matrix is the confusion and ambiguity it creates in terms of authority structure. It is often the workers in the middle who bear the brunt of this and are subject to considerable stress. Such a problem is not a just modern issue; it was known about in biblical times prompting Matthew (6:24) to observe that 'No one can serve two masters, for either he will hate the one and love the other; or else he will be devoted to one and despise the other'.

There are also other very practical details that render this structure less attractive. There are, for instance, twice as many managers as the two conventional structures. This not only impacts directly on the overheads of the organization but just involving more people in decisions and communications creates additional complexity.

What, then, is the big advantage that outweighs all of these drawbacks and persuades so many organizations that this is the structure for them?

The answer is that it is the only solution that addresses the conflicting demands made upon those organizations who engage in activities which are neither pure projects nor pure operations. The disadvantages of the two idealized structures discussed above render them unacceptable for such mixed endeavours and inevitably the Matrix is favoured since it offers a compromise that mitigates the impact of these significant disadvantages.

The pros and cons of the Matrix structure are summarized in Table 2.3.

Table 2.3   Pros and cons of Matrix Organizations

	Pros	Cons
Matrix (Note: most of the pros and cons lie in the fact that the Matrix is a compromise between the two other organizational types. For instance a Matrix is better at retaining expert knowledge than a Task Force but not as good as a Functional Organization etc.)	• Honest representation of the blend between the routine and the unique aspects of the work of real organizations.	• Conflict and stress associated with members reporting to two or more managers. • Poor team identity. • Additional costs associated with 'doubling up' of managers associated with function and project.

MAKING THE MATRIX WORK

How then are the problems of the Matrix to be overcome? The solution does not lie in structure. As suggested the Matrix is an incoherent structure. To address its shortcomings we must look to other aspects of the organizations, specifically the behaviour of the incumbents and how they seek to influence each other. Such aspects are best addressed in the context of organizational culture and the next chapter addresses this.

OTHER MATRIX OPTIONS

Implicit within the descriptions above is the assumption that the two types of organizational structure combined with the Matrix are defined by the roles, i.e. whether they are responsible for a function or a task. This is the most important scenario and the only one addressed in the text above but it should be acknowledged that there are other scenarios that give rise to Matrix Organizations, for instance geography.

Consider an international company that has facilities in a number of different countries. Collectively these different facilities form a coherent structure that allows the organization to offer a full range of functions, even though each country on its own may offer a limited functional capability. From a legal perspective, however, these organizations need to be companies incorporated in their host country and this requires them to have a local authority structure. An incumbent can find themselves reporting to their functional manager who may be located in another country and yet have a line manager located in the same building.

Further, this introduces the prospect of a Matrix of multiple dimensions. The author recalls working on a project being managed in one country, belonging to a function that was managed in a second country, whilst having to report for legal reasons to a director of his host country; a three-dimensional Matrix in action.

This complexity is an increasing aspect of organizations as globalization gathers pace and is largely facilitated by sophisticated electronic-based communication and the evolution of Virtual Teams. In turn this is creating some very real challenges for organizations.

Reference

Weber M., 1947. Legitimate Authority and Bureaucracy. In D.S. Pugh, ed., 1990. *Organizational Theory Selected Readings*. London: Penguin Group. Ch. 1.

Chapter 3
The Clash of Cultures Within a Matrix

In contrasting Functional and Task Force Organizations it is straightforward to point out the harder, structural aspects which differentiate between them, and hence the different types of work they are best suited to, as we have done in the previous chapter. However, to fully appreciate the differences between these two types it is necessary to look a little deeper and specifically at softer behavioural aspects, and hence the type of people who are attracted to each.

The reality is that these different types of organization operate in different environments, respond to different types of challenges and represent different paradigms. They pose very different attractions and detractions to potential members. Accordingly, we can expect each will attract like-minded people.

The effect of this over time is that very different sets of attitudes, instincts and behaviour emerge within the two organizations that are not revealed simply by reference to an organizational chart. These softer aspects are encompassed within the expression 'culture' and the two organizations nurture profoundly different cultures.

An understanding of these different cultures not only assists in the understanding of Task Force and Functional Organizations, but of the Matrix also. This is the case because the Matrix represents not only a hybrid of structures, but a hybrid of cultures too.

Task-Orientated Culture

PHILOSOPHY

What is the purpose of a group defined within a Task Force Organization?

It can only be to complete the task.

Once this is achieved there is no reason for the group to exist. The ethos can therefore be summarized as 'deliver and disband' and this is entirely consistent with the temporary and transient aspects of projects.

To satisfy this ultimate purpose, the commercial imperative becomes one of effectiveness. By this, the focus is on doing what is necessary to make this one endeavour successful, and negate that which would threaten this outcome. In such an 'all or nothing' scenario, mitigation of risks that threaten the overall endeavour tends to be of more concern than achieving localized efficiencies.

As stated in Chapter 1, all projects ultimately deliver some kind of change and so it is not surprising that a willingness to embrace change and innovation is often associated with cultural aspects of groups delivering such work. Indeed, since they exist only for the duration of the project, there is no loyalty to a past way of working nor commitment to a future way of working. This leaves them free to innovate and embrace whatever is necessary to deliver the task at hand.

In these respects, the efforts of the group are very much aligned to the specific requirements of the customer, and the team delivering the task often enjoy a very strong rapport. On the positive side, this perception of a 'customer-focused team' provides great comfort to the ultimate owner of the product in question. This can however have some drawbacks. In extremis it can be perceived that some team members can 'go native' and become more loyal to the customer's interests rather than their employer (the product can sometimes offer better long-term prospects to technical experts than the organization creating it).

NATURE OF THE WORK

Although projects are one-off endeavours they are long-cycle activities. Whereas each washing machine took less than a day to create, the Olympic stadium will take years. The former is a short cycle, the latter a long cycle.

In the first instance, the production line starts again each day with new products and what happened yesterday has little relevance. In the second example, the work of each day builds on that created previously and will support that which will be done tomorrow. This imposes a huge obligation for forward thinking and planning and an ability to defer satisfaction of completion. Discipline, dedication and patience are the order of the day.

Also, with the best will in the world, after all this dedicated and patient preparation, sometimes the task is not successful. As stated earlier, projects are very risky endeavours. It is difficult to overestimate just how sickening it can be to devote months or years of work to an endeavour that ultimately fails. A willingness to buy into this gamble is a fundamental trait of the culture.

The risk of failure is often directly attributable to the uniqueness of project work and in particular the uncertainty that this generates and how it inhibits a rule-based approach to management.

To many, the challenge of doing something new and making decisions uninhibited by rules is exhilarating. To others it is the stuff of nightmares, especially without the support and advice of 'old hands' further along the learning curve (pure task-orientated cultures do not retain them).

STABILITY OF DEMAND

The demand for resources within a project is unstable.

Those engaged in this work must respond in terms of the design of the organization (to facilitate the 'revolving door' discussed earlier), the techniques adopted, and also in the culture of the individuals.

The expression 'feast or famine' is often used to describe the workload within a task-orientated culture whereby, often, the demand is seemingly either too much or too little but never just right. There must be an acceptance of the need to 'pull out all the stops' at times (including sacrifice of weekends and evenings), but also recognition that there are times when there will be very little to do. (It is a difficult task to explain to someone steeped in a function-orientated culture that it is acceptable for personnel in a task-orientated culture to spend protracted periods of time 'at work' but 'on the bench' and allowed to simply read the newspaper or otherwise amuse themselves. Such inefficiency is anathema to them.)

Similarly, those who embrace task-orientated cultures accept the lack of job security. Many workers within these are 'contractors' whose careers consist of a sequence of short-term assignments. In many ways these people are the epitome of task-cultured individuals. Not only are they happy to undergo an interview in the morning with the prospect of being appointed and working at a desk in the afternoon, but will do so with minimal termination notice.

Good 'contractors' are prized for their ability to quickly assimilate to new scenarios, working patterns and peer groups whereby they can swiftly settle into productive activity and start adding value almost immediately.

This requires the new incumbent to be technically competent since, whereas a Functional Organization will consider investing in training of recruits, a Task Force Organization will not. Why should they when they can simply buy in a fully trained incumbent for the brief period, albeit at a slightly higher rate?

INCENTIVIZATION

The absence of any job security or long-term commitment beyond the current task is reflected in the reward and incentive schemes typically involved. Parties (individuals or sub-groups) are typically engaged on a contract basis that lasts only for the duration of the task. Reimbursement methods are usually simple and revolve around a rate, often a generous rate, based on a 'piece-rate basis' and perhaps even accompanied by a completion bonus. Employees are encouraged to work hard and fast but they are not encouraged to hang around afterwards.

CAREER PROSPECTS

Task Force Organizations offer very little in terms of promotions and a clear career progression, certainly in comparison to a functional structure.

This is largely due to their chaotic and unstable nature but it is also related to the lesser focus on specialist knowledge. Whilst specialist knowledge is valued, within a project team there is often little tolerance of prima donna behaviour. Members who do what is needed to get the job done, regardless of what their formal job description is, are generally highly valued. Many readers will be familiar with the expression 'a jack of all trades and a master of none'. Whilst there are obvious limits to this approach, especially when addressing complex and potentially dangerous projects, it does convey the flexibility, adaptability and 'can-do' attitude that is valued with project workers.

Function-Orientated Culture

PHILOSOPHY

What is the purpose of a group defined within a Functional Organization?

The equivalent question for a Task Force Organization was straightforward but it is not so clear-cut for a Functional Organization.

Functional Organizations are associated with the delivery of routine operations, i.e. short-cycle procedures repeated for numerous and identical products. Our washing machine factory is a typical example, but what is the purpose of the factory? It is not simply 'to make washing machines' since, if it became more profitable to manufacture televisions, it is likely that the owner would choose to do that instead (the Shell oil company started in business importing sea shells). Ultimately, manufacturing organizations are concerned with the making of money, but it is not just short-term profit. Such organizations also invest in training and preventative maintenance, all of which have a negative impact on short-term profit, but critically will increase the likelihood of making profit in the future. The overarching requirement of these organizations is not only to make a profit in the short term but to sustain the ability to do that into the future. Accordingly, the imperative becomes 'survival of the organization'.

Organizations will ultimately sacrifice a favoured product to ensure the survival of an organization. This is a characteristic of almost all successful commercial organizations, they are prepared to adapt to survive but the key thing is that survival is more important than loyalty to any product. In this sense we can see that they are diametrically opposed to a task-orientated culture and their 'deliver and disband' ethos.

There is a huge irony here because although there is a need to adapt over the long term to ensure survival, the function-orientated culture is characterized by its resistance to change in the short term.

Although the washing machine production line could be changed to one manufacturing televisions, in practice this will represent a major and hugely expensive change. Production lines, by their very nature, are designed to create just one type of product and once the investment has been made, there will be a huge commitment to sustaining it and any change will be strongly resisted.

NATURE OF THE WORK

The workers on the production line will do the same work as yesterday and will do the same tomorrow; another day, another washing machine.

The short-cycle repetitive, low risk, rule-based environment stands in stark contrast to that of a task-orientated culture. This stability and consistency often enables the 'de-skilling' of positions; incumbents need not understand, they need to just follow the instructions.

To many, the comfort and security this offers is very appealing, for others it is an horrendous prospect.

STABILITY OF DEMAND

Aggregation of many short-cycle repetitions creates a very stable and predictable resource demand. For instance the demand for washing machine packers is the same today as it was yesterday as it will be next week.

In these circumstances it is possible to create a resource pool that fits very closely to the demand, with very little surplus. One consequence of this is that working hours and rotas are very stable. A second is that minimal surplus renders the operation very efficient in its use of resources. This is in contrast with the project environment where resource utilization is often surprisingly inefficient.

It is important that it is so since, in the stable and mature market for washing machines, cost of production is a major point of competition and there is much focus on efficiency. Efficiency is often more of an immediate concern than the risk of a washing machine not performing. In a project environment the reverse is true and the risk of overall failure is usually more of an immediate concern than any local efficiency.

INCENTIVIZATION

In keeping with the survival aims of the organization, share ownership schemes, pension schemes, loyalty bonuses and health schemes are all commonplace and each encourages employees to commit to the organization into the long term.

Further, Functional Organizations provide excellent environments for learning and training opportunities which can be a major attraction to potential recruits (graduate training schemes, for instance).

CAREER PROSPECTS

The stability and permanence of Functional Organizations provide an opportunity for an established career path. Working your way up the organization hierarchy is a realistic aim.

This can be a long-term gamble, especially in smaller organizations, since opportunities may not come along very often and promotion may be into 'dead men's shoes'. However the path upwards is clear.

In organizations that celebrate stability, promotion can be as much a recognition of long service as recognition of managerial potential. Further, in a true Functional Organization, such linear promotion ensures that the manager and team share a functional expertise. For this reason, one's manager used to (and probably still can) do your job. This is often in contrast to a Task Force structure where the chances of a manager and subordinate sharing a function is far less likely.

Also, in an organization that resists change, those members who think beyond the confines of the Functional group, for instance by promoting new ways of working, are often thought of as mavericks and not necessarily favoured by their peers. There is an enormous irony here since these cross-functional instincts are the very qualities needed by those who reach the uppermost reaches of the Functional structure, yet those who exhibit them lower down are often 'weeded out' of the organization by their own promotion policies.

SUMMARY OF CONTRASTS BETWEEN POLEMIC CULTURES

These contrasts between the two cultures are summarized in Table 3.1.

Table 3.1 Contrast of task-orientated and function-orientated cultures

	Function-orientated culture	Task-orientated culture	Notes
		Philosophy	
Purpose	Survival of the organization	Deliver and disband	The organizations, and hence cultures, are fundamentally different
Commercial imperative	Efficiency (cost reduction)	Effectiveness (reduce risk of failure)	In a project environment, cost of failure, and the risk thereof, generally eclipses any short-term efficiencies
Attitude to change	Very averse	Raison d'être, natural habitat, procedures in place to manage this	Very significant!
Customer focus/responsiveness	Medium/poor	Good	The 'big picture' perspective of the customer is more obvious to those in a Task Force structure
		Nature of work	
Type of work most suited to	Routine operations	Projects	
Risk of 'getting it wrong' (in terms of the product)	Low	High	Consequence of a project's 'uniqueness'
How check acceptability of product	Compare to previous examples. Established tests. Reliance on systems (checking)	Reliance on individuals' perceptions of what it should look like (thinking)	When making a unique product, there is no 'norm' to compare it to. Far greater reliance on diligence of staff
Authority referred to on technical matters	Supervisor	Peer group	In a functional organization the supervisor is an experienced specialist in the function in question
Position on learning curve	End	Beginning	This is associated with the high degree of uncertainty associated with project work

Table 3.1 Continued

	Function-orientated culture	Task-orientated culture	Notes
	Nature of work (cont.)		
Attitude to rules/procedures	Gospel	Advisory	There are limits to the 'procedurizing' of project-related work
Purpose of rules/procedures/techniques	Exert control. Substitution for expertise or wisdom of operative. Avoid operator having to think	Tool to be selected and used by craftsman at their own discretion	Those working on unique products must be afforded a high degree of discretion
	Organization		
Production cycle	Short and repeated	Long and a one-off	Projects can last many years. Routine operations typically last a matter of hours
Stability of structure	Stable/dependable	Transient/variable, constant state of flux/shifting sand/organized chaos	A direct consequence of the repetition of non-project work
Basis of departmentalization	Function (verb)	Task (noun)	This is consistent with the classic Matrix structure
Number engaged	Constant	Variable	Consistent with the 'revolving door' aspect of Task Force Organizations
Responsiveness	Slow	Fast	The presence of rule-based governance is one feature that inhibits the response time of Functional Organizations
Activity levels	Constant	Always changing/'feast and famine'	It is normal for staff engaged in projects to alternate from being over-worked, to under-worked

Table 3.1 Continued

	Function-orientated culture	Task-orientated culture	Notes
		Personnel	
Favoured attributes in employees	Steady, reliable, conformity, does as told	Adaptable, high energy, ideas source/originality, imagination	Different organizations attract very different people
Incentives	Health schemes, pensions (encourage long service)	Completion bonus (encouraged to leave)	A direct consequence of the 'Purpose' addressed above
Job security	High	Low ('building pharaoh's tomb')	A direct consequence of the 'Purpose' addressed above
Terms of engagement	Salaried	Contractors	Consistent with the permanence of the two types of organization
Organization's features attractive to employees	Dependable Defined hours/effort Stable environment Career structure Training/plan/develop for future	Exciting Challenging New and varied demands Breadth of involvement Creativity	Different people are attracted to different types of organizations

A Clash of Cultures

Both of these cultures are represented in the Matrix, and inevitably they will clash.

- Consider a well-established functional manager, probably older, a true expert in how the functional techniques have been deployed over the last 20 years. How will he respond to some project co-ordinator, probably younger, perhaps not long out of college, insisting that these previous practices upon which his reputation and authority are based are not compatible with the new product as specified by the customer?

- Consider an eager project co-ordinator wanting some individuals to work late, on overtime rates, to achieve a critical delivery milestone. How will they respond when, despite there being money in the project budget, the functional manager refuses on the basis that it will set a dangerous precedent for others in the department also wanting overtime?

- Consider a 'contractor' being employed on a short-term 'no-notice' basis to assist on a specific project. How will the permanent workers feel when they learn that, despite their years of dedication to the company, their salary is equivalent to a lower daily rate than the new arrival?

- Consider a functional manager faced with a looming under-utilization of their resource and asking for a new order to be released for manufacture. How will they respond if the project co-ordinator for the new order refuses permission on the basis that the client has not conveyed approval of the design?

In each of these situations, the instincts of those individuals steeped in a function-orientated culture will take them in the opposite direction to the instincts of those steeped in a task-orientated culture. In each instance submitting fully to one or the other will cause significant problems.

MAKING THE MATRIX WORK

How are these problems to be overcome? A number of approaches are suggested.

Recognition of the Inherent Flaws

A precursor to an effective operation within a Matrix is to recognize that it is flawed.

The unitary chain of command associated with both the Functional and Task Force Organization is compromised. Despite everyone's best efforts there will still be inconsistencies, failures and contradictions within the system authority structure and incumbents must learn a degree of tolerance.

Within bureaucracies, especially functional bureaucracies, you may not like where you stand but at least you do know where you stand. By contrast, within a Matrix, life maybe exciting and varied but you are never really sure where you stand and where your obligations end.

Respect Different Cultures

In the same way that harmony is achieved in a multi-cultural society only if each respects the culture of others, within a Matrix, harmony is reliant upon an acceptance and respect of other cultures.

Project managers must have a respect for the production manager's need for early notice and minimizing of any changes or disruptions.

Production mangers must have a respect for the project manager's need to respond to the particular wishes of a client, even if it disrupts existing manufacturing arrangements.

Avoid Total Reliance on Formal Authority

Chapter 2 described how the pattern of hierarchical structures is based upon the devolution of formal authority. However, as also mentioned, formal authority is not the sole method of influencing people within an organization.

Other factors can be brought into play and we can exert influence over others by using our personality, our charisma, our powers of persuasion.

Figure 3.1 offers a description of the Matrix that includes this aspect. In this, formal authority flows downwards, as indicated by the 'Authority Vector'.

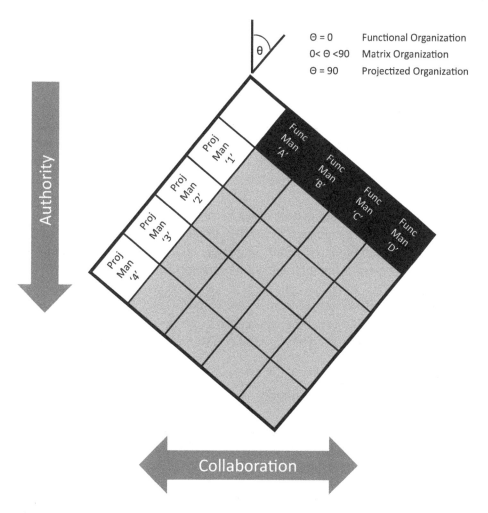

Figure 3.1   Exerting influence within a Matrix structure
Source: Adapted from Wearne (1993).

The organization is represented by the two-dimensional matrix, and its position along the 'Organizational Continuum' is indicated by the value of the angle theta. If theta is 0º then all of the formal authority flows through the functional managers and the result is a pure Functional Organization. If, however theta is 90º then all of the formal authority flows through the task (project) managers, and the result is a pure Task Force Organization. If theta is anywhere between these two extremes, then the result is a Matrix structure.

The influencing by dint of charisma and persuasion is recognized in a 'Collaboration Vector' lying at right angles to the 'Authority Vector', and flowing left to right for project managers and right to left for functional managers. It crosses the lines of formal authority and is consistent with the Type B communication discussed in Chapter 2.

The influence to be secured from collaboration complements that derived from formal authority and successful Matrix Organizations contain managers that are proficient in the use of such soft skills. Further, they are populated by workers who are receptive to such approaches, and will not simply rely on formal authority associated with a linear chain of command.

Readers are encouraged to consider the importance of the soft skills required of project managers in Matrix Organizations, in the light of this. Projects are ultimately delivered by people, and if project managers cannot influence people they simply will not be successful.

As we shall discuss in Part 4, the value of very many of the project management skills are best appreciated by the degree to which they facilitate collaboration. This is particularly the case with the planning techniques discussed.

Match Responsibility and Authority

There is no point in holding someone responsible for that over which they have no authority. I cannot be held responsible for the weather tomorrow if I do not have the authority to influence it.

This much is obvious yet very many Weak Matrix Organizations hold the project co-ordinator solely responsible for the performance of the project, even though they are offered minimal authority over it. Similarly, authority without responsibility is destructive within an organization.

Whatever type of Matrix is selected (i.e. whatever angle of theta) there must be a consistency whereby responsibility for success or failure is apportioned in the same measure as authority.

Reference

Wearne, S., 1993. *Principles of Engineering Organization*, 2nd edn. London: Thomas Telford.

Chapter 4

The Life of a Project

Like projects, our own lives are only temporary. We are born and then, sometime later, we will die. But again, like projects, we are transient: we change throughout our lives.

Our physical strength, for instance, changes. As newborn babies we have very little strength (apart from the lungs!) but as we are nourished and exercise, our strength grows. It grows throughout adolescence, reaches a maximum in early adulthood, and then starts to decline through middle age, slowly at first but perhaps a little faster in our later years.

Consider the amount of help and support we need from others. This is the opposite to the above, being very high in our early years, dropping to very little in our adult years, before rising dramatically as we pass into old age. We can represent these trends pictorially (see Figure 4.1).

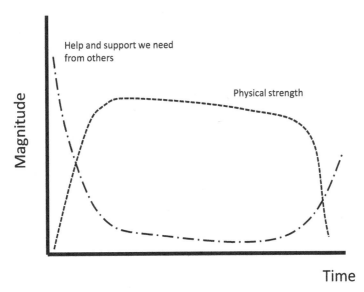

Figure 4.1   Trends during our own lifecycle

Even though each of us is unique, these (and other) changes apply to us all and an awareness of them allows us to predict the future with some confidence, and hence to manage our own lives a little better. For instance, these two changes show the wisdom of pensions and the need to put aside some resources during our productive years to cater for our later years.

The same applies to projects. Each is unique, but the changes over its life are not and, by studying previous projects, it allows us to understand, and manage, projects better.

Consider the following.

How Projects Change Throughout Their Life

The following significant trends of a project over time are the principal examples of the transient aspects of projects discussed in Chapter 1.

RATE OF EXPENDITURE

The rate at which we spend money, i.e. the amount of money spent per day, per week, per month, changes throughout the life of a project. Further, since most of the money we spend on projects is ultimately spent on reusable resources, predominantly people[1] (either directly or indirectly via suppliers) the trend of the parameter 'Total Number of People Engaged on Project' follows the same shape as the trend of 'Rate of Expenditure'.

Consider a project like the 2012 Olympic Games in London. When the decision was made to put in a bid for the Games very few people were involved. Having made this decision, many more were involved subsequently in writing up the bid. However, this number was tiny compared to the huge number of people engaged in the subsequent planning and designing of the new facilities. In turn this huge number was dwarfed by the colossal numbers involved in constructing the facilities. However, one year after the Games, how many are engaged? A very small number.

This pattern of an initially upward arching curve that levels out at a maximum after about two thirds of its duration, before undergoing a dramatic

---

1   Ultimately, all expenditure is for the engagement of people since all material comes out of the ground (either mined or harvested) and at this point is free of charge.

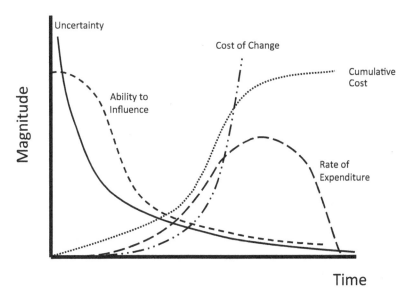

Figure 4.2   Trends during a project lifecycle

drop-off, is characteristic of projects. It can be described as a bell curve that is distorted to the right (see Figure 4.2).

This demonstrates that the busiest time of the project, when most of the money and most of the human effort is being spent, is actually in the later parts of a project.

Although the parameter 'Total Number of People Engaged on Project' follows the same trend, it should be acknowledged that this understates the volatility of the resource demand. If we were to disaggregate this total into the individual types of resources we would see a more complete and complex picture of the project team continuously changing in its make-up as different sub-groups joined and left the project. This 'revolving door' aspect of those organizations that deliver projects has enormous implications for the dynamics of the team and also the practicalities of resource management discussed in Chapter 15.

CUMULATIVE EXPENDITURE

The rate of expenditure should not be confused with the 'total spent so far', known as the 'cumulative expenditure'.

This is the sum of all costs up to that date; the amount that we have spent in this time period, plus the amount we have spent in all the preceding periods.[2]

The graph for this parameter is a very characteristic shallow S-shape and is often referred to as an 'S-curve'.[3] The cumulative expenditure (both planned and actual) features very heavily in the planning and control of projects, for example, within the Earned Value Management technique.

COST OF IMPLEMENTING CHANGES

Consider again the construction of the new Olympic stadium, and imagine making a change whereby the stadium is to be relocated 18 inches to the east. What would be the cost implication of this, if the change was effected?

- When the decision to bid for the Games was made?

- When the plans were finalized?

- When the foundations were concluded?

- When the stadium was complete?

- Six months before the opening ceremony?

The costs associated with making a change depend upon when in the life of the project the change is initiated. The later it is, the more work there is that will need to be corrected, so, as can be seen in Figure 4.2, the relationship is represented by a dramatically upward arching curve.

It is well that anyone involved in projects is familiar with this curve. It demonstrates how a change, even a modest change, when implemented in the early parts of a project, can have minimal implications and yet, making the same change later in the project, can be wholly ruinous to the whole endeavour.

---

2   For the mathematically minded it is the integral of the earlier curve (area under the curve) and its gradient, or steepness is equal to the value of the previous curve, at any individual point in time.

3   The name derives from 'S' being an abbreviation for 'Summation', since these curves are most properly referred to as 'Summation Curves'. This explains why, very often, real 'S-curves' do not look much like an 'S'. The important features are, firstly, that it is always ascending (the cumulative expenditure never reduces) and, secondly, the gradient, on a large scale, is shallow–steep–shallow, even though locally, on a finer scale, there may be some variation in gradient.

The mechanism whereby changes are so destructive, and hence why they must be managed, is such that it warrants careful attention and Chapter 11 is dedicated to this purpose.

ABILITY TO EXERT INFLUENCE

When, in the life of a project, is it most important to 'get things right'?

Unsurprisingly, it is the inverse of, and wholly influenced by, the 'cost of implementing change'. Because the cost of change 'sky-rockets' upwards in the later stages of a project, the rationale and opportunity for such changes diminishes.

Therefore, the ability to influence a project is very high at the start of the project but drops off dramatically as plans are enacted (see Figure 4.2).

Many project managers still greatly over-exaggerate their ability to influence events late in a project. The practical reality is that once enactment of the plan commences, the 'die is cast'. The corollary of this is perhaps the most important perspective, namely, to influence a project one must maximize the efforts at the start of the project, during its conception and planning.

This logic extends to any phase, work package, fragment or task within a project. There is nothing cheaper and quicker than 'getting it right first time around' when implementing the project, however 'getting it right first time around' requires time, money and effort to be invested at the start.

Failure to sufficiently conceive and plan a project results in an ever-increasing number of problems emerging during the later stages, with a consequential ever-increasing demand for the project management resource. Such a scenario can be described as 'Crisis Management' and is a depressingly frequent reality for projects.

UNCERTAINTY

Chapter 1 described how the project environment is characterized by a high degree of uncertainty, however this level of uncertainly does not remain constant throughout the project. It follows a trend whereby it is very high at the very beginning and drops off exponentially during the project lifecycle (see Figure 4.2).

The rate at which this uncertainty is reduced is not just a feature of the project and its inherent characteristics, but also the skill of the project manager.

Good project managers are always striving to reduce the amount of uncertainty as much as possible, as quickly as possible; to pull the shape of the curve downwards.

The optimum scenario is to pull the curve into a right angle whereby, at the very start of the project, all uncertainty disappears. This, of course, is the reality of those engaged in routine operations, such as the assembly of the washing machines when, at the outset, everything is already known. This is not a realistic prospect for projects. By their very nature it is not possible to remove so much uncertainty so quickly. However, that is not an excuse not to try.

Almost all of the efforts of project management can be described in terms of how they seek to reduce this amount of uncertainty. This gradual and managed erosion of the uncertainty is sometimes referred to as 'progressive elaboration'. A consequence of this is, that as the project manager takes the project forward, they are able to offer estimates of parameters, such as final cost and duration, with increasing precision.

Strategic Control of Projects

The interplay between the 'ability to exert influence' and 'uncertainty' provides a very valuable insight into projects, the difficulties they pose and how crucial the early stages are.

It shows that the decisions that exert most influence over the project are made at the very time when uncertainty is at its highest, and hence most likely to be erroneous.

This simple fact explains why projects are so difficult to manage.

It also provides the rationale for so many project management techniques but perhaps the most significant of these is the use of Decision Gates.

THE RATIONALE FOR DECISION GATES

Consider being asked to endorse a proposed project to develop a new product.

Reject the project and you may be depriving yourselves of a very profitable new revenue stream.

Sanction it and you may be committing to a very expensive and damaging white elephant.

No decision made later in the project will have a greater impact and yet this is the time of highest uncertainty, when the key pieces of information that will indicate the final costs and benefits of the project are known in only the vaguest terms.

This represents a significant risk to the organizations that sponsor projects since there is a high likelihood that the chosen decision will be the wrong one, not due to any incompetence on behalf of the decision-maker, but because the information has such high uncertainty associated with it.

Reducing the uncertainty requires work to start on the project but this will consume precious money and resources, the waste of which the decision, fundamentally, is trying to avoid. However, basing the decision on such uncertain data carries enormous risk.

This represents an inescapable conundrum to sponsors of projects and the appropriate response is to proceed by a series of 'Decision Gates'.

Here, the word 'gate' is interpreted in a very literal sense. The project cannot pass through a gate without stopping and opening it, and this can only be done with the permission of the gatekeeper.

By these, permission for the project to proceed is given, but only sufficient funding is released to allow the project to proceed up to some defined point in the near future, at which time the decision whether to proceed will be reviewed.

As we have seen, the costs associated with the early stages of the project are relatively low, in stark contrast to the erosion of uncertainty which is fastest at this time. Consequently, when, at some later point, the decision to approve

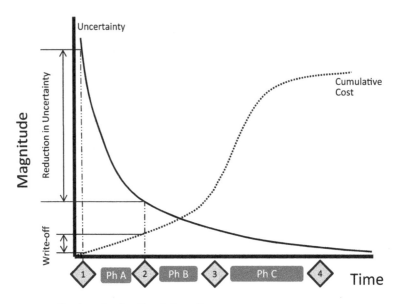

Figure 4.3   Rationale for Decision Gates

the project is reviewed, it will be with the benefit of significantly superior information and after only modest expenditure (see Figure 4.3).

It may well be that the erosion of uncertainty about the likely costs and benefits[4] reinforces the rationale for the project in which case it can progress to the next Decision Gate.

Alternatively, the erosion of uncertainty may wholly undermine the rationale for the project, in which case it must be stopped.

Such early termination is not necessarily a symptom of poor project management. More often than not the reverse is true.

For an organization, it is more important to ensure that they manage the right projects than it is to manage a project well. Proceeding in the manner described, with the robust use of Decision Gates, is the safest way of protecting its investments.

---

4   The decision made at the gates involves the marginal benefit and marginal cost. Actual expenditure to date is ignored on the basis that it is a 'sunk cost' and cannot be recovered in any case. This is a reason why, especially at the later Decision Gates, a project may be continued with, even though the total benefits may be exceeded by the total costs.

However, in practice, strong management is required to enforce these decisions because, understandably, early termination can be emotionally challenging; often akin to putting the family pet to sleep.

Project teams and managers must be tenacious, persistent and wholly committed to the success of a project, otherwise they will not prevail. Sustaining this whilst simultaneously maintaining the neutrality required for objective decisions about whether the project is viable, is an unpleasant conflict of interest.

This conflict of interest is one reason why projects are controlled at two levels – a strategic and a tactical level – and have both a sponsor and a project manager.

THE DESIGN OF A 'PROJECT LIFECYCLE' MODEL

The divisions of work between the Decision Gates are known as 'phases' and the series of phases and Decision Gates are known, collectively, as the project's 'lifecycle'.

The design of the lifecycle model is directed by the need to abort unattractive projects as early as possible and to minimize the expenditure that may have to be written off.

This can be achieved by minimizing the period between the Decision Gates but since each requires the updating of the business case and the reconvening of the steering group or executive board, there are practical limits to the frequency of Decision Gates that a project can accommodate. Also, overly frequent Decisions Gates have the effect of 'micro-managing' the project manager.

A compromise is therefore required and early in the project the 'gatekeepers' will identify when they want the Decision Gates to occur. Also, they will decide what information (and hence documents) and deliverables they wish to have available at each of those Decision Gates. This will be done with a view to defer spending on expensive work as late as possible, whilst simultaneously reducing the uncertainty as quickly as possible. This will both improve the quality of early decisions and minimize any write-off cost (see Figure 4.3). Accordingly, inexpensive measures that dramatically reduce uncertainty, such as feasibility reports, are associated with the early Decision Gates.

The items required at each Decision Gate are created in the preceding phase. They are known as 'phase products' and they define the work required within the phases. Early phases will have 'phase products' such as investigation reports, the mid-point phases will have designs and plans, and the later phases, the actual project deliverables.

STRATEGIC AND TACTICAL CONTROL OF PROJECTS

Lifecycle models assist organizations to differentiate between 'strategic' and 'tactical' control over projects.[5] 'Strategic control' is exercised by the sponsor and project steering group (the gatekeepers) at the Decision Gates. It is concerned primarily with the protection of the sponsoring organization.

'Tactical control' is the day-to-day control of work within the individual phases, exercised by the project manager.

The former is more important than the latter. It provides the ultimate sanction and without it misconceived projects, perhaps with the potential to bring down the whole of the sponsoring organization, cannot be cut away. History offers many examples of the consequences of such failure.

As well as the project itself, strategic control will consider its commercial environment and the other projects being sponsored by the organization. Sometimes the strategy of a sponsoring organization changes such that the output of the project is no longer required; sometimes the innovation of a competitor renders a project redundant; sometimes it is better to divert the limited resources of an organization in pursuit of a more attractive project. Each of these are reasons to terminate a project even when, intrinsically, it is in good shape.

In addition to deciding whether to proceed or not with the project, Decision Gates offer senior management an opportunity to verify the tactical control of the project manager, for instance by checking that all phase deliverables have been completed to a satisfactory degree. In this respect the gates can start to become an exercise in progress evaluation, and whilst a degree of this is inevitable, care should be taken to prevent the steering group being drawn into a level of detail that can and should be managed by the project manager.

---

5   Further detailed analysis and comparison of strategic and tactical control is offered in Chapter 16.

STRATEGIC PLAN

A well-conceived lifecycle is best thought of as a strategic plan. It becomes a link between those commissioning and those executing the project and is an important element of an organization's project governance.

Once established it allows the steering group to step back and let the project manager and team get on with the tactical management of the project.

For the project manager, it also allows them to let go of the bigger picture and manage the project one phase at a time; an altogether more manageable parcel of work. This is particularly relevant for large projects that may last many years.

It is important therefore that the lifecycle is well conceived.

THE LIFECYCLE AS THE BASIS OF A 'METHOD'

Many organizations are established not just to deliver one project, but a series of projects, for example a construction company. Very often these projects are sufficiently similar to each other that the same lifecycle, or strategic plan, can be applied to each.

This offers many potential advantages to an organization. These advantages are associated with economies of scale (each project does not have to design their own), speed of initiation (the strategic plan is already there), familiarity and consistency (everyone in the organization already understands the process and their role), ease of comparison of projects, and it also aids the adoption of 'lessons learned' from previous projects by refining what should be done and when.

Many organizations choose to maximize the potential for these benefits by supplementing the common lifecycle with standard forms, documents, roles and responsibilities and the like. The combined effect of these is that they become a protocol that lays out how a project is to be delivered. This protocol is known as a project management method (sometimes as a 'methodology').

Readers may wish to observe that the adoption of such a method serves to reduce the 'uniqueness' of the project and has the effect of moving it downwards in the continuum offered in Figure 1.1. Potentially, this offers many advantages but again the caveat remains that all projects are unique and there are limits to how far the same approach can be applied to different projects. Many readers will have experienced the intense frustration of being obliged to follow a management protocol which is simply inappropriate for their project. It can be disastrous.

For this reason, each method tends to apply only to one specific environment. Publicly available methods are available, e.g. PRINCEII, but most methods are specific to projects within just one type of industry (e.g. the Guide to Railway Investment Projects (GRIP) in the UK rail sector), or projects just within the one company.

In practice there is a great skill involved in designing a 'method' that is sufficiently rigid such that the desired benefits can accrue, and yet remain sufficiently flexible such that it can be applied easily to a number of different projects.

GENERIC LIFECYCLE MODELS

As implied above, there is some latitude in the precise design of a project lifecycle model and different practitioners choose to 'slice and dice' projects differently.[6]

This becomes evident when considering projects in just one sector of industry or commerce; in just one organization; or indeed just one type of project. When considering such a subset of projects it is possible to tailor the lifecycle model to the specifics that appertain.

However, behind this is a broad pattern and flow of activities that is common to all projects, so much so that we can entertain the idea of a generic lifecycle model; one that can be applied to all projects.

The next chapter describes such a model.

---

6   There is again an analogy to our own lives. Shakespeare once famously wrote about the 'Seven Ages of Man' and yet Hinduism talks about the four stages of man. Each is describing the same life; the same journey from cradle to grave, and yet they choose to decompose it in different ways, each to reflect their own understanding and their own emphasis.

Chapter 5
A Generic Project Lifecycle Model

This chapter is concerned with the description of a generic lifecycle of a project. Such an exercise provides a very valuable insight into the nature of projects.

Firstly, we shall consider how a project comes into being.

Genesis of a Project

Do our lives start at birth or conception?

The question is posed to indicate that, although we conveniently bracket our lifecycle with the events of birth and death, the story is a little more involved. Similarly, although we may recognize the start of the project as the signing of a formal mandate (a Business Case or a charter) there is actually a lot of work required to get to this stage.

All projects have some form of genesis when someone perceives of an opportunity or threat that should or could be addressed. However, that is not to say that all ideas become fully funded projects, and it is not to say that absolute clarity about the idea exists at this stage.

Often, responses to a number of threats or opportunities come together as one initiative. Alternatively, some fragment into a number of separate initiatives. Sometimes, different people will have different ideas and perceptions of how a specific threat or opportunity should be addressed, whilst others may view different opportunities as being more urgent. In such instances, they may launch what may be referred to as 'counter-moves' (Miller and Lessard, 2000).

Estimates and predictions made during these earliest timers are the most unreliable and imprecise and it is rarely clear which is the best way to proceed.

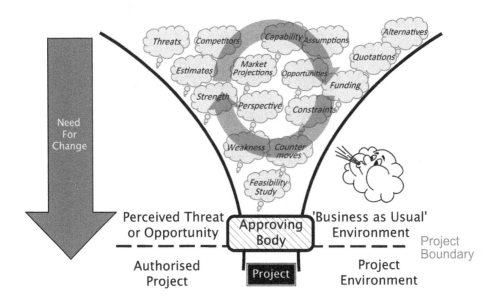

Figure 5.1   Project genesis

The chaotic nature of this early 'ideas stage' of a project is depicted in Figure 5.1 above, with competing ideas and environmental factors being stirred and churned as organizations strive to find the most advantageous way forward.

Although all projects start with this stage, most of us would not recognize that a project exists until there is an authorized budget, an appointed delivery team and a clear objective. This implies some form of approval or authorization threshold, across which the project has to pass.

Establishing the exact position of this threshold is a difficult prospect for an organization because crossing the threshold requires decisions to be made about which ideas and options to pursue. But, before an idea can be assessed, its rationale must be demonstrated. But, to demonstrate this rationale, work must be done, and this requires time and resources. But, before resources for this work can be released, authorization is required … and so the cycle repeats.

This 'chicken and egg scenario' is predominantly managed via the phases and Decision Gates of a lifecycle, as discussed in the previous chapter, but it does make it difficult to decide exactly when a project is deemed to have started.

In a practical sense, the threshold demarcates between the project environment and the 'business as usual' environment and within individual organizations is often established on the basis of which budget is being spent. After the threshold, a dedicated and authorized project budget is available, but prior to this, the early feasibility and scoping work is funded from an annual budget established by each department for initiatives they identify.

Project Lifecycle

Figure 5.2 describes the generic lifecycle model offered by the APM (2006).

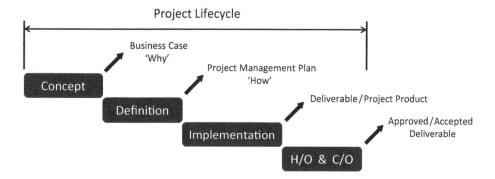

Figure 5.2   The project lifecycle
Source: Adapted from APM (2006).

Although other models exist, this model is selected for discussion because of its generic nature and hence applicability to a very wide range of projects.

It divides the project into four phases with Decision Gates in-between. Each of the four phases has an output, usually a tangible output, referred to as a phase product.

CONCEPT PHASE AND THE BUSINESS CASE

The first phase is 'Concept' and it addresses the chaotic genesis described above. Whereas the end is a very definite point, its start is vague since projects seemingly condense out of their atmosphere. Accordingly, although drawn as a solid bar for convenience, the phase is better represented as a taper, indistinguishable from its background at first but gradually becoming more definite.

The phase is dedicated to the creation of the Business Case and if we were to summarize in one word the question about the project that this document answers, it is 'why?'.

This question 'why?' is the most fundamental question that must be answered for any endeavour and for this reason the Business Case is the single most important document in any project. Everything else in the project flows from, and is dictated by, it.

If there is not a reason, a business rationale, for the project that is consistent with the overall strategy of the sponsoring organization then no matter how well it is being delivered, how enjoyable it is, how high-profile it is, it must be stopped. It is impossible to argue against this obvious logic and readers may assume, therefore, that instances of projects proceeding without a current Business Case are almost negligible – sadly, they would be very wrong in this assumption.

In a practical sense the Business Case assumes major importance by dint of the signatures it bears, since approval of the project by the project steering group is conveyed by their signing of the back page. The signed document is a mandate, empowering the project team to spend the company's resources in pursuit of the project's aims. Thus, the act of endorsing the Business Case[1] signifies the crossing of the threshold described above; the passing of the first Decision Gate of the lifecycle; and the end of the Concept phase.

The activity conducted within the Concept phase is best considered by reference to the contents of the Business Case.

Content of the Business Case

The Business Case is the ultimate project document and must facilitate authorization and control decisions. This requires the contents as follows.

Firstly, the Business Case must provide a rationale for the project. In the context of commercial projects, this is a 'cost–benefit' analysis that contrasts the cost of establishing and operating the new asset or capability, with the benefit that will accrue from its use and ownership. In doing so it must identify and

---

1   Readers may wish to note that in some countries, most notably the United States, the mandate document that bears the authorizing signatures is a 'Project Charter'. This is a standalone and separate document that will refer to a Business Case.

quantify those benefits. This is not straightforward since, whereas costs are relatively easily quantifiable, many benefits are intangible, and therefore not easily quantified. Due to the very high levels of uncertainty associated with this early period of the project, the quantification of both parameters is inevitably offered with caveats relating to risks, assumptions and constraints and it is important these are recorded so that they can be monitored.

Secondly, it is vital to establish the criteria upon which success is going to be judged. Although this will ultimately relate to the magnitude of benefits realized (less cost), it is also very helpful to identify 'success criteria' for the actual asset or capability (the project product or deliverable) being created, in terms of technical capability, cost and time to create and their relevant priority. Establishing such criteria is necessary for subsequent control of the project but also because the act of setting them focuses minds. If you do not know what success looks like then it is most unlikely that you will achieve it!

Thirdly, very often projects are not isolated endeavours. Organizations frequently deliver projects in parallel with other projects or ongoing activities within their commercial portfolio. Individual projects are often affected by and affect these other activities and this must be recognized when decisions are being made.

A summary of typical Business Case contents is offered within Table 5.1.

Table 5.1   Typical Business Case contents

The purpose of the project	To include a business rationale aligned to the organization's strategy.
Commercial justification of the project	To include an investment appraisal model containing identified and quantified benefits and costs.
	Such models will include provision for uncertainty and risks and will therefore refer to:
	• Identified risks.
	• Mitigation strategies.
	• Assumptions.
	• Constraints.
	• Dependencies.
	Investment appraisals may also contain evaluation of alternative options and hence demonstrate why the favoured option was chosen.

Table 5.1   Continued

Success criteria	Typically these will relate to duration, cost and/or performance of the product and the relative prioritization between them. (In some instances the product will be known and can be wholly technically specified at this point.)
Portfolio considerations	To include: • Relative priority of project. • Impact on ongoing business. • Dependencies on other project's outputs. • Opportunity cost.
Provisions for strategic control	To include: • Phases and phase products. • Identity of steering group and sponsor. • Stakeholder analysis and appropriate provision (this may include securing the buy-in of resource owners).
Provision for tactical control	To include preliminary and high level baseline estimates for scope, time and cost.
Signatures of steering group	The document is a mandate to spend the company's resources and so must bear authorizing signatures.

Roles Involved with the Business Case

It is far more important to ensure that the right projects are being undertaken than it is to ensure that they are being managed well and the skills and insight required to select a project are different from those required to deliver it. This is yet another reason why projects have both sponsors and project managers and it is the former who owns the Business Case and hence selects projects: they are the most important person in any project.

The sponsor will act as a champion of the project. They will be a permanent and senior person within the organization, be intimate with the organization's strategy and have sufficient influence and credibility with those in authority to take the project through the initial and subsequent Decision Gates, up to the point when the intended benefit is realized.

Although the sponsor owns the Business Case, this does not mean that they must physically write it. For a very large project, like the creation of a new power station, establishing the Business Case is an enormous task in itself and it is inconceivable that the sponsor would do it on their own. In practice it will be managed as a project in its own right with a dedicated 'project' manager and team so although the sponsor must ultimately own the result, they may not manage its creation on a day-to-day basis. To help avoid confusion, some organizations have Development Project Managers and Delivery Project Managers who are engaged before, and after, Business Case approval, respectively. There is no absolute need for the subsequent project manager to be involved before Business Case approval. The Business Case will be approved by the project steering group who are the 'gatekeepers' for this and subsequent Decision Gates.

Sub-phases

For very large projects, such as the power station discussed above, because the act of establishing the Business Case is such an enormous commitment in its own right, it will require pre-authorization.

In these instances the single Concept phase discussed is, in effect, being divided into smaller sub-phases with appropriate gates in-between. Such an approach can be appropriate for larger projects when lifecycles of more than four phases are frequently adopted.

DEFINITION PHASE AND THE PROJECT MANAGEMENT PLAN

The second phase is 'Definition' and the phase product is the 'Project Management Plan' (PMP). If we were to summarize in one word the question about the project that this document answers then the answer is 'how?'.

This document is owned by, and produced under the direction of, the project manager. It contains the output of the planning activity and so anticipates the project work to be done, the method by which this will be controlled, the time and cost that it will consume, how the team will behave and relate to each other, and the like.

Planning is synonymous with project management and its importance is such that Chapter 14 is wholly dedicated to the techniques involved.

The scope and detail of the investigation carried out in this phase leads to a dramatic reduction in uncertainty, most easily recognized by the increased precision of estimates, especially in relation to the key parameters of cost and duration. Also, the detail within the PMP will better indicate the risks and other implications of the project. This improved data is used to update the Business Case, especially the cost–benefit model.

With the superior information to hand at the Decision Gate at the end of this phase, the steering group is well placed to revisit their earlier decision as to whether it is appropriate for the project to proceed.

IMPLEMENTATION

The third phase is 'Implementation' and, having planned the work in the previous phase, this plan is now enacted to create, as a phase product, the new asset or capability. The phase is associated with managing and controlling performance against this plan and administering to any changes that may be required.

In terms of money and resources spent (see Figure 4.2), this is by far the most significant phase. However, from a purely project management point of view, it is surprisingly unimportant since, as discussed, the ability to influence the project has diminished rapidly by this stage. Only rarely can a poorly conceived and planned project be recovered in this phase.

Since the new asset will be available at the end of this phase, some may question the need for a Decision Gate. Abandoning a project at this stage would involve the writing-off of a considerable investment, but it is not unheard of. (Just because money has been spent it does not mean it is worth persevering.)

The decision more often relates to whether all the work of this phase has been completed and the timing of subsequent handover activities.

HANDOVER AND CLOSEOUT

Although this is addressed as just one phase, two separate strands of activity occur in parallel.

The activities associated with 'Handover' relate to the formal acceptance by the sponsor of the main deliverable (the new asset or capability) and its ancillaries such as documentation. If we consider a project such as that delivering a new power station, the process of accepting the asset involves very extensive testing and proving lasting many months, sometimes years.

'Closeout' activities involve disbanding of the team; disposal of the project facilities, apparatus and materials; closing accounts; and archiving data. As part of this process it is usual to carry out some reflection of how the project performed and what could be improved should a similar endeavour be embraced again. These 'lessons learned' activities, as we shall discuss, are extremely valuable to both the sponsoring organization and project personnel.

The Decision Gate is mostly concerned with ensuring that all these activities have been completed and hence allowing the formal closure of the project.

The project manager is responsible for the delivery of the new asset or capability and this point represents the conclusion of their involvement in the project. Their performance will be judged against the success criteria associated with time, cost and performance identified within the Business Case.

Extended Project Lifecycle (Product Lifecycle)

Since the project manager and the delivery team finish their involvement in the project at the end of the Handover and Closeout phase, it would seem appropriate to consider the end of the project has been reached. However in many respects the four-phase model is inadequate.

The fundamental reason that organizations invest in projects is to realize a benefit and this is not achieved during these early phases. So, whereas the four-

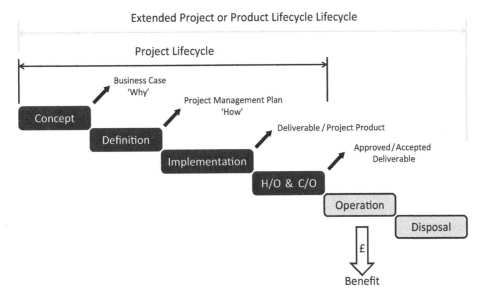

Figure 5.3   The extended project lifecycle
Source: APM (2006).

phase model is relevant to the delivery team, the perspective of the sponsoring organization requires further phases. This gives rise to the 'extended project lifecycle' (sometimes referred to as the 'product lifecycle'; see Figure 5.3 on the previous page).

This consists of six phases, the first four of which are identical to the earlier model. The two additional phases are 'Operation' and 'Termination'.

OPERATION

This phase involves the new asset or capability (the project product or deliverable) being put into operation to realize the benefit that was identified in the Business Case as being the reason for the project.

If benefits are not realized then the work to date has been a waste of time and resources.

The sponsor is ultimately responsible for the realization of this benefit and their performance will be judged on this basis.

If the asset in question is, say, a new factory then this phase will be very much longer than the sum of that required by the preceding phases.

This is usually the case but not always. Consider the project addressing an open air concert. It may take months to design and create the stage, seating and site facilities, even though the actual concert takes only a few hours.

TERMINATION

'Termination' involves the decommissioning and safe disposal of the asset. For many projects this is inconsequential and may even result in a further benefit, for example, the scrap value of machinery. For others, however, it can be the costliest phase. Consider the decommissioning of a nuclear power station.

The costs associated with such disposal should be incorporated within the cost–benefit model of the Business Case.

References

Association for Project Management (APM), 2006. *APM Body of Knowledge*, 5th edn. High Wycombe: APMKnowledge

Miller, R. and Lessard, D.R., 2000. *The Strategic Management of Large Engineering Projects Shaping Institutions, Risks and Governance*. Massachusetts: The MIT Press.

PART 2

The Perspective of the Supplier

Organization Upon Projects

Chapter 6
The Contrasting Predicaments of Owners and Suppliers

So far, we have discussed the nature of projects and the cultures and structures of the organizations that deliver them. Also, we have identified the primary objective of the project as being the realization of a benefit from the utilization of an asset or capability that is established during the initial period of the project.

Whilst this is true, for further analysis and understanding to occur we must differentiate between two types of organization, both of which are engaged in delivering the project but who are subject to very different influences.

The distinction required is between that of Owner Organizations and Supplier Organizations.

Owner Organizations: The Opportunities and Risks

Owner Organizations (OO) are those that commission the project. It is they who will own the completed asset or capability (the project's product or deliverable) and reap the reward of the benefits realized from its operation. Examples would include the local water authority commissioning a new treatment works, a car manufacturer commissioning the construction of a new factory, a bank commissioning a new IT system.

These organizations have huge freedom. Outside of their obligations to their shareholders (to increase shareholder value) and to obey relevant laws, they are free to do whatever they like and invest their resources where they please. They can choose whether or not to run any particular project and to decide what that project will encompass.

A car manufacturer may choose to build a new plant or they may choose to spend their money updating an existing one. And, if they do decide on the new plant, then they can build it within any country whose laws will allow them to do so. The options are almost boundless.

However with such freedom comes confusion. Faced with such a wide variety of choice we can foresee a situation within the organization where there is a bewildering collection of ideas and initiatives, each offering opportunities and risks, each with supporters and detractors and each competing for the company's resources. The confusion is heightened by the attendant uncertainty about the future and what it may hold, especially in terms of emerging technology, market preferences and competitors' moves.

This situation is the complex and difficult environment that accompanies the genesis of a project, described in Chapter 5. But, propelled by the commercial imperative to improve and change, eventually, through this fog of political machinations, will emerge the favoured idea; the one that offers most reward for the least consumption of resources. This comparison, quantified as a 'cost–benefit ratio', is the critical measure of any project and is the heart of the project's Business Case.

On approval of this Business Case, the Owner Organization (OO) will create and fund a dedicated 'project delivery team'; a temporary structure existing only for the duration of the project.

Despite the protection offered by the Decision Gates, it must be acknowledged that projects are very risky undertakings. The Owner Organization (OO) will see no reward until the final asset or capability is complete and operating, and hence realizing the much sought benefits. Much can, and very often will, 'go wrong'. They face two types of risk; those that affect the deliverable (new asset or capability) and those that affect the environment within which it will operate. For convenience we will refer to the former as 'product based risks' and the latter as 'Business Case based risks'.

If we consider our new car plant project suggested above, product based risks would include risks such as wrongly specified concrete being poured into the foundations requiring subsequent excavation and replacement. Such risks will impact upon the cost, duration or technical performance of the completed product.

Business Case based risks do not impact on the product but they do impact on the realization of benefits. Imagine, for instance, during the construction of the car plant another oil crisis occurred which trebled the cost of petrol causing a collapse in the demand for new cars. Accordingly, even though the new car plant may be completed ahead of time, under budget and produce cars superbly, it may well never deliver sufficient benefit due to a collapse in the market demand.

Owner Organizations (OO) are exposed to both these types of risk and their implications can be punitive.

It becomes clear that for the OO, a project is a speculative investment with no guarantee of success.

However, on the positive side, sometimes events turn out to be much more beneficial than first anticipated and, for the OO, the speculative investment can lead to it reaping a reward that greatly exceeds its hopes. Who amongst us would not have been happy to have been part of the organization that invested its resources in pursuit of the idea that telephones did not need cables?

As we have established, projects represent something different, something unique, and it is most likely that early in their lifecycle, a piece of work will be required, perhaps just a fragment of the overall project work scope, that demands specialist equipment or personnel that the Owner Organization (OO) does not possess in-house. At this point it is obliged to secure access to such resources by entering into a contract with a company that does. In doing so, we start the creation of the larger project team and the involvement of Supplier Organizations.

Supplier Organizations: The Opportunities and Risks

Typically, Supplier Organizations (SO) are permanent organizations that, over a period of time, have nurtured an expertise and capability within a specialist skill or function.

An example may be an architect's practice, and within the example of the car plant above, it may be engaged by the Owner Organization (OO) to design the building for the new facility.

Within this scenario the Supplier Organization (SO) undertakes a defined piece of work. Very often this work involves the creation of a physical product which is then delivered to the client, but it can also relate to a service, in which case the product is abstract.

Supplier Organizations (SO), therefore, are engaged in the work of a project, in collaboration with the relevant Owner Organization (OO), but this does not mean their positions are identical.

In contrast to the OO, the SO is more constrained in terms of the types of projects it becomes engaged with. Its involvement is generally predicated on its expertise in a given area, expertise largely honed over many years of experience; or alternatively, because of its access to specific apparatus or facilities (a transport company which owns a fleet of specialist vehicles, for instance). These fundamental advantages cannot be easily changed and as such Supplier Organizations (SO) seek out those projects (and hence OO) that require access to those facilities or expertise.

Consequently, their prelude to a project is different. Whereas the Owner Organization (OO) has the freedom to become involved in whatever it likes, there is a practical constraint on the Supplier Organization (SO) that means it only becomes involved in similar projects (usually those with a similar technological topic). Whereas for the OO the initial confusion and uncertainty can apply to many aspects of the project, for the SO, there is usually only little confusion over the actual technology or processes to be adopted. For the SO, its uncertainty is primarily associated with a unique client or a unique location.

Like Owner Organizations (OO), Supplier Organizations (SO) also endure a complex and difficult environment associated with the genesis of their share of the project, but, unlike the OO, this environment is a market, and their engagement with it an exercise in marketing and selling.

If successful in this endeavour the Supplier Organization (SO) is well placed to secure its reward, but its reward is different to that of the Owner Organization (OO). Rather than retaining ownership of the product and the benefits that accrue from its operation, the SO will exchange its deliverable for a consideration, i.e. payment. Its entitlement to such consideration will be established within a contract.

In many respects this makes the life of a Supplier Organization (SO) easier than that of the Owner Organization (OO) since, rather than waiting for any eventual realization of benefit, the SO need only satisfy its obligations stated within the contract[1] and it will become entitled to its reward of payment.

---

1   Some care is required here because there are some obligations of the SO that may not be explicitly stated in the contract. For instance, in any case, the SO is obliged to provide goods of 'merchantable quality' and this will confer 'implied terms' on the SO.

This immediately releases it from exposure to the Business Case based risks discussed earlier because, excepting any exotic contractual clauses, whether the OO realizes its benefit or not, it is obliged to honour the contract and pay the SO on receipt of the deliverable.

Whilst this is good news for the Supplier Organizations (SO), any rejoicing is tempered by three further aspects.

Firstly, whereas SO are generally immune to Business Case based risks, they cannot easily insulate themselves from product-based risks. Indeed, much of the reason why Owner Organizations (OO) engage Supplier Organizations (SO) in the first instance is because the SO is better able to manage the product-based risks. Most likely, the contract will be so written as to ensure that the SO is fully exposed to them, so as to insulate the OO from them.

Secondly, if the speculative investment realizes vastly more benefit than anticipated, the Supplier Organization (SO) will not benefit. It has insulated itself from this risk and that cuts both ways.

Thirdly, the Supplier Organization (SO) incurs another risk, namely that of the Owner Organization (OO) not honouring its obligations to make payment. As we shall discuss later, mitigating this risk of client default often is not straightforward.

However, being in receipt of a contract confers another advantage on the Supplier Organization (SO) and this relates to the definition of what is to be supplied. Much of the uncertainty associated with the early phases of a project is to do with defining exactly what the product will be. In committing to a contract the Owner Organization (OO) is obliged to take a view on the answer to this question. In doing so it incurs considerable commercial risk and by doing so insulates the SO from much of the risk inherent in the project. Should the OO mistakenly describe its requirements within the contract then such mistakes will need to be addressed by varying the detail of the contract. In such instances the agreement of the SO will be required, and in practice this will entitle it to compensation in the form of increased payment or a relaxation of its obligations.

This is an example of when the interests of the Owner Organization (OO) and the Supplier Organization (SO) are in opposition. Disputed changes, claims and counter-claims usually set the SO and OO in direct opposition to each other. It is not always the case, but more often than not, that the SO benefits from changes whereas the OO is harmed by them. Such is the importance of the management of changes that Chapter 11 is wholly dedicated to the topic.

CAVEAT IN RELATION TO TYPES OF SUPPLIER ORGANIZATIONS

In Chapter 1 we discussed the mass manufacture of identical, non-bespoke, standard products such as washing machines. Every project will consume some such standard products and also commodities such as raw materials.

Although, technically speaking, the suppliers of these meet the criteria for a Supplier Organization (SO), they are not the type of organization that this text is concerned with since such organizations have no need to embrace project management techniques. This is because the specification of the product is fixed. The Owner Organization (OO) will simply accept them as they are, or not, and there is no added risk exposure on behalf of the SO just because the product is to be used on a particular project.

A useful differentiator between the types of Supplier Organizations (SO) relates to the sequence of selling and creation of the product. For standard products, such as washing machines, the product is made first and then sold.

Table 6.1   Different organization types

Owner Organization	**Asset management companies, e.g. utility company** (commissioning construction of a new asset)	**Service providers, e.g. hotels** (utilizing services of other suppliers such as a grocer)
Supplier Organization	**Specialist supplier, e.g. architects, engineers, software writers** (providing bespoke products or services)	**Commodity suppliers, e.g. grocers, steel suppliers, washing machine factory** (providing non-bespoke products or services)
	Projects	**Routine operations**

Notes: 1. Organizations can occupy different locations in different instances. For example a car plant occupies the bottom right-hand quadrant in the context of supplying cars but if it was procuring a new factory it would be located in the top left. The text within the brackets clarifies the context.

   2. Although Figure 1.1 expressed the division into project and routine operations as a continuum, it is simplified here to just two classifications.

   3. Complex projects have extensive supply chains such that many Supplier Organizations (SO) that are involved in project work do not have the ultimate OO as their direct client. There may be one or more other SO in the chain, between the two parties.

For a SO supplying bespoke items, by necessity, the selling must occur first, before manufacture.

Further clarity regarding different types of organization is offered by Table 6.1, on the previous page. This text concerns those that lie on the two left-hand quadrants and in particular those within the bottom left-hand quadrant, i.e. those SO engaged in project work.

Chapter 8 offers a more detailed analysis of differing types of Supplier Organizations (SO).

Practical Divergence Between Owner Organizations and Supplier Organizations

The differences in the predicament of the two types of organization described above leads to a divergence in the practical problems faced by them, and hence their responses. The following describes the more significant of these.

Such an analysis, however, must come with the caveat that it is a generalist view that applies to most OO–SO relationships, most of the time. The precise relationship between any Supplier Organization (SO) and Owner Organization (OO) is defined within their contract and whereas the following assumes such contract terms are conventional, there is ample opportunity for the parties to conceive of, and agree to, exotic terms that seek to erode some of the aspects suggested.

CONSTRAINTS ON BUDGET AND TIMESCALE

It is usual that there are more potential Supplier Organizations (SO) than there are Owner Organizations (OO) and so the chosen SO secures the contract in the face of competition from other SO. This puts the OO in a very strong position and able to choose between the competing SO and select the one that offers the most favourable solution.

Consequently the selling process for a Supplier Organization (SO) (and hence procurement process for the OO) usually involves some form of tendering process where its offer is judged on criteria such as (1) the time it requires to complete the work; (2) the minimum amount of consideration it is prepared to accept; and (3) the quality, or performance, of the deliverable to be supplied.

For the favoured SO, acceptance is subsequently formalized by the signing of the contract which will clearly state these offered values.[2]

From this point onwards these values become constraints upon the Supplier Organization (SO); within the timescale it must complete a product that meets the quality and performance criteria laid down. However, there is no such constraint on how much the SO will spend.

Cost and consideration are two very different things. The latter determines how much payment the Supplier Organization (SO) will receive, the former is how much it will spend. Whilst it is very common for the latter to be constrained within the contract, not so the latter. Clearly though, for the SO to remain solvent and in business its consideration must exceed its cost. The commercial imperative for the SO is to ensure that the margin between the two (its profit), is as large as possible. It does this by imposing internal restrictions on how much it will spend, but it can only do this to the extent that its obligations to supply a satisfactory deliverable are not compromised.

This conflict is well known to anyone who has worked in a Supplier Organization (SO) but it is worth clarifying that whereas timescales and specification of the deliverable are usually externally imposed on the SO, the budget, with due regard for required profit, is usually internally imposed by the SO.

PREMATURE TERMINATION

This scenario of unbounded costs and bounded consideration (as in a Firm Price contract) pose the biggest risk to the Supplier Organization (SO).

Acceptance by the SO of the consideration quoted in the contract is predicated on its estimate of the actual cost, made when preparing its bid. Any error in this estimate is to be borne by the SO and such errors can be catastrophic in their impact.

In Chapter 4 we discussed Decision Gates where those with executive control of a project decided whether to proceed by reference to likely cost and benefit. We further discussed that this decision is repeated at the Decision Gates throughout the lifecycle, each taking advantage of the improved

---

2   The analysis is more straightforward if we assume the contract is of 'Firm Price' type (see Chapter 13).

information and estimates available as the uncertainty reduces. This scenario better reflects the Owner Organization's (OO) predicament because once the Supplier Organization (SO) has passed through the Decision Gate that accepts the contract, it incurs a contractual (and hence legal) obligation to complete its portion of the project. The decision cannot be reversed at a subsequent Decision Gate. In those instances where the SO substantially underestimates the cost of a project, the implications of not being able to opt for premature termination can lead to bankruptcy.

This is in stark contrast to the Owner Organization (OO), which can terminate the project at any time. Most likely, this will involve writing-off substantial amounts of money (to include the costs incurred to date and also additional money to meet its contractual obligations to the SO) but nonetheless, it can terminate and limit these losses. It is not nearly so straightforward for the SO.

As we shall discuss in Chapters 12 and 13, the ability to accurately, and cheaply, estimate the costs of work is of particular relevance to the Supplier Organization (SO), especially prior to its acceptance of the contact.

RESOURCE MANAGEMENT

In Chapter 4 we discussed how the demand for resources fluctuates through the project lifecycle. This poses a problem since retaining resources for periods when they are not needed for productive work incurs considerable cost, however, having insufficient resources available at a critical time will impede the project.

This is a dilemma for all those managing projects but the implications are disproportionately felt by the Supplier Organization (SO) rather than the Owner Organization (OO).

For the Owner Organization (OO) the project is usually[3] a one-off event and, most likely, it does not carry sufficient resources, in terms of both numbers and specialism, to meet the project's demands (otherwise there would be no need for SO). By engaging the Supplier Organization (SO), the OO is making

---

3   Some OO manage major assets and infrastructure (rail, water and telecommunication networks) and are constantly commissioning projects to create or refurbish assets. For them, projects are an ongoing feature, but they are the exception. For most OO their involvement in projects is sporadic.

the available resource pool elastic and hence able to respond to the fluctuating demands of its project.

In doing so, however, it is passing the problem on to the SO and, unfortunately, its opportunities for dealing with the problem are limited.

The SO can simply engage another tier of SO, and so pass on the problem. To varying degrees, all organizations do this and, in turn, their suppliers engage sub-suppliers. However, as we descend through the procurement chain, the option becomes progressively less attractive to the SO for a number of reasons.

Firstly, the Supplier Organization (SO) is often engaged only because it can offer specialist and rare resources. In such instances there is no one else to pass the problem on to.

Secondly, engaging resources on a temporary basis incurs a higher charge-out rate than if they were to be engaged permanently and, since the SO at each tier of the procurement chain takes some profit, the option simply becomes less commercially viable.

The effect of these, and other reasons, is that the resource pool for SO tend towards being inelastic and the managerial responses discussed in Chapter 15 are of more relevance to them.

STAKEHOLDER MANAGEMENT

Earlier, we discussed the complex and confusing environment associated with the early stages of project. Whilst this is true for both Supplier Organizations (SO) and Owner Organizations (OO), there are differences. For the SO this is a time of selling and marketing activity whereas for the OO it is associated with securing approval for the endorsement of a Business Case.

From a purely political perspective, the situation is more complex for the OO.

Supplier Organizations (SO) only decide whether or not to accept a contract, it is the Owner Organization (OO) that decides whether the larger endeavour will proceed. If we consider a contentious project like building a radio antennae near a school, it is not the SO supplying the electrical equipment who is obliged to defend the project in the face of opposition, it is the OO.

In project management terms these activities to promote the project and deal with those who object to it, are known as stakeholder management. It is a very difficult and time-consuming business and one that, by and large, the Supplier Organization (SO) can leave to the Owner Organization (OO).

TECHNICAL EXPERTISE

Owner Organizations (OO) often engage Supplier Organizations (SO) because they have specialist knowledge or capability that the OO does not have. This conveys different risks onto the two parties.

On the face of it, simply engaging a SO enables the OO to outsource part of their work and so avoid the costs of maintaining a permanent internal resource. But, in avoiding the costs, they also lose in-house expertise and if the subject matter relates to a fundamental aspect of the OO's business, and if the capability of the SO in question is very specialist and rare, then the OO can find themselves in a very weak position. Specifically there is a risk that they will become a 'dumb client' with insufficient expertise to maintain appropriate oversight of a SO upon which they are wholly reliant (see Chapter 8).

For the Supplier Organization (SO) there is no option other than to retain the expertise since their business is wholly dependent upon it. However, maintaining expertise for use on future potential projects often involves retaining key resources when there is no current demand for its services. Having a significant part of its workforce 'on the bench' is a problem strongly associated with SO engaged in project work.

CONTINUOUS IMPROVEMENT

To secure ongoing reward after the project product is complete the Owner Organization (OO) must simply utilize the product and realize benefit. The Supplier Organization (SO), by contrast, must secure another contract with another OO.

Whereas the OO only may be engaged in a continuous sequence of projects,[3] for the SO it is an imperative and so the need to continually improve one's capability at project management is more relevant to the SO than the OO.

It is for this reason that the 'lessons learned' type activities discussed at Chapter 18 can have more immediate relevance to Supplier Organizations (SO) than Owner Organizations (OO).

The Supplier Organization's Project Lifecycle

The fundamental trends of a project lifecycle, discussed in Chapter 4, apply equally to both Owner Organizations (OO) and Supplier Organizations (SO), as do the concept and importance of Decision Gates. However, the differences discussed above are such that the generic project lifecycle model offered in Chapter 5 is not wholly relevant to the project activities undertaken by the SO.

The activities of the Supplier Organization (SO) are a special case and they warrant a lifecycle model of their own. This is addressed in the following chapter.

Chapter 7

The Supplier Organization's Project Lifecycle

In the previous chapter it was stated that the differences between Supplier Organizations (SO) and Owner Organizations (OO) were such that the SO warranted a lifecycle of their own that addressed just their perspective. Figure 7.1 offers just such a lifecycle and it is further described in this chapter.[1]

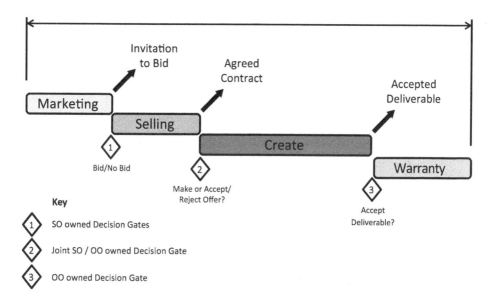

Figure 7.1   Supplier Organization's project lifecycle

---

1   Like the lifecycle offered in Chapter 5, the lifecycle offered here is a model. To be useful, models need to be simple, however their principal weakness is always their simplicity. The nature of procurement is such that there are a great many combinations and permutations of payment terms, contract types, and the like that can result in variation in the exact Decision Gates and phases that apply. The model is offered as a generic model to assist in the understanding of what appertains to most SO, most of the time. Real examples may, and will, vary.

Comparisons and Contrasts of the Lifecycle Models for Owner Organizations and Supplier Organizations

The above lifecycle model is consistent with the models offered in Chapter 5 in that it consists of phases and Decision Gates.

The two are different in terms of the identity of the phases and the phase products, and also that the Decision Gates are not always owned by the organization in question. Whereas the Owner Organization (OO) owns all the decisions made within its lifecycle, it is not the case here where only one is owned outright by the Supplier Organization (SO). This is evidence that, unlike the OO lifecycle, the SO lifecycle cannot exist in isolation. A SO needs an OO but an OO does not necessarily need an SO.

This joint ownership of Decision Gates, and the phase deliverables identified, allow for the very necessary interaction and connection between the Owner and Supplier Organizations to be made. The practicalities of this interaction will be discussed in Chapter 9.

In terms of content, the most obvious difference of the Supplier Organization's (SO) lifecycle is the early phases of Selling and Marketing, and they warrant the following observation.

MARKETING AND SELLING AS PROJECT MANAGEMENT ACTIVITIES

Selling and marketing are not considered to be part of classic project management. Neither the fifth edition of *A Guide to the Body of Knowledge* (PMBOK® Guide), by the Project Management Institute, nor the sixth edition of the *APM Body of Knowledge* include them as standalone topics. Whereas they are referred to in the fifth edition of the *APM Body of Knowledge*, this is only in the context of them being a soft skill that can be applied to persuade stakeholders of the merits of a project.

In both these publications, the establishment of contracts between Supplier Organizations (SO) and Owner Organizations (OO) is addressed as 'Procurement' and is therefore addressed from the point of view of the buyer, i.e. the OO.

In the context of project management, selling and marketing are not something the Owner Organization (OO) need worry about. Indeed if the project is to be delivered using in-house resources only, then there will be no need for the OO to consider the establishment of contracts at all, not even from just the perspective of a buyer.

Clearly this is not an approach that is acceptable to a Supplier Organization (SO). By definition these parties must engage in contracts, and hence markets, and specifically they must do so from the perspective of a seller since it is the receipt of the consideration, the payment that they will secure from a contract, that is their prime pursuit and objective. If the Supplier Organization (SO) does not sell then it will not survive.

Further, whilst divorcing the selling effort from the delivery process is a relatively safe option for those Supplier Organizations (SO) that supply standard off-the-shelf components, this is not the case for the SO delivering bespoke goods or services. In such organizations the selling and marketing disciplines are not minor competences that a project manager should just have some passing knowledge of. To a SO, the skills of selling and marketing become intrinsic to the work of its project manager for the following reasons:

1.   They are a vital link in establishing the continuity between what the OO wants and what the SO is to supply. This continuity is at the heart of the OO–SO relationship.

2.   As discussed in Chapter 4, the early phases of a project have a hugely disproportionate effect on the subsequent project and hence when most influence can be exerted. Accordingly, in the SO project lifecycle the activities within selling and marketing are the time when most influence over their overall performance is exerted. This has particular relevance to the quality of the relationship between the parties.

3.   They tie individual projects to the strategic objectives and commercial predicament of the SO.

Marketing and selling are not practices unique to Supplier Organizations (SO) just within the sphere of projects. All commercial organizations sell something and readers will find many books that address them as standalone disciplines. However, they are not often discussed specifically in the context of projects and project management competences.

In an effort to make up this shortfall, they each have dedicated chapters in Part 4.

The Supplier Organization Lifecycle Phases and Decision Gates

The phases and Decision Gates within the Supplier Organization (SO) lifecycle shown in Figure 7.1 are described as follows.

'MARKETING' PHASE

Marketing can be described best as ensuring one puts 'the right product in front of the right customer at the right time'.

As discussed earlier, the Supplier Organization (SO) retains permanent ownership of, or access to, specialist resources and expertise. Owner Organizations (OO), by contrast, have a demand for such resources and expertise only when a suitable project has been commissioned. Typically, this demand is significant but infrequent.

With such spasmodic demand, it is unlikely that SO and OO have an ongoing relationship, indeed they may well be unknown to each other prior to the project, and putting them in contact with each other in the first instance is not straightforward.

For a successful relationship there must be an overlap between what is required by the Owner Organization (OO) and what the Supplier Organization (SO) is happy to supply but, at the outset, it is often very difficult to recognize such an overlap exists. Firstly, the OO may not understand precisely what it wants. Secondly, by necessity for those addressing bespoke requirements, there is flexibility about what a SO is prepared to offer.

This vagueness and uncertainty often characterizes these early exchanges and just like that of the Owner Organization's (OO) project, the exact starting point of the Supplier Organization's (SO) project lifecycle is often indistinct.

Also, at this early point in the SO lifecycle, the ability to exert influence is at its highest. Much SO effort is directed at influencing the OO such that it is persuaded to specify its requirements in such a way that it suits what the SO can offer and also, preferably, such that it can put the SO's competitors at a disadvantage.

In some instances a particular Supplier Organization (SO) will be the only party capable of satisfying the Owner Organization's (OO) requirements. Alternatively, the SO will be able to establish such a strong relationship with the OO that the latter elects not to involve any other competing SO. Such instances, when no competition is involved, are sometimes known as 'single tender actions' and can be very favourable to the SO (and also the OO).

However, in most instances there is more than one Supplier Organization (SO) in competition for the work and so, to ensure fairness, a formal and publicized procurement process is adopted. This process can vary in its complexity but will involve each interested SO submitting a bid that details the technical and commercial package that it is offering in response to the stated requirement of the Owner Organization (OO). This brings the SO to the first Decision Gate.

'BID/NO BID' DECISION GATE

The logic of the Decision Gate, as described in Chapter 4, applies here and for the Supplier Organization (SO) this early decision is the most important.

If the SO submits to the selection process by putting together a bid, it will incur the considerable financial and opportunity cost. It is only appropriate to do this if there is a very real prospect of successfully securing profitable work. If a SO gets into the habit of preparing expensive bids for work which it stands no chance of winning, or alternatively, for work that is not sufficiently profitable, then it will not be in business for very long.

However, unless the SO submits bids it cannot secure work and so will not survive.

As with the OO, selection of the correct project is more important than how well it is managed and the ability to make the correct decision at this gate is a major determinant of how commercially successful the Supplier Organization (SO) will be.

'SELLING' PHASE

Selling is the process of persuading a prospective customer to buy your product from you, for the maximum price and on the most favourable terms.

Having decided to submit a bid, the Supplier Organization (SO) must go about preparing the same and simultaneously persuading the Owner Organization (OO) of the superiority of its offer such that the OO will be prepared to pay a premium to secure it.

The significant amounts of work and expense required to prepare such a bid are justified by the need to mitigate the inherent risk. This is especially the case when the commercial terms on offer relate to a 'Firm Price' (see Chapter 10) since if the offered price is too high it is unlikely the work will be won in the face of cheaper competitors; if it is too low it increases the risk that it will be exceeded by the actual costs.

To avoid either of these outcomes, activity within this phase seeks to precisely understand (and maximize) the price the Owner Organization (OO) would be prepared to pay and also to precisely understand (and minimize) what the actual cost of the work is likely to be.

The former of these involves the SO seeking to influence the OO. Inevitably this will involve the arts, sometimes the darker arts, of salesmanship. The latter involves the SO undertaking estimating; a difficult, expensive but crucial activity for every SO.

'MAKE OR ACCEPT/REJECT OFFER' DECISION GATE

This Decision Gate leads to the creation of a contract or else, if not favoured by the Owner Organization (OO), the termination of the Supplier Organization's (SO) involvement. There is a legal requirement whereby, for a contract to come into being, one party must make an offer and the other must unconditionally accept it. This process needs the consent of both the OO and SO and so, inevitably, it is a jointly owned Decision Gate.

This is why the making of an offer represents a major legal commitment on behalf of the SO since, after this point, the OO need only accept it and a contract is formed. It represents a significant surrendering of the ability of the SO to influence future events. It may be that, for whatever reason, after compiling the bid, the SO elects to abandon the process without making the formal offer. This, however, is less than ideal since the considerable costs of compiling the bid will have been incurred.

The simplest scenario involves the Owner Organization (OO) receiving bids (offers) from the various potential Supplier Organizations (SO), making a judgement as to its preferred partner, and unconditionally accepting their bid, at which point the contract is formed. In practice it may be more complex. For instance, the OO may ask for a price reduction or some other type of concession from the favoured SO. From a legal perspective, this represents a counter-offer and the effect of this is to put the SO in the position of having to make a decision whether to accept it or not. Accordingly the final decision of the Selling phase may be to either make an offer to the OO, or accept (or reject) an offer from the OO.

Once an unconditional acceptance is made the contract is formed and the existence of a contract has very significant implications for each party.

'CREATE' PHASE

The Supplier Organization (SO) is obliged to perform the work scope called for in the contract. This will involve the provision of some service or the creation of some goods.

In return, the Owner Organization (OO) is obliged to fulfil its duties specified under the contract. This may involve providing access to facilities or information or providing equipment or resources. It will also, ultimately, involve the payment of the contractual consideration, i.e. money.

Although represented diagrammatically in Figure 7.1 as a simple rectangle, in practice this phase may include separate tranches of work that may be arranged sequentially or in parallel. An example of the former would be a 'design and build' contract whereby the SO must first design the products and secure acceptance of the design before proceeding to build. An example of the latter would be a haulage contractor transporting a number of different loads whereby the tranches of work are performed at the same time and each subject to a separate acceptance.

'ACCEPT DELIVERABLE' DECISION GATE

In a very simple scenario, the completed goods are assessed by the Owner Organization (OO). If it deems them to be acceptable and in accordance with the requirements of the contract, formal acceptance of them is conveyed, ownership of the goods is transferred, and final payment is made.

In a strict legal sense the contract has jurisdiction over this activity (the OO is entitled only to that specified therein) but in a practical sense the Decision Gate is owned by the OO and the SO is at its behest.

In addition to the division of work into tranches, other practicalities may ensure that this Decision Gate is not so much a one-off event, but a series of events. For the reasons discussed in Chapter 18, this gate is far harder to define than the others.

'WARRANTY' PHASE

After 'Accept Deliverable', most likely there will be ongoing obligations to the Owner Organization (OO) such as delivery of the accepted product or documentation; demobilizing of contract facilities; settling of claims and counter-claims; closing of accounts; receipt of final payment, etc.

There is also much work to be done that is not for the benefit of the project in question, but for future projects that the Supplier Organization (SO) may embark upon. 'Lessons learned' activities are an example of such work. Other examples include recording of customer details so as to secure any future 'Spares and Service' contracts.

The end of the phase, and hence the end of the SO lifecycle (though not necessarily its legal obligations to the OO[2]) occurs on the conclusion of this work, or else the expiry of the 'Warranty Period' (often known as a 'Defects Liability Period'), whichever is the later (usually the Warranty Period).

The Warranty Period starts immediately after the goods are accepted and put into operation by the OO, and any failures occurring within this time not directly attributable to misuse are to be made good by the SO, at its cost.

Uses and Benefits of the Supplier Organization Project Lifecycle

As described in Chapter 4, the project lifecycle, with its attendant Decision Gates, forms a strategic plan for a project. As such it provides a framework for both the strategic and tactical control of a project and, if appropriate, can form the basis of a project method for the organization involved.

Further, the drawing up of a lifecycle requires the participants to engage in the act of planning and, as discussed in Chapter 14, this conveys very many advantages.

---

2   Some legal obligations of the SO do live on beyond this point, for instance its obligations for latent defects.

Chapter 8

The Role of a Supplier Organization Within a Project

By the simplest analysis, the expression 'Supplier Organization (SO)' can include an enormous range of different types of organization.

The relationship between the project and the Supplier Organization (SO), and the degree to which the SO should embrace the principals of project management, differs for these various different types.

These points were acknowledged in Chapter 6 but this chapter explores further the different types of SO and their relationship with the Owner Organization's (OO) project.

The Supplier Organization as a Member of the Owner Organization's Project Team

The classic approach to the planning of a project involves decomposing the work to be done into a series of discrete Work Packages. This is usually achieved with the aid of a Work Breakdown Structure (WBS): a hierarchical structure that sequentially decomposes the totality of the project work into smaller and smaller fragments. 'Work Package' is the name given to those fragments that exist at the lowest level of the Work Breakdown Structure, the so-called Work Package Level (see Figure 8.1 on the next page).

Ownership of each of these Work Packages is given to an individual party, and they are then responsible for ensuring the work contained therein is completed. An owner can own more than one Work Package.

Many readers will be familiar with a structured approach to this apportioning of Work Packages that involves a Responsibility Assignment

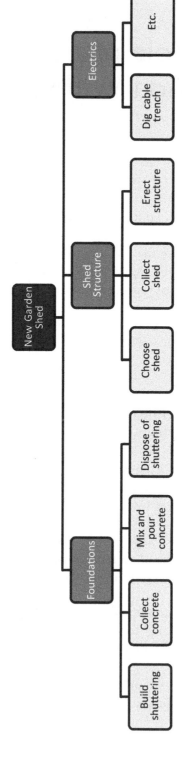

Figure 8.1   A Work Breakdown Structure

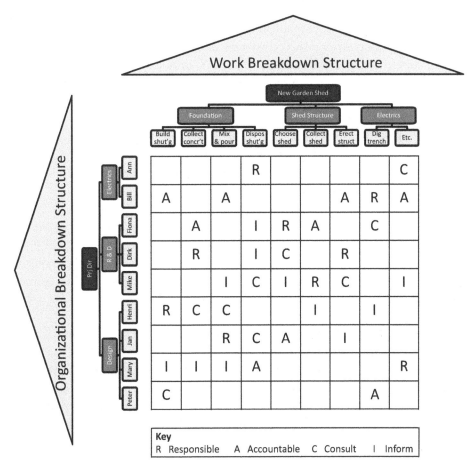

Figure 8.2   A Responsibility Assignment Matrix (RACI) Chart

Matrix, of which the RACI Chart is the most popular example (see Figure 8.2 above). This RACI Chart is a two-dimensional matrix that links between the Work Packages and those involved in the project. The former is the bottom row of the Work Breakdown Structure whereas the latter is the bottom row of an Organizational Breakdown Structure (OBS) (a hierarchical structure that identifies all the parties involved in the project).

If the project is very modest in size, and completed using just the Owner Organization's (OO) in-house resources, then the Work Package Owners will be individual employees. However, outside of these caveats, it is most likely that Work Package Owners will also consist of external organizations; Supplier Organizations (SO).

By defining the project organization thus, such that it includes SOs, we see further clarification around the 'temporary and transient' nature of the project organization discussed in Chapter 1. The SO is only involved whilst its Work Package is active. Once it is complete it will drop out of the project organization of the OO.

Also, we see here the relevance of the Task Force Organization discussed in Chapter 2, and its ability to accommodate the 'revolving door' phenomenon whereby new parties constantly join and leave the project organization as their Work Packages commence and complete.

In this respect the Task Force organizational structure is more relevant to the amalgamation of all those parties engaged in a project, rather than just one commercial entity. That is to say, parties that are connected by purchase contracts and not just employment contracts. This scenario is what some commentators, for example Lock (2002), refer to as a 'Contract Matrix'.

Project Team Members: The Trouble with Semantics

Since the Supplier Organization (SO) is a member of the Organizational Breakdown Structure (OBS) of the Owner Organization (OO), it becomes tempting to describe the SO as a 'team member', but some care is required here since we quickly become drawn into a maelstrom of conflicting syntax. Consider the following.

Figure 8.3, on the next page, describes the classic structure that helps to define project roles such as the roles of sponsor and project manager. Within this, there is a distinction between 'suppliers' and 'team members'; a distinction that relates to the employing organization.

The implication is that the sponsor and the project manager are employees of the same organization (the Owner Organization (OO)) and if the Work Package Owner is also an employee of this same organization, then the expression 'team member' can be applied to them. If, however, the Work Package Owner is employed by another organization, i.e. a Supplier Organization (SO), then within the constraints of the model they are 'suppliers'. Seemingly, to be a member of the 'project team' individuals must be employees of the OO.

The distinction becomes questionable if we embrace the growing habit of organizations to engage individuals on a freelance basis and referring to them as 'contractors'. Step into many offices of an Owner Organization (OO) that

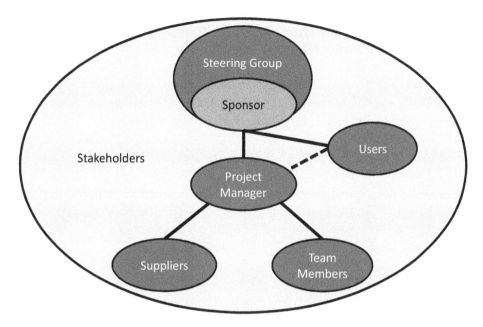

Figure 8.3   Project roles

is delivering a project and you will see a group of men and women, doing identical work, wearing identical clothes and behaving in identical ways. However, whereas most will be employees of the organization, the rest are engaged on a 'contract' basis and for a limited duration, such as the lifetime of a specific project. Strictly speaking within the constraints of the above these are 'suppliers'. The situation becomes further complicated when we consider long duration projects which can result in the 'contract' staff being more permanent than the 'permanent' staff. (Incidentally, this distinction is a problem for the tax authorities as well. Contractors in the UK may be familiar with IR35 legislation.)

A simple definition of a 'team member' as being someone who 'does the work required of the project' becomes unworkable if it is to include every individual who has contributed to the project, even down to the individual who drove the digger that loaded the iron ore into the truck that eventually formed the steel beam that became part of the roof of our new car plant. Individuals at that level have no concept of themselves working on an individual project.

This confusion does serve to show that not all Supplier Organizations (SO) are the same and the degree to which they can claim to be members of the overall project team varies. The following section offers a practical classification for this.

Classifying Supplier Organizations as Members of the Owner Organization's Project Team

In considering the degree to which the Supplier Organization (SO) can be classed as a member of the Owner Organization (OO) project team, two aspects are significant and each relate to what they are supplying.

THE SIZE OF THE FRAGMENT (BREADTH OF INVOLVEMENT)

Within the simple analysis offered by Figure 8.3, and further presuming that no SO owns more than one Work Package, the co-ordination between Work Package Owners is wholly undertaken by the project manager. Often, however, the SO will own more than one Work Package of a project.

In this case, for economies of scale and other matters of convenience, it is most likely that there will be just one contract between the Supplier Organization (SO) and the Owner Organization (OO). Consequently, the fragment of the project that the SO retains responsibility for can be very large and consist of many Work Packages. This being the case, a portion of the co-ordination duties will be transferred to the SO, decreasing the role of OO project manager but increasing the burden of project management borne by the SO.

To take this scenario to the extreme, if all the Work Packages were owned by just one Supplier Organization (SO) then the concept of project management will be more associated with this SO rather than the Owner Organization (OO).

THE NATURE OF THE FRAGMENT (INTIMACY)

In addition to its size, the nature of the Supplier Organization (SO) fragment also has an influence on the degree to which the SO can be classed as a member of the Owner Organization's (OO) project team.

If, for instance, we consider a construction project, in terms of the total man-hours the involvement of the architect may be relatively modest. 'Create drawings' may be just one Work Package, but just the number or size of the Work Packages does not fully recognize its importance to the project and hence the relationship with the SO that is required.

The designer of the building must be intimate with the uniqueness of the project and their work will have significant implications on how the other Work Packages and Supplier Organizations (SO) will be defined.

The extreme of this will involve the engagement of a SO just to carry out the project management function on behalf of the OO. This is largely consistent with role of the 'Consultant' within traditional procurement strategies commonplace within the UK construction industry, as defined by Smith (2003).

TYPES OF SUPPLIER ORGANIZATION

Reference to these two aspects enables us to offer a basis of classifying different types of Supplier Organization (SO).

By adopting each of the considerations described above we have the following two-dimensional matrix (see Table 8.1).

Table 8.1   Types of Supplier Organizations (SO)

		Low Breadth	High Breadth
Intimacy with the project	High	**Bespoke item suppliers** Consultant, architect, supplier of highly bespoke components	**Turnkey suppliers** Broad range of bespoke equipment
	Low	**Commodity suppliers** Supplier of single standard components	**Bespoke cluster suppliers** Supplier of range of standard components
		Low	High

Breadth of involvement

The matrix offers four different types of Supplier Organization (SO), described as follows.

Turnkey Suppliers

The Supplier Organization (SO) located in the top right-hand corner would be those undertaking a very large portion of the work scope and also undertaking work that was intimate to the project. This category would include 'turnkey' suppliers. This expression relates to the idea whereby at the end of the contract the SO simply hands over to the Owner Organization (OO) the keys to a new facility that has been created by the SO. The involvement of the OO is minimal and restricted to indicating the performance required of the deliverable (and making payment on completion). In these circumstances the SO will undertake everything required including design and management of the project.

Accordingly they are not so much a member of the Owner Organization's (OO) project team: they are their project team.

Commodity Suppliers

The Supplier Organization (SO) that would be located in the bottom left-hand corner would be those undertaking a modest and defined portion of the work scope and also undertaking work that was not intimate to the project. This category would include those providing standard 'off-the-shelf' equipment such as a pump, a crane, a printer as well as simple commodities. The component may be very complicated, such as a television, but since it is not modified to any degree for the project in question, and especially if the equipment is selected by the buyer, then there is little need for the supplier to be engaged with the specific aspects of the project in hand.

They have minimal claim to be treated as a member of the Owner Organization (OO) project team.

They would not meet the requirements described in Chapter 6 for those organizations that should embrace project management techniques.

Bespoke Item Suppliers

The Supplier Organization (SO) that would be located in the top left-hand corner would be those undertaking a modest portion of the work scope but work that was intimate to the project. This category would include the type of consultants described above, within the construction arena. Such a SO would need to be fully conversant with the specifics of the project and produce a bespoke product that responds accordingly.

It would also include those organizations that supply highly bespoke components. An example here would be the supply of a turbine for use in a hydro-electric project. The apparatus would be very carefully designed to suit only the geographical aspects, such as pressure and flow rate of the water, of that particular application. As such the designers would need to be wholly familiar with the specifics of the project and would share a considerable amount of communication with the Owner Organization (OO) team. This is the case even though the work to produce the turbine is only a very small part of the entire project effort in terms of expenditure.

They have a strong justification for being regarded, and hence treated, as a member of the Owner Organization (OO) project team.

Bespoke Cluster Suppliers

The Supplier Organization (SO) that would be located in the bottom right-hand corner would be those undertaking a large portion of the work scope but work that was not intimate to the project. This category would include those supplying a wide number of standard components and where the size, and hence value, of the work warrants special attention.

By way of example, let us imagine the supply of security scanners for the recent Olympic Games. The Olympic Games utilized a large number of venues and each contained an extensive security facility featuring numerous airport type scanners that each customer was obliged to pass through. These scanners were not designed specifically for the Olympic Games, they were standard components, however, there were a great many of them, in a variety of locations.

This imposes an additional burden on the Supplier Organization (SO) in terms of managing the coordination of their extensive scope of supply and also the degree of liaison required with the OO. It would be expected that the SO in question would treat this as a special and unique event and would look to manage the overall supply as a project.

They have a very good justification for being regarded as a member of the Owner Organization's (OO) project team.

The Relevance of Project Management

The closer a Supplier Organization (SO) towards the top right-hand corner of Table 8.1, the greater its claim to be regarded as a member of the Owner Organization's (OO) project team and also the greater its need to embrace aspects of project management.

We would expect a degree of consistency between the location of an individual SO in Table 8.1, its location on the 'Continuum of Creative Endeavours' (Figure 1.1), and also its location on the Organizational Continuum (Figure 2.4).

As the SO approaches the top right-hand corner of Table 8.1, the top of Figure 1.1 and the right of Figure 2.4, there will be an increase in its obligations for communication externally with the OO, and internal cross-functional integration. This can be indicated by the authority given to the nominated individual within the SO, responsible for the contract.

More often than not, this individual is given the name 'Project Manager'. Since Owner Organizations (OO) usually engage more than one Supplier Organization (SO) we can immediately see that for any one OO project there could be a large number of individuals with the title 'Project Manager' and yet there will be only one bearing this title within the OO.

It is a premise of this book that most practitioners of project management are employed by Supplier Organizations (SO) rather than by Owner Organizations (OO).

The Supplier Organization as the Owner Organization's Project Manager

Consider those Supplier Organization (SO) who lie at the extreme top right-hand corner of Table 8.1. As stated above, they take on considerable responsibility for the management of the project, so much so that the role of a project manager within an Owner Organization (OO) diminishes.

If we refer to the classic model offered in Figure 8.3 we see the distinction between a sponsor and a project manager.

There are variations in practice here but again within the context of a 'classic model' the two roles are differentiated thus.

The sponsor commissions the project, secures the funding, owns the Business Case (and the answer to the question whether to proceed with the project) and is ultimately accountable for delivering the benefits specified in the Business Case.

The project manager manages the project and the team on a day-to-day basis, monitors and controls progress, owns the project management plan (and the answer to the question how to proceed with the project) and is ultimately accountable for delivering the product (deliverable) to the success criteria relating to time, money and quality.

Within these definitions, and as implied earlier, it is wholly realistic for the project manager so described to be part of a Supplier Organization (SO). Indeed this becomes inevitable when either the SO is a single 'turnkey supplier', or alternatively, when the SO is a 'bespoke item supplier' and the Work Package involved is explicitly 'project management'.

The attraction to the Owner Organization (OO) of dispensing with an in-house project manager can be strong, particularly when the project in question demands specialist knowledge or capability that the OO does not have and also when this specialist knowledge or capability is not intrinsic to the core business of the OO.

However, the arrangement becomes less safe when the frequency of such projects change, or if the nature of the work is intrinsic to the core business of the OO.

Imagine, for instance, a mail order company embarking on a project involving the replacement of its IT system. The IT system of any modern company is crucial to its business and this is especially so for one involved in mail order.

The Owner Organization (OO) may choose to simply engage a Supplier Organization (SO) on a 'turnkey' basis to undertake the project. Whilst there may be a simple short-term numerical business rationale for this, there are risks. Specifically, there is a risk that the OO becomes a 'dumb client'. This expression is reserved for those OO who have insufficient expertise even to maintain appropriate oversight of a SO. It is a point that is difficult to define but many with experience of working within an OO will have experience of having passed beyond it and being wholly at the behest of the SO.

To their cost, too many OO have failed to recognize the danger of subcontracting functions that are the soul of their business.

Procurement Chains and the Supplier Organization as a Subcontractor

We have focused on the Supplier Organization (SO) only insofar as it being directly in contract with an Owner Organization (OO).

This is overly simplistic and many readers will have experience of SO offering bespoke equipment for use on a project when their organizations are not in direct contract with an OO. Instead they are in contract with another SO who in turn may be in contract with the OO.

For any project of moderate size or greater, there exists a procurement chain. At the apex of this is the Owner Organization (OO), immediately below are the Tier 1 suppliers (with whom the OO is in contract directly), immediately below them are the Tier 2 suppliers (with whom Tier 1 suppliers are in contract directly), and so on through the remaining tiers.

The need for a Supplier Organization (SO) to embrace aspects of project management is not reserved just for Tier 1 suppliers. The need exists below this level but as we move down through the tiers of the supply chain this need reduces and the type of SO involved migrates towards the bottom left-hand corner of Table 8.1.

References

Lock, D., 2002. Organisation Structure. In M. Stevens, ed., *Project Management Pathways*. High Wycombe: The Association for Project Management. Section 66.

Smith, N., 2003. Roles and Responsibilities in Project Contract Management. In R. Turner, ed., *Contracting for Project Management*. Aldershot: Gower Publishing.

PART 3

Aligning the Interests of Owner and Supplier Organizations

Chapter 9

Connecting Supplier and Owner Organizations

Interconnection of the Two Project Lifecycles

As discussed in Chapter 7, a useful way of contrasting the differing perspectives of the Owner Organization (OO) and the Supplier Organization (SO) is by reference to their different lifecycle models, namely Figure 5.3 and Figure 7.1.

In bringing the parties together, these two lifecycles must become connected (see Figure 9.1).

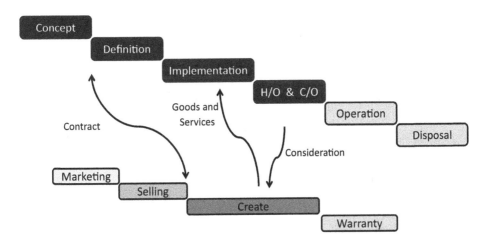

Figure 9.1   Interconnection of Owner Organization and Supplier Organization lifecycles

Source: Adapted from APM (2006).

Whereas the Owner Organization's (OO) involvement in a project is truly 'cradle to grave' (from the initial 'lightbulb moment' to the final disposal of the asset), the involvement of the Supplier Organization (SO) relates only to the life of its fragment of the project. If the fragment of the SO in question is large then its lifecycle model may approach the length of the OO lifecycle, but most often the lifecycle of the OO is considerably longer than that of the SO.

If the fragment of the Supplier Organization (SO) relates to, say, a feasibility report then its whole lifecycle may overlap with just the Concept phase of the Owner Organization (OO). If it relates to supply of test equipment it may overlap just with the Handover and Closeout phase.

Interaction between the two organizations starts when it becomes clear that the project may require something that the SO can supply. Such early interaction is only informal in the sense that just information is being exchanged. Firm coupling of the lifecycles occurs when a contract is agreed between the two parties. The point of subsequent disconnection is not so straightforward. Exceptional instances (such as *force majeure* conditions) can lead to premature termination, but these are rare. A practical approach assumes disconnection occurs when goods and services are delivered by the SO and the consideration is received, though, as shall be discussed in Chapter 18, the point when the SO liability expires is actually more complicated than this.

There are other transfers between the two parties, usually documents (specifications, drawings, progress reports) but sometimes hardware (specialist material made available to the SO) but in all cases it is the contract that fundamentally determines the relationship between the two parties and what is to be exchanged.

A contract is an agreement that obliges one party to swap something they have for something they want, with another party, in a prescribed way. In very simple terms the first party is an Owner Organization (OO) that wants goods or services and is prepared to offer a consideration (money). The second party is the Supplier Organization (SO) that is prepared to supply these goods and services in exchange for the consideration. The 'prescribed manner' will detail how the two parties are to behave in relation to each other, how certain risks are to be shared and managed, and also the detail of the minor items to be exchanged, i.e. the contract's 'terms and conditions'.

Though a contract is simple in principle, there are a number of different types, each of which is designed to satisfactorily administer to different variations of the scenario. Further, the coupling of parties allows for very many different arrangements that allow the Owner Organization (OO) to link with a very large number of Supplier Organizations (SO). As such the SO can find great variation in the manner in which it is connected to the OO and its project.

Design of the Procurement Chain

Chapter 8 referred to a procurement chain and the various tiers involved. There are actually a number of combinations and permutations and they are best explored by reference to an example.

Imagine you have just won the lottery and your biggest problem is how to spend your money. You already have the mansion of your dreams but still there are those few spare millions burning a hole in your pocket. Whilst reclining in the sun on the southern terrace one afternoon you fall on the idea of building a swimming pool.

The work scope for this can be divided into the four Work Packages, 'Clear area', 'Dig hole', 'Line pool' and 'Fit pump'.

SIMPLE CONTRACTS

A simple procurement chain would involve you (the OO) seeking out four parties (the SO), one for each of the Work Packages. The project fragment for the first Supplier Organization (SO) is 'Clear area'. When it has finished the second SO could address its fragment, 'Dig hole', and so on. This arrangement is shown in Figure 9.2, on the following page, and the contracts involved are just simple contracts.

There are advantages to this arrangement. Specifically the Owner Organization (OO) retains full control over who is doing the work and when it is done, but there are drawbacks.

Firstly, the OO is obliged to set up and administer four contracts. This requires time and resources and, also, a degree of technical understanding such that it can understand and communicate appropriately with each SO over what is to be supplied and how.

Secondly, the OO is exposed to significant risks associated with co-ordinating the work of the parties. If, for instance, the SO responsible for 'Line pool', on arrival at site, realizes that the pool has not been dug to the proper

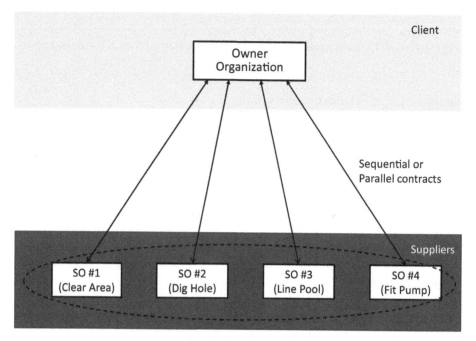

Figure 9.2   Simple procurement chain

dimensions, who is responsible for sorting out the problem? In the first instance it lies with the OO.

INVOLVEMENT OF LEAD CONTRACTORS

An alternative arrangement has the Owner Organization (OO) engaging a Supplier Organization (SO) as a lead contractor, whose fragment is the whole pool construction project. (This arrangement is consistent with the 'turnkey supplier' located in the top right quadrant of Table 8.1.)

Consider the OO engages 'Acme Pool Services' in this role. It may be that this SO is just a one-man operation who, in turn, engages the other SOs described above to carry out of each of the Work Packages, but the situation is fundamentally different from before. Figure 9.3 applies.

The contracts between Acme Pool Services and the Supplier Organizations (SO) in the lower tier are referred to as sub-contracts. The 'sub' relates to the fact that they are subordinate to the contract between the Owner Organization (OO) and Acme Pool Services. This latter contract can be known by many names. Turnkey contract, prime contract, principal contract, comprehensive contract

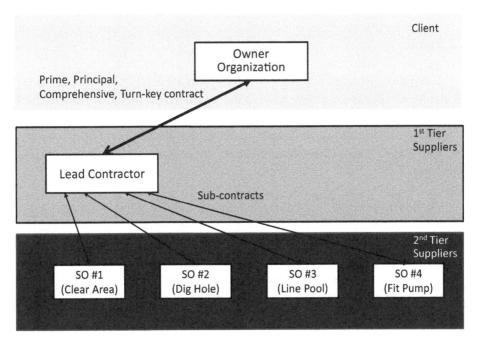

Figure 9.3   Procurement chain involving a lead contractor

are all examples. The organization in the position of Acme Pool Services can also be referred to as the principal contractor.

From the perspective of the OO, the situation is much simpler since, now, there is just one contract for it to establish and administer to. This both frees it from the burden of having to deal with each SO, and insulates it from the risks associated with co-ordinating them. Now, if the hole is found to be dug incorrectly, it is Acme Pool Services that is obliged to sort things out.

Though this makes the life of the Owner Organization (OO) easier, it is at the expense of Acme Pool Services, which now incurs the added administrative burden and risk, and for this it must be compensated. One could expect that, all other things being equal, this second arrangement (Figure 9.3) would cost the OO more than the first scenario (Figure 9.2).[1]

---

1   It should be noted, however, that this is not always the case. Acme Pool Services is selected on the basis that, unlike the Owner Organization (OO), it is experienced in the construction of pools. It has skills, equipment, knowledge, expertise and contacts that enable it to manage the building of the pool far better than the OO, such that it may well be able to do the work for a considerably cheaper sum and some of this saving may be passed onto the OO in which case the second scenario is both easier and cheaper for the OO.

Although this arrangement offers great potential, there are drawbacks for each party.

From the perspective of the Owner Organization (OO), it loses influence. Consider waking one morning to see a workman from a tiling contractor fitting tiles different to those you agreed with Acme Pool Services. On remonstrating with them, the individual may well point out that his company does not work for you, that they work for Acme Pool Services and that they had not specified any type.

Obviously you, the OO, have recourse via Acme Pool Services (so long as the contract with them was explicit about tile type) but nonetheless, your ability to directly influence the work is diminished. This is an example of privity of contract. By this a party can have rights over, or obligations to, another party only if there exists a contract between the two. Here there is no contract directly between the OO and the tiling contractor and so the former cannot instruct the latter.

The effects of this become very pronounced when there are many tiers to a procurement chain. For the Owner Organization (OO) at the top, to influence the behaviour of a party at the bottom (a SO), requires instructions to pass through a large number of parties. These delays and administrative burdens can become extreme and, in some instances, deemed as unacceptable, requiring the OO to design a flatter procurement chain (or in extremis bring work back 'in-house').

For Acme Pool Services, a significant drawback of the arrangement shown in Figure 9.3 relates to its exposure to commercial risk. By the arrangement there will be a number of organizations in contract with Acme Pool Service that will want to be paid once their work is completed. In turn, Acme Pool Services will expect to be paid by the OO. All will be well if this happens but there are opportunities for disaster here.

Foremost is the risk that the Owner Organization (OO) will not honour its commitment to pay. Bankruptcy could be a cause of this or, alternatively, the OO may not be happy with the performance of Acme Pool Services and withhold payment accordingly. This dispute may not affect all the suppliers to Acme Pool Services, in which case the latter may well be faced with the prospect of having to pay its suppliers yet not have been paid itself. Even if the OO does eventually make the payment, a protracted delay may have the same effect as default. Without access to significant reserves Acme Pool Service may find itself having to borrow money, with all the attendant interest costs, to cover the cash-flow crisis. Very many contractors have been unable to survive such a crisis and bankruptcy has been the result.

Organizations in the position of Acme Pool Services are very keen to protect themselves from these types of problems, for instance by adopting 'back to back' terms and conditions whereby the contracts between themselves and their clients are as identical as possible to those with their suppliers. By this, any sanction available to their clients become the same sanctions that they can impose on their suppliers, allowing problems to be simply passed down the procurement chain. Also, consistent with the adage about 'possession being nine tenths of the law', timing of payments becomes important and it is likely that Acme Pool Services will have insisted on payment being made by the OO in stages, through the life of the contract. Ultimately, however, there must be a degree of trust between the parties and if Acme Pool Services has reservations about the credit-worthiness of the OO then it should simply not enter into a contract with it.

A company like Acme Pool Services may not be prepared to accept a commercial risk of this magnitude, but there is a way whereby its skills and expertise can be available to the Owner Organization (OO) without it being

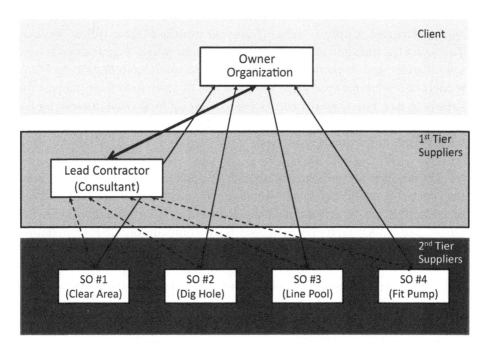

Figure 9.4   Simple procurement chain with consultant

involved as a lead contractor. The fragment of the project for which Acme Pool Services is responsible can be restricted to the provision of advice only. Such advice may extend to which suppliers to favour and what their contracts should consist of but, crucially, the contract with the suppliers on the lower tier of the chain is with the OO directly. Figure 9.4 applies (see the previous page). In this instance the involvement of Acme Pool Services is consistent with the top left-hand corner of the matrix in Table 8.1.

There are other types of contractual relationship between these parties.

CALL-OFF CONTRACTS

Doubtless, your new pool will be an architectural triumph in which case Acme Pool Services could expect further orders from your jealous neighbours. As such, Acme Pool Services would look to engage its suppliers with a contract that includes this follow on work, as well as the current project, in which case the parties may choose to establish a 'Call-off' contract (also known as 'Term' contract, a 'Framework' contract or an 'Alliance' or 'Partnership').

These contracts include all the details of the earlier contract, including rates, except the quantity to be supplied. Once established, to access the services of the supplier, there is no need for Acme Pool Services to negotiate another contract, simply, it 'calls off' another tranche of the goods or services. This saves the time and expense of having to renegotiate a contract each time a need arises, and so reduces the burden on procurement departments. Many readers will work for an organization that has in place such a contract for the supply of, say, hire cars. The contract can be set up in the first instance by the procurement experts, and then simply used by others in the organization that have a need for the goods or services.

The implicit favouritism towards the Supplier Organization (SO) once the contract is established is a major advantage since it may increase volumes of trade. This can be enhanced by an exclusivity clause whereby the Owner Organization (OO) agrees not to approach any competitors of the SO. In return, the SO may offer a reduced rate compared to that for a one-off supply.

By their nature, these types of contracts tend to favour the supply of large quantities of simple goods, services or commodities. Supplier Organizations (SO) associated with the bottom right-hand corner of Table 8.1 may well find this type of contract attractive.

SYNDICATE CONTRACTS

Looking at the situation described in Figure 9.2 we can imagine that those in the lowest tier of the procurement chain have cause for concern. Specifically, Acme Pool Services is a 'middleman' between them and the Owner Organization (OO), creaming off profit which may otherwise be available to themselves. They have a vested interest in dispensing with the middle tier and contracting directly with the OO.

Imagine, therefore, representatives of these Supplier Organizations (SO) put an offer to you, the OO, to do the work for less if Acme Pool Services is dispensed with. You are perhaps attracted by this better price but unwilling to proceed since Acme Pool Services was brought in primarily to avoid the need for you, the OO, to have separate contracts.

There is a mechanism whereby the Owner Organization (OO) can have just one outgoing contract and yet not involve a lead contractor. The mechanism involves the Supplier Organizations (SO) in the lowest tier coalescing into a single entity; a syndicate. Figure 9.5 applies.

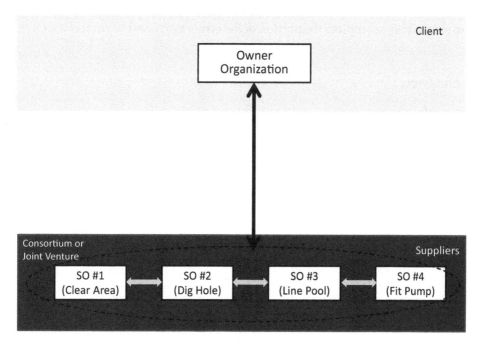

Figure 9.5   Procurement chain including syndicates

In this scenario your main concern as the Owner Organization (OO) is how to ensure that each of the syndicate members behaves themselves. For instance, the last thing the OO would want is for one of the syndicate members to disappear and the other members simply shrug their shoulders and absolve themselves of any duty to resolve the disappearance.

Accordingly, for this scenario to be acceptable there is normally an insistence on behalf of the OO to bind the syndicate members together that would cater for, and protect the OO from, a default on behalf of one the members. There are two popular ways of doing this which in turn creates either a joint venture or a consortium.

In the instance of the joint venture, a new company is created with each of the syndicate members as a shareholder. This protects the Owner Organization (OO) since its contract is with the new company and inherent within this structure is a mechanism that commits the shareholders.

In the instance of a consortium the individual members retain their identities as separate organizations but agree a 'joint and several liability'.[2] By this, each of the parties are obliged to complete their portion of the work but, crucially, should a member of the consortium default then the other members are also liable to complete the portion of the errant party and so protect the OO.

Reference

Association for Project Management, 2006. *APM Body of Knowledge*, 5th edn. High Wycombe: APMKnowledge.

---

2   There are variants that do not contain such an agreement but are less attractive to the OO.

Chapter 10

How Much to Pay
the Supplier Organization?

A fundamental aspect of any agreement between a Supplier Organization (SO) and an Owner Organization (OO) is how to calculate the amount of consideration the SO is to receive.

Although there are many options, there are two basic approaches which can be considered as being opposites and whose contrast offers valuable insight.

'Firm Price' Versus 'Cost Reimbursable' Models

A 'Firm Price' contract involves both parties agreeing a figure at the outset. Then, regardless of what it actually costs the Supplier Organization (SO) to complete the work, the consideration they will receive is the amount agreed previously. This is the simplest and most popular of mechanisms. Terminology is a bit fluid here but we shall refer to it as a Firm Price contract (though many will refer to it as Fixed Price contract – see below).

In stark contrast to this is a Cost Plus contract. By this, at the completion of the work, the Supplier Organization (SO) lays out its costs and the Owner Organization (OO) reimburses the SO these costs, plus an additional fee to cover profit. Such a fee can be determined as a percentage of the costs, in which case it is known as a 'Cost Plus Percentage Fee' basis (CPPF).

The selection has a gross influence on the behaviour of both parties and, to ensure that the SO is incentivized to meet the real objectives of the OO, it is vital that the correct choice is made.

Returning to the scenario depicted in Figure 9.2, and just the contract for the digging of the hole, is it in the best interests of the OO and the SO to favour a Firm Price, or a Cost Plus contract? In reaching a decision, the following should be considered.

RISK AND REWARD

The 'knee-jerk' response of many Owner Organizations (OO) in this scenario is to favour a Firm Price contract, since, on the face of it, it insulates them from risk.

For instance, consider the Supplier Organization (SO) estimates a cost, and hence price, for the work on the assumption that the soil to be dug is sandy. However, when the hole is actually started, an enormous rock is discovered that dramatically increases the cost of the work. If the OO had agreed a Firm Price contract then the additional cost is to the account of the SO, so holding the OO immune from the problem.

By the corollary of this, we would imagine that the SO would favour a Cost Plus arrangement.

However, on closer inspection, we see that a Firm Price contract is not wholly good news for the Owner Organization (OO) since, although it does reduce exposure to the consequences of the risk, it obliges the OO to pay for the privilege. It pays for this mitigation via a margin, between the cost and price, which is determined by any astute SO to cover for such eventualities. This margin is to be paid irrespective of whether the risk actually materializes into an event. Accordingly the OO is paying a fee to reduce its exposure to uncertainty; an insurance policy by another name.

If the OO is risk averse, in its eagerness to transfer the risk, it may be prepared to pay a considerable margin. If, in turn, the risk of the rock does not materialize then the SO can release this margin to its profit; an attractive prospect for all SO. For this reason it may well be worth the SO accepting this risk since a Firm Price contract does actually maximize its opportunity for profit margin.

Adoption of a Firm Price contract will favour the Supplier Organization (SO) only if: the Owner Organization (OO) is risk averse; there is little competition to the SO; and/or, the SO in question is in a good position to manage the risk. Ability to manage the risk may include local knowledge revealing that the likelihood of there being a rock is very small. Alternatively, it may have access to skills and equipment that allow it to deal with any rock better than others.

If the opposite of these exist, the OO may well be better off with a Cost Plus arrangement.

It is worth reflecting here, that, although contracts are usually referred to as an exchange of goods or services for a consideration, at their heart is the trading of risk, and the amount of risk each party carries is dominated by the selection of reimbursement type.

The presence of competition is important because Supplier Organizations (SO) will compete with each other by reducing their prices, which often involves reduction in the margin they deem necessary to cover their risks. The opposite is also true in the absence of competition. Whereas this is often to the benefit of the Owner Organization (OO) there is an element of 'caveat emptor' (buyer beware). If the SO incurs risks which ultimately it cannot bear then it will pass into bankruptcy and the work will not be completed, ultimately to the cost of the OO. In reality the OO can never wholly insulate itself from risk and it is advised to ensure, as far as is possible, that it does not impose a risk on a party that is unable to bear it.

In choosing between Firm Price or Cost Plus contracts, both the Supplier Organization (SO) and Owner Organization (OO) are managing the risk by pushing it into the ownership of the other party. A better solution would involve them examining the risk with a view to actually managing it directly, by reduction (or elimination) of likelihood or impact. This may involve the drilling of test bores, for example, by the SO under a separate contract, which could then inform the subsequent decision about the main contract.

Even after this direct management, it is likely that there will still be some latent risk and this should remain with the party best able to bear it, and they should be rewarded financially for doing so.

A final point here relates to the 'risk averse' nature of many organizations. For cultural reasons, many organizations find it very difficult to deal with the inherent uncertainty associated with projects. At a fundamental level, they struggle to accept that at the outset of the endeavour, the final cost of a project, or fragment thereof, cannot be predicted with absolute certainty. They put their personnel under great pressure to avoid it and a practical way of dealing with this, when buying, is to favour Firm Price contracts since this does give some (though not absolute) certainty about what the final bill will be. This, of course, is 'manna from heaven' for many profit-hungry and risk-seeking SO who are only too happy to assist the risk averse OO. In reality many OO pay a very high price to satiate their risk aversion.

SUPERVISION AND INCENTIVIZATION

Having engaged a Supplier Organization (SO) to dig the hole, what would the concerns of the Owner Organization (OO) be if they had to leave site for a while?

If the SO is engaged on a Firm Price contract then there is little to be concerned about because any time wasted is its own time, and the cost is to its account. Apart from the delay, the OO is not exposed to the cost of tardy performance by the SO.

The opposite is the case when a Cost Plus contract is embraced. In such instances, the OO will pay for the time of the SO regardless of how productive that time is. Indeed, it can be argued that Cost Plus contracts, especially those where the fees are calculated as a percentage of the costs, actually incentivize the SO to delay the work and ramp up the costs, and hence its profit, as much as possible.

The choice of reimbursement type has implications for the incentivization of the Supplier Organization (SO) and, if an Owner Organization (OO) chooses a Cost Plus contract, it may choose to make provision for additional supervision, despite the added administrative and cost burden.

Although a Firm Price contract has an intrinsic incentivization effect, this is not always helpful since there are instances when an OO is anxious that the SO is not encouraged to complete the work as quickly as possible. Imagine, for instance, that as part of the new swimming pool complex you had commissioned a sculptor to create a stunning marble statue as the centrepiece of the facility. Would you really want them to rush the work? This is an instance where a Cost Plus Percentage Fee contract may be appropriate since it would incentivize the sculptor to take every care, regardless of time.

LIKELIHOOD OF CHANGES

Imagine having established a Firm Price contract for the digging of the hole for your new rectangular swimming pool whilst your partner was away. Further imagine that on hearing of your news they are distraught since, as they remind you, you had promised them a round swimming pool.

To rectify the situation you ask the Supplier Organization (SO) to fill in the corners of the hole and widen the sides to accommodate the round profile. However, unless special provision is made in the contract, one party is not at liberty to alter the agreed terms of a contract without the consent of the other party and the SO is not obliged to comply with your request.

Being aware of this, an astute SO may use the situation to their advantage, even if the additional cost of the modification is modest, say £2,000.

The Supplier Organization (SO) knows that so long as it is prepared to dig the original hole then, by the terms of the contract, it is entitled to the original price of £10,000. Since the Owner Organization (OO) no longer wants the original hole, it is unlikely that it will want the SO to proceed. A categorical refusal by the SO to make the change will probably result in it being sent off site but with the payment of £10,000. The OO must then find another SO to come and complete the round pool, for a price of, say, £10,000.

The astute SO will know that without its consent to the change, the OO will be faced with a final bill of £20,000. Therefore, it offers to accept the change for a new total contract price of, say, £19,500, resulting in an additional profit of £7,500.

In reality it is unlikely that the situation will be as stark as this. Most Supplier Organizations (SO) like to retain a good reputation in the marketplace so as to facilitate further work and it is unlikely that the Owner Organization (OO) will have offered a contract that does not contain some provision for instructing variations. However, the scenario does serve to illustrate a very important point; namely, a Firm Price contract severely impedes the ability of the OO to vary the work once the contract is agreed.

If there is a strong likelihood of the Owner Organization (OO) wanting to instigate change during a project, the relative attraction of a Cost Plus contract, over a Firm Price contract, increases. If you, as the OO, wanted an architect to work with you to develop a design for the new pool complex, it is likely that you will want them to come up with different ideas and sketches in the first instance, which you could use to help decide how the design should evolve. In this situation the OO would want to reserve the right to change its mind as the process advances and it is inconceivable that the SO would not insist on a Cost Plus contract.

For the Supplier Organization (SO), the practical consideration when contemplating a Firm Price contract is ensuring that it is never in a position of having to vary works without securing additional revenue. Such a scenario in the above situation could have occurred if only the volume of the hole had been specified in the contract, and not the shape. Although the Owner Organization (OO) may be adamant that it did refer to a round pool in earlier discussions, the SO may insist that it had only ever envisaged a rectangular pool. This is a dangerous situation for the SO since, before payment, it is in a very weak negotiating position and in all likelihood will have to fund the change.

CLARITY OF SCOPE DEFINITION

In all situations, but especially in those involving Firm Price contracts, the exact scope of the work to be done must be clear to all concerned. For the Supplier Organization (SO) this is important for a number of reasons, including the following.

Firstly, the SO is obliged to cover from its account any amount that the cost exceeds the price and it is a risk that can have catastrophic consequences. To avoid this, prior to agreeing price, it estimates the cost. The estimate must be a good one and this can only be achieved with an accurate and explicit statement of what is to be done. In the example offered, as well as the likelihood of rocks in the earth, the SO will need to consider access routes to site, restrictions on site working hours, the off-site tipping of spoil and many other facets that will impact on the cost and duration.

Secondly, as addressed above, an explicit description protects the Supplier Organization (SO) from the impact of changes since entitlement to additional payment is dependent upon demonstrating that the Owner Organization (OO) is now asking for something different, i.e. that a change has actually taken place. If the original description was not sufficiently explicit to facilitate this demonstration, then the SO is in danger of not being rewarded for the extra work.

Thirdly, an explicit description of scope will reduce likelihood of conflict between the parties and ease final settlement. 'Scope creep' describes the habit, often an unconscious habit, of increasing the scope of work during execution. During the life of a contract many OO change their minds as to what they believe they asked for originally. Without an explicit description it can be hard for a SO to demonstrate compliance with original instructions and justify final payment.

Responsibility for drawing up such an explicit description usually lies with the Owner Organization (OO). This can be problematic and not just because it is a very expensive and time-consuming exercise. In many instances, the OO is simply insufficiently experienced to do it properly. Another very real problem is that, especially at the outset of the project, the degree of uncertainty is such that an explicit description of the work scope is just not possible.

A consequence of this is that Firm Price contracts tend to be more prevalent in the later stages of the project lifecycle, when less uncertainty prevails, and Cost Plus contracts tend to dominate earlier on, as in the case of the architect, above.

ADMINISTRATIVE BURDEN

A further drawback to Cost Plus contracts is that sufficient evidence of actual costs must be collated and presented to justify payment. This imposes an administrative burden on the Supplier Organization (SO) to collate it, and the Owner Organization (OO) to endorse it.

Imagine doing the weekly shop at a supermarket and all the goods were to be bought on a Cost Plus basis. Clearly, just the thought of the paperwork involved demonstrates that it would be wholly unworkable. The simplicity of a Firm Price arrangement ensures its appeal.

There is also an aspect of confidentiality here since most commercial organizations prefer not to share with others what they have paid to their suppliers. A Cost Plus arrangement denies the SO such confidentiality and obliges it to operate on an 'open book' basis whereby the OO has full sight of its costs.

Other Payment Terms

As discussed, the Firm Price contract and Cost Plus contract have very distinct attractions and detractions. In practice, many parties embrace hybrid arrangements that seek to combine elements of each such that risk is shared more equitably between the contracting parties.

Very many such arrangements exist, many highly evolved for a specific application, but the following are the more common examples. They each represent different risk exposures and can be arranged loosely on a continuum (see Figure 10.1).[1]

---

1   The exact sharing of risk is determined by the wording and quantifications within each specific contract. The arrangement within a continuum offers an approximate guide only.

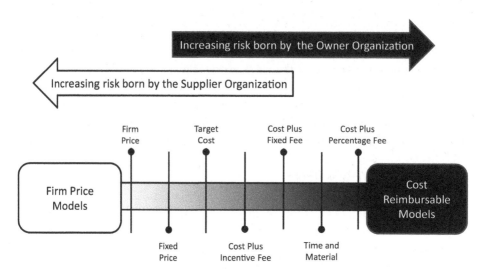

Figure 10.1   Risk sharing within differing reimbursement types

COSTS PLUS FIXED FEE (CPFF)

In a Cost Plus Percentage Fee contract the fee to which the SO is entitled is calculated as a percentage of the cost incurred. This is seen to be very favourable to the Supplier Organization (SO) since it will benefit from any increase in cost. A variation of this approach has the fee fixed at an agreed sum. This provides a modest incentive to the SO to limit the costs since, although the SO will not lose money, its profit calculated as a percentage of the whole reimbursement, will reduce as the costs increase.

COST PLUS INCENTIVE FEE (CPIF)

Alternatively, payment of the fee can be contingent upon some measure of satisfactory performance of the Supplier Organization (SO). For instance, imagine a grand opening party is being planned for your pool, on 1 August. For this to happen, the hole must be dug by 1 May. The contract with the SO could provide for the SO to be reimbursed the costs but only to receive a fee if it completes the work by this date. Again the SO will not lose money but clearly it is incentivized to expedite the work.

TIME AND MATERIALS

This is a very popular approach to adopt, especially when the scope of the works is uncertain. In essence it is a Cost Plus contract.

By this, the Supplier Organization (SO) is reimbursed the costs associated with any material purchases. (In some instances a small handling fee may be added to this to cover administrative costs.) Costs associated with labour are reimbursed at a fixed rate such as a cost per hour, or per day, or per month.

The appeal to the SO is that it exposes it to minimal risk and that the administrative burden is simplified, relying mainly on time sheets.

The appeal to the Owner Organization (OO) is largely in relation to the ease with which it can subsequently vary the work. On the downside, it can prove expensive if the number of hours increases substantially beyond that originally envisaged since the SO tends to 'over recover' fixed overheads.

TARGET COST CONTRACTS

There are variations on this theme but they all seek to share the burden of excessive costs between the Supplier Organization (SO) and the Owner Organization (OO) in an agreed ratio. This ratio is sometimes known as the 'pain: gain' share.

Applying this to the scenario above it may be agreed that the 'Target Cost' of digging the pool is £8,000; that the SO would be entitled to reimbursement of the costs; a fee of, say, £2,000; and a share of any savings between the Actual and Target Cost in a ratio of, say 80:20 OO:SO.

If the Actual Costs were £6,000 the SO would receive £8,400 which represents a percentage profit of 28.6 per cent. By contrast if the Actual Costs were £12,000 then the SO would receive £13,200 which represents a percentage profit of 9.9 per cent. The calculation of these is laid out in Table 10.1 on the next page.

The Target Cost is a genuine estimate of what the actual price will be. It is possible to reach this through competition whereby each competing SO offers a Target Cost. Changes can be accommodated, subsequently, by altering the Target Cost figure.

This option promotes close collaboration between the parties since both parties share an incentive to reduce costs. Helpfully, the degree of the risk can be apportioned directly on the basis of what each party is able to bear.

It does, however, incur an administrative burden on both parties since it requires an 'open book' policy on behalf of the SO.

Table 10.1   Target cost contract reimbursement calculation

Target cost	£8,000	
Fee	£2,000	
Pain: gain share (OO:SO)	80:20	
Scenario	I	2
Actual cost	£6,000	£12,000
Reimbursement		
Cost	£6,000	£12,000
Fee	£2,000	£2,000
Pain: gain	20% of £8,000 – £6,000 = £400	20% of £8,000 – £12,000 = -£800
Total	£8,400	£13,200
Profit as a percentage	28.6%	9.9%

FIXED PRICE CONTRACTS

As mentioned above, many adopt this expression for what has been referred to above as a Firm Price contract. In contrast, some readers will have come across it being reserved to describe the following, slightly different, arrangement.

The contract is essentially a Firm Price contract, however, part or all of the contract price can be varied in accordance with some index that is beyond the control of either party.

The most common example of this is when a provision is made for inflation. If the contract is to last a long time, or alternatively the currency of the consideration is subject to high levels of inflation, it may be appropriate for the Supplier Organization (SO) to be allowed to inflate its prices in accordance with a publicly available rate.

The use of this arrangement is prevalent in the construction industry where a myriad of published indices facilitate its use. Examples of these include the Construction Price and Cost Indices produced by the UK government.

A more exotic use of the method can cater for fluctuations in raw material costs such as the price of copper which grossly affects the buying or selling of electrical equipment with a high copper content. In such instances the copper element of the deliverable can be weighed and the price to be paid is determined by the spot price for copper on the London Metals Exchange at the point of transfer of ownership.

EXOTIC CONTRACTUAL RELATIONSHIP

Another element that can influence decisions over reimbursement relates to the ability of the parties to fund the work. For significant projects, especially public projects, providing the capital to pay for the work is problematic.

Solutions can involve the Owner Organization (OO) paying the Supplier Organization (SO) over a protracted period of time. Simple versions are similar to the credit arrangements offered in many retail situations and can involve a third party to provide funding and to bear the risk of an OO default.

Over recent years more exotic arrangements have come into being that allow the OO to obtain the benefit they seek from a project without actually owning the product or paying the SO directly for it. Instead they pay the SO for the service offered by the product.

There are many combinations and permutations. For instance 'BOT' (Build Operate Transfer) contracts have the SO building an asset and then enjoying the operational benefits before transferring the asset over to the OO at some defined point. 'BOOT' (Build Own Operate Transfer) is a variation that involves the SO owning the asset.

In these arrangements the Owner Organization (OO) is often a public body and the Supplier Organization (SO) a private body hence expressions such as 'PPP' (Public Private Partnership) and 'PFI' (Private Finance Initiatives).

Paying for the benefit of ownership rather than the asset is not restricted to public projects. Rolls Royce, for instance, secures half of its revenue and 70 per cent of its profits from its 'Totalcare' business model that focuses on a 'power by the hour' approach rather than the conventional supply of their aircraft engines (Coates, 2014).

Reference

Coates, D., 2014. *Growth Champions Rolls Royce*. [online] Available at: http://growthchampions.org/growth-champions/rollsroyce/ [accessed 10 April 2014].

Chapter 11
Management of Changes

Irrespective of whether your organization is a Supplier Organization (SO) or an Owner Organization (OO), anyone involved in projects must develop a keen understanding of change; the causes of change, its enormous potential for wreaking havoc and how it must be managed carefully.

In Chapter 4 we discussed how, the later in the project lifecycle the change is made, the higher the cost.

This relationship is sometimes referred to by the formula $1:n:n^2:n^3$ (Turner, 2007) and relates to the cost of implementing change during Feasibility, Design, Execution and Closeout. Within this, 'n' is an integer that depends upon the type of project. Turner offers n=3 for shipbuilding and n=10 for information systems giving ratios of 1:3:9:27 and 1:10:100:1000 respectively. Dramatic numbers indeed!

How Changes Affect Projects

This increase is easily understood if we consider what is involved at the various stages of, say, a commercial construction project. Imagine changing the type of brick used to face the building with another brick type of similar cost.

The change instigated during Feasibility would involve only minor changes to drawings and will be of negligible cost. The same change during Design would not be catastrophic but would involve the revision of many more documents and drawings. Making the same change during Execution would not only involve changing all the earlier documents but also actual construction work would need to be abandoned and reworked. The same changes during Closeout would be truly catastrophic since in addition to all the earlier costs, most likely, there will be the cost of dismantling earlier work before rework can commence and, since so much of the costs will be time-based (in, say, maintaining the construction site infrastructure), the additional delays would have a further impact. Such delays will also probably delay the operation of the new asset and hence impact on revenue.

However, even this brief description understates the cost of change since many of the costs are not immediately visible. Consider the following.

On receipt of a request for a change such as that suggested above, it is most likely (and highly advisable) that a prior assessment of the implications would be carried out. Imagine calling a meeting to do just this, but who should be involved? To ensure a thorough understanding we would need the architect, the site manager, the procurement manager, etc. In short, we would need to invite all the key members of our project team.

Immediately after the meeting starts let us pause to consider the implications of our actions, regardless of what the eventual outcome of the meeting is.

Firstly there are the direct costs. Have you ever sat in a meeting and worked out how much the direct cost of the meeting is in terms of the salaries of the attendees? Add in their on-costs and travel and accommodation at the venue and the figure is colossal. Someone has to pay that cost!

Secondly, what would they be doing if they were not at the meeting? They would, of course be carrying out the jobs they are paid to do; coordinating the designers, controlling the site, managing the suppliers. Whilst they are at the meeting the project is deprived of their services. This is the 'opportunity cost' and is the value we forgo by taking the chosen option. In respect of employees, their opportunity cost is always greater than their direct cost, otherwise it would not be worth employing them.

Thirdly, what will happen on the site as soon as the manager leaves to discuss a change that will render further work abortive? Have you ever done some fantastic work only to be asked afterwards to tear it down because someone gave you the wrong specification? Changes, even just the threat of changes, destroy motivation, team spirit and, perhaps most importantly, faith in the leader. What will happen next time the team is asked to do something by the same person who gave the wrong instructions last time?

Fourthly, in considering the change, new versions of drawings and specifications will need to be created. Despite the best efforts of the finest configuration librarians, the more versions there are of a document, the more opportunity there is for confusion and serious technical errors.

All these have a detrimental impact on the project that will be incurred regardless of whether the change is actually approved or not, and are in addition to the cost of the actual rework.

More often than not, the advantages of change are overestimated and the costs underestimated, especially since, as discussed, even the mere threat of change has enormous capacity for damaging projects. Especially in the later stages of a project, changes should be resisted.

Avoiding the Need for Changes

With this in mind it would be helpful to avoid the need for changes in the first instance. Chapter 4 first introduced the trends of 'Uncertainty' and 'Cost of Implementing Change' shown in Figure 11.1.

The sharp upward turn of the 'Cost of Implementing Change' at 't_i', is associated with the commencement of the Implementation phase since after this point it is hardware and not just paperwork being changed. For the project, there is nothing cheaper and quicker than 'getting it right first time' during the Implementation phase.

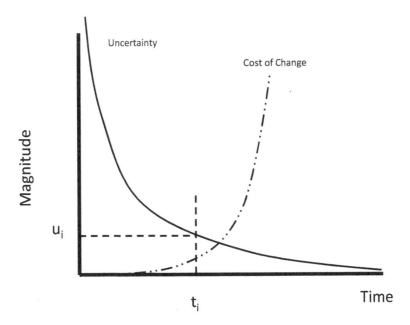

Figure 11.1   Avoiding the need for changes

However, the likelihood of not 'getting it right first time' and hence the need for change, is indicated by the degree of uncertainty 'u_i' appertaining at the start of Implementation.

There are a number of ways in which this uncertainty 'u_i' can be minimized. Firstly, the Implementation can be delayed. The reduction in 'Uncertainty' is primarily associated with the planning activities during the earlier phases. Simply increasing the amount of prior planning, by delaying the start of Implementation (or bringing forward the start of planning) ensures Implementation commences with much diminished residual uncertainty. Readers may be more familiar with the correlation of this, with those projects deemed to be super urgent and prematurely pushed into Implementation. Chaos, change, cost overruns and delays are inevitable.

Secondly, the profile of the 'Uncertainty' curve can be altered. Selectively increasing the resources devoted to planning activities and risk mitigation will erode uncertainty quicker. Thus reducing the uncertainty at Implementation to '$\bar{u}_i$' and hence risk of change (see Figure 11.2).

In both these instances prolonged and diligent planning should be viewed as being an active risk mitigation strategy.

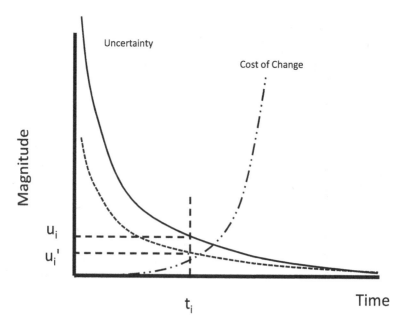

Figure 11.2   Accelerated erosion of uncertainty

There is a third option whereby the profile of the curve of 'Cost of Implementing Change' can be altered by delaying significant and expensive work until later in the project. Although this has the same effect, it is more complex to manage.

Two further points are worthy of note here.

Firstly, a change can only be recognized as such if there is a discernible difference between what is happening and what was expected to happen. It can seem, therefore, that vague plans are a good thing, but this is not the case.

Secondly, the frequency of change requests can be as important as the magnitude of individual requests. An excessive rate may indicate that the project has too much latent uncertainty and has been implemented too soon. In such instances it may be worth suspending the current phase and repeating the previous phase.

Change and the Supplier Organization

Management of changes is especially important to the Supplier Organization (SO) since it can have either a negative or positive effect on profit, depending upon whether responsibility for the instigating change lies with the SO or with the Owner Organization (OO).

It was suggested above that, from the perspective of the OO, the need for making a change during an Implementation phase is largely mitigated by diligent planning in the preceding phase. Such linkage across sequential phases is the case for the SO too. Specifically, diligent work in the pre-contract phases of Marketing and Selling is crucial to the successful avoidance or management of changes post-contract. This is especially so in relation to the work concerned with clarifying scope.

The Inevitability of Change

Given the destructive nature of change it would be convenient to eliminate it, but, unfortunately, there are practical limits to the degree to which uncertainty can be reduced prior to Implementation.

The rate of uncertainty reduction decreases over time (the gradient of the curve in Figure 11.1), so, since many project costs are time-based, eventually the cost of further delays to Implementation will exceed the benefits to be had from the marginal reduction in uncertainty.

There are consequences of this.

Firstly, there is an optimum period of planning for a project. Secondly, there will always be a residual element of uncertainty at the commencement of Implementation.

Consequently, changes are an inevitable feature of a project implementation and so a process to manage changes is essential.

Change Control Processes

SIMPLE PROTOCOL

Irrespective of whether one is a project manager in an OO or a SO there are two golden rules when it comes to managing changes:

1.   Do not implement any change without appropriate authorization.

2.   Do not implement any change until the consequences have been thoroughly considered.

Both of these objectives are addressed in a change management process. Figure 11.3 describes a basic example of such a process. It would be suitable for an OO managing a modestly sized project using 'in-house' resources only.

Firstly, a potential change is formally recognized by completion of a Change Request Form with a description of the proposed change and why it is thought to be a good idea. All suggested changes are usually recorded in a second document, a Change Log, which simply tracks each suggested change and the decision reached. It will reference the serial number on the Change Request Form and so the need to duplicate all of the information is avoided.

No one has a monopoly on good ideas and so it is usual that any stakeholder is entitled to raise a Change Request Form, though the obligation of completing the form, helpfully, does tend to filter out frivolous requests.

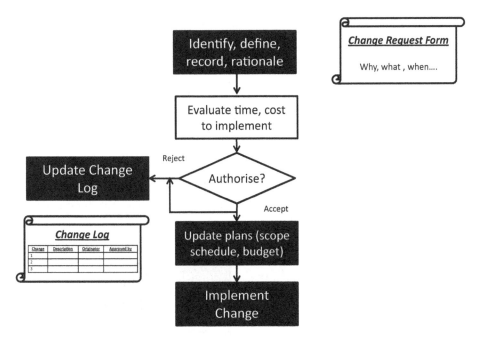

Figure 11.3   Simple change control process

Secondly, an assessment of both the costs and benefits of the change is made. These costs are not just financial. They will also include the impact on duration, the opportunity costs of the resource, the risk exposure and the performance of the project product.

Thirdly, a decision is made as to whether the change should be accepted or rejected.

If the decision is to reject the requested change then the log is updated and the matter closed.

If the change is accepted, then the log is updated, the project plans are modified and the change is implemented.

CONSIDERING THE IMPLICATIONS OF 'CONSIDERING THE IMPLICATIONS'

If the project in question is large or complex then the protocol offered above would become problematic.

As suggested earlier, it is not only the cost of making the change that is damaging to the project; the actual process of considering the implications of the change is also damaging.

In the simple example above, all requested changes will be assessed fully, but it is unlikely that this would be acceptable since a colossal amount of time and resources may be committed to just considering changes.

To prevent this, further steps are required such that before the implication of a change is considered, the implication of considering the implication is considered. This may well seem like bureaucracy gone mad but there is good reason for it (see Figure 11.4).

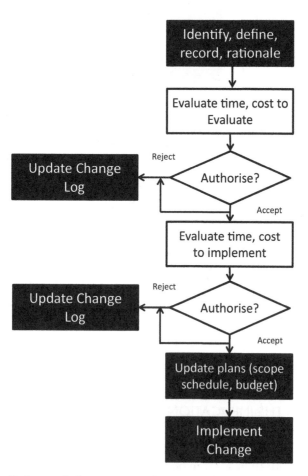

Figure 11.4   Enhanced change control process

AUTHORISATION OF CHANGES

The decision whether to approve or reject changes requires familiarity with a number of disciplines and project topics. For modest projects, the sponsor is capable of the decision but for larger and more complex projects, the decision is often too complex for just the one person. In such circumstances a 'Change Control Board' representing a range of expertise becomes appropriate.

Managing Changes that Cross Contractual Boundaries

These considerations emphasize how complex the management of changes is. However, this complexity increases by an order of magnitude when we consider changes that migrate across contractual boundaries. When this happens it requires a party to do something which they were not originally contracted to do, or alternatively, accept something less than what they are contractually entitled to. Such changes have profound implications and need special treatment.

THE INTERESTS AND RIGHTS OF THE PARTIES

Firstly, what entitles the Owner Organization (OO) to instruct the Supplier Organization (SO) to make changes? If we order a meal at a restaurant and, just prior to it being served, we change our minds and order another dish, is the restaurant obliged to concede to our request? In all likelihood they would insist that we meet our obligations under the original agreement and pay for the first meal, before entering into a new agreement for the second meal.

There is no right enshrined in law that allows one party to unilaterally vary the terms of a contract. A contract is a deal and the whole point about a deal is that it commits each party to do that which they have promised to do.

This creates a difficulty.

The difficulty is particularly acute with Firm Price type contracts when both the scope and consideration are predetermined amounts.

Such changes can be made to the contract if both parties agree to the change, but this has drawbacks. Principal amongst these is the relative negotiating power of the Owner Organization (OO). As discussed in Chapter

10 the practicalities of the situation usually ensure that the OO is in a very weak position when trying to negotiate necessary late changes.

The problems are not just restricted to money. Often, when the need for a change is recognized, progress must be stopped until the change is implemented. Delays associated with negotiations can be devastating to the OO's project, which can further weaken its position.

Many readers who work for an OO will recognize this predicament and the frustration and commercial detriment that it can represent.

Similarly, many readers who work for a SO will also recognize this predicament, but from a different perspective; one that recognizes the very significant commercial opportunity that such changes provide for a SO.

However, it is not all good news for the Supplier Organization (SO) since it is within the context of changes that it can be at its most vulnerable. Very careful management is required and many well-intentioned SOs, whilst attempting to be helpful and courteous to an OO, have put themselves in serious commercial peril.

RESERVING THE RIGHT TO INSTRUCT CHANGES

This weak position, when instructing change post-contract, can represent an unacceptable risk to the Owner Organization (OO) and so most insist that a mechanism is included within the contract allowing them to vary the works, with immediate effect and without the prior consent of the Supplier Organization (SO).

In turn, this poses considerable difficulties for the SO. How can it ensure that it will be rewarded appropriately for such work? What resource planning and provision should it undertake in response to a contract that obliges it to conduct some, as of yet, undefined work at some unknown point in the future?

These very real concerns are addressed by further clauses that offer some protection to the SO, for example, by imposing limits on the magnitude of changes that the OO can instruct.

These clauses, that seek to ensure equitable treatment to both parties, can become complex and whereas there are common themes there are differences in the exact wording of them in different contracts.

Ability of the Supplier Organization to Manage Changes

Managing changes across contractual boundaries imposes significant burdens. Both parties, but especially the Supplier Organization (SO), will need to respond with specific facilities, skills and instincts. Consider the following.

OFFICE ADMINISTRATION

Many aspects of a contract's execution require significant administrative effort but prominent amongst these is the management of change.

In the first instance, contract clauses that address change, seek to ensure clarity of communication. They often require that formal variations and other significant notices are addressed in writing, in a predetermined format, between nominated individuals.

Further, to ensure the changes do not impose delays, there is usually a time limit within which replies must be sent.

It is said, especially by the experienced, that the party that triumphs in any contract dispute is the party with the best record. At minimum, the project manager (PM) of a Supplier Organization (SO) must ensure that the correspondence and information in relation to changes are documented and archived contemporaneously, and that this is not compromised by a desire to keep the Owner Organization (OO) happy nor to uphold progress with the work at hand. There are many heart-breaking stories of SO who, with the best of intentions, have neglected to defend their own position in favour of servicing the immediate needs of the OO and its project. More than a few have been rendered bankrupt as a result.

Suitable provision must be made within the resource plans of Supplier Organizations (SO) to service this administrative burden and many SO who are moving from the routine operations to the project arena are taken aback at its magnitude.

COMMERCIALLY ASTUTE PROJECT MANAGERS

Some Owner Organizations (OO) manage projects using just in-house resources and in these cases the OO PM need have no requirement to administer to contracts but, by definition, this is not a luxury that can be afforded to Supplier Organizations (SO). The PM of a SO will always be responding to an incoming contract and (in common with the project managers from OO who are engaging SO) they will need to be comfortable with the administration of contracts and be commercially astute.

For instance, the exact alteration to the scope, price and duration of any individual change will need to be negotiated and agreed. This will often involve the SO submitting an offer, to which the OO will offer a counter-offer or acceptance.

It becomes clear that the negotiation of change becomes an exercise in selling and buying. For the Owner Organization (OO) this requires its PM to have a capability in the discipline of buying, and for the Supplier Organization (SO) this requires its PM to have a capability in the discipline of selling.

Further, the PM within a successful SO will be sufficiently commercially astute to recognize the opportunities for further work. This requires the skillset of the PM to include aspects of marketing.

However, the PM for both an OO and a SO must recognize the potential threat from changes. They must be diligent in what they say and do. The OO must be careful not to inadvertently lay itself open to a claim for compensation by asking for something outside of its contractual entitlement. The SO must resist the desire to 'keep sweet' the OO by simply acceding to OO requests even though they may seem innocuous.

CLAIMS AND COUNTER-CLAIMS

There is often an overriding need to maintain progress with the Owner Organization (OO) project and so the rights reserved in the contract, by the OO, to instigate change usually allow for such changes to be made immediately. This postpones much of the administration, including calculation of the compensation to which the Supplier Organization (SO) is entitled, until well after the event. Accordingly the presentation of the various claims and counter-claims, and negotiation of the final settlement between the parties, often occurs after acceptance of the final product.[1]

The PMs of both parties must be sufficiently competent so as to be capable of undertaking these major negotiations. Apart from the soft skills involved

---

1   Ideally such negotiations should be embraced as early as possible and not wait for the final phase but practicalities often result in them being held to the end.

there must be sufficient knowledge of the technical aspects of the work; knowledge of the contract; and also the legal framework within which it operates. In extremis, the settlement may require the involvement of a third party such as an adjudicator and in these circumstances the PM will need to be able to write a case that articulates their claims, or defence against a counter-claim, and is capable of withstanding legal scrutiny. Whilst both parties have an interest in these settlements, the outcome is often more significant for the Supplier Organization (SO) since its profit is directly affected; the sole reason for engaging in the project in the first place.

MANAGING SUBCONTRACTORS

Many Supplier Organizations (SO) engage other SO as subcontractors. A SO that is obliged to accept changes instigated by its client must consider how, in turn, it can secure the same rights over its own suppliers, since having to reimburse one's suppliers for changes and not being able to recover this from one's client is a potential disaster for the SO.

A simple response is to use identical contract terms and conditions with its own suppliers, i.e. a 'back to back' arrangement, though in practice it is rarely as straightforward as this. As discussed in Chapter 8, as we descend through the procurement chain, in terms of both product and also contractual agreements, there is a move away from the bespoke and towards the routine. The lower in the chain they are, the less able is the Supplier Organization (SO) to respond to requests for exotic contractual terms and also to bear risk.

SUPPLIER ORGANIZATION ORIGINATED CHANGE

When supplying goods in response to a contract, the Supplier Organization (SO) loses a degree of autonomy in deciding the fate of changes it instigates itself.

If the changes have no impact upon whether the requirements of the contract are met then the processing and authorization of the change can remain within the SO, but if this is not the case, then the matter must migrate across the contractual boundary.

Imagine that the manufacture of a complex part has a minor accident whereby one dimension is slightly less than that required by the drawing. If the dimension in question does not compromise the performance of the item, and especially if the cost and time required to remanufacture the part are excessive, then the SO may request that the OO accept the part as it is. A reasonable OO may accede to the request in which case it becomes an authorized change.

Such requests are not rare when making complex bespoke equipment and are referred to variously as Concession Requests or Derogations, and the protocol for managing them is often dictated by the terms of the contact.

These become far more complex when the error is not inconsequential; when they involve the Owner Organization (OO) performing significant extra work to assess the implications of the proposed change; or when they require the OO to provide extra facilities within the project to accommodate the change. In such instances the SO may be required to compensate the OO.

SUB-SUPPLIER ORIGINATED CHANGE

The Supplier Organization (SO) will also become involved in processing changes requested by its own suppliers. In turn these may need to be passed up to the Owner Organization (OO) for final approval.

Sophisticated Change Protocol

As can be seen from the above, managing change is problematic enough in any case but managing changes which cross contractual boundaries is both complex and fraught with difficulties.

The relatively simple protocols addressed within the flowcharts earlier will need significant further enhancement to accommodate the differing contracting parties.

Firstly, they will need to reflect any processes specified within the contract in question.

Secondly, since for the Supplier Organization (SO), changes can originate from within its own organization, the Owner Organization (OO) or from the suppliers, any protocol must deal with the source of change (and hence liability for it).

Especially in the context of the latter point we can see how correspondence in relation to changes may flow up or down many tiers within the procurement chain, involve a great many individuals and account for a considerable consumption of resources. The cost of these must be met and, whereas some costs can be recovered from the party responsible for necessitating a change, it is unlikely that all such costs can be recovered.

NEC Family of Contracts

Change can set Owner Organizations (OO) and Supplier Organizations (SO) in direct conflict. Historically, the management of contracts, particularly those in engineering and construction, secured a reputation for significant adversity between the two parties.

This was seen by some as a major impediment and one individual, Dr Martin Barnes, set out to improve the situation. The result was the NEC (originally known as the New Engineering Contract).

The NEC is now a comprehensive family of contracts, covering many diverse sectors and widely applied around the world for the management of relationships between the parties engaged on major projects.

These contracts differ from the more traditional contracts in that they were drawn up specifically to promote good project management techniques and ensure the relationship between the parties is one of collaboration rather than conflict. This was achieved via three characteristics (NEC, 2009):

1.   It stimulates good management of the relationship between the contracting parties.

2.   It is flexible so as to allow its use in a wide variety of commercial situations.

3.   The language and structure of the document is clear and simple.

A consequence of this is the moving of change resolution away from retrospective management associated with post-contract claim resolution, and towards a proactive approach. For example, Owner Organization (OO) instigated changes are described as 'Compensation events' and rather than being managed largely after the fact, changes must be dealt with immediately. This is achieved by a strict system of rapid notification and by requiring the Supplier Organization (SO) to provide quotations for the new work within a strict time frame and before they are enacted.

Whereas this maintains the pace of the project and the currency of the documentation, it does impose significant obligations upon the parties, particularly the SO to maintain an administrative capability that can deal with the communication duties imposed upon it.

Further alignment with good project management practices is an inherent encouragement for the parties to avoid the need for changes by diligent prior planning and preparation, especially pre-contract. As Dr Barnes (2012) puts it:

> *[There is a mechanism built in from the 1st edition of NEC that] every time somebody gives a new instruction to the contractor there is the potential for costing the client money ... [so the] pressure to get it right before you went out to tender would be stronger.*

The widespread adoption of the NEC family of contracts and its inherent approach is a glowing testament to how it improves the management of relationships between parties managing projects. However, the management of changes is still a complex and difficult topic and one that requires attention and resources.

References

Barnes, M., 2012. *The NEC Story*. Interviewed by Robert Gerrard, 11 July 2012. [online] Available at: http://www.neccontract.com/about/index.asp [accessed 11 April 2014].

NEC, 2009. *Procurement and Contract Strategies: An NEC Document*. London: NEC.

Turner, R., 2007. Managing Scope – Configuration and Work Methods. In: R. Turner, ed., 2011. *Gower Handbook of Project Management*, 4th edn. Farnham: Gower Publishing.

PART 4

Selected Project Management Techniques for Supplier Organizations

Chapter 12
Marketing in a Project Environment

If a company does not have a market they do not a business; this holds true irrespective of the technical excellence of their product or indeed the quality of their management team. It is a truism for any business.

Marketing ensures organizations put the right product in front of the right customer at the right time, and its success is essential to any ongoing business.

The traditional activities of marketers involve identifying potential customers, establishing a relationship with them, understanding their needs and directing product development.

All these apply to marketing within the project environment but as we shall see there is a particular emphasis on the establishment of customer relationships and facilitating the communications that are so essential to effective project management.

Marketing in Project and Non-Project Environments

Firstly, let us consider marketing in a non-project environment. By way of an example let us recall the washing machines discussed in Chapter 1. The product is highly evolved and mature, having been refined over many years of experience of servicing, and listening to, the same type of customers.

The customer base for washing machines is made up of individual customers, as opposed to businesses. These customers will be knowledgeable about the product and its use. They will also know the supplier and its competitors and many will exhibit 'brand loyalty' and favour our supplier with repeat business.

In turn the supplier knows a great deal about the buyers; the typical ages, gender bias, what magazines they read, what television they watch and websites they visit. This enables them to know how, and where, to contact them. Each sale will be an entirely private affair between supplier and customer and although the value of each transaction is modest, there will be numerous transactions.

Contrast this with the unique products and transient relationships of the project environment, again, discussed in Chapter 1. By way of an example let us return to the creation of a major sports stadium. The customer base for such a product consists of a small number of varied businesses and commercial enterprises that could be located anywhere in the world. Orders are small in number but of enormous individual value. Since purchase of such a product is infrequent, the experience and knowledge of the individual customers, most likely, will be low in relation to both the product and also the market and potential suppliers.

Similarly, in the absence of regular business, the potential suppliers, most likely, will know little about individual potential customers, including their identity. Further, given the size and nature of sports stadia, we can expect the relationship between the parties, and the nature of the work, to become a matter of enormous public interest, especially if public money is involved. The job of a marketer within a project environment is a very different challenge to that faced by one within a non-project environment and the contrast is summarized in Table 12.1.

Table 12.1   Contrast of typical market environments for project and routine operations

Environment	Project	Routine operations
Trade type	Mostly B2B	B2C and B2B
Nature of product	Bespoke/unique	Standard/off-the-shelf
Frequency of ordering	Low	High
Value of contracts	High to very high	Low to medium/high
Likelihood of repeat orders	Low	High
OO–SO relationship	New	Long established
Buyer knowledge	Often low	Often very high
Environmental influence, i.e. political	Often high	Usually very low
Roles and structure of actors	Often vague and transient	Established
Funding provided by	Often a third party	Client

Putting Potential Owner Organizations and Supplier Organizations in First Contact

As with all marriages, in the very first instance, the parties have to make contact with each other. As we have indicated, this can be very difficult.

For very large public projects, at the outset, it may be clear that there will be a project but unclear who the parties, such as the Owner Organization (OO), will be. The perception of a need, for example for enhanced airport capability, exists way before developers and other actors are identified. In such instances who does the Supplier Organization (SO) approach to express their interest?

For more modest and private projects, e.g. a manufacturer building an extension to its factory, the identity of the client is clear but the existence of the potential project may not.

This is the situation that prospective SO find themselves in and to a marketer their most precious asset is their network. Through this informal web of contacts they are constantly on the lookout across this unstructured and vague environment for first clues as to the identity of potential projects and OO. It is this activity that has been described by some as 'scanning the milieu' (Cova et al., 2002).

As with single boys and girls looking for prospective partners, it is helpful to go where you think other like-minded parties go and this often involves clustering around a common interest.

For prospective Owner Organizations (OO) and Supplier Organizations (SO) there are two important types of clusters; technology and geography.

Civil engineering, IT and transport are examples of different technologies that have dedicated magazines and trade fairs.

The second cluster, geography, can involve magazines and trade fairs but can also involve trade missions sponsored by the governments of respective countries. For more modest SO, local trade organizations and Chambers of Commerce can also help sustain the vital network of contacts.

Advertisements, articles and trade stalls provide the Supplier Organization (SO) with opportunities to demonstrate their achievements with previous projects in the hope of attracting Owner Organizations (OO) with relevant projects or, alternatively, to encourage potential OO to sponsor new projects requiring the SO special skills. Magazines have the advantage of a wider coverage, whereas trade fairs have the advantage in that they facilitate early face-to-face dialogue.

Although it is usually the SO who instigate first contact via advertisements, it is customary in some industries for the OO to advise of a new project in the appropriate magazine.

The geographical context becomes particularly important for those SO supplying very high value products, for which the demand is very intermittent. The need for their prospective market to be as large as possible can involve them operating on an international scale, requiring them to establish sales and marketing offices, or agencies overseas. This presence facilitates 'face-to-face' meetings and 'word of mouth' communication, and the establishment of personal relationships; a vital precursor to business in many cultures. Large organizations can invest enormous sums of money servicing such a facility, over many years, before even the merest hint of a major project comes along.

There are other mechanisms that help introduce prospective Owner Organizations (OO) and Supplier Organizations (SO). Consider the following.

The Internet is having a dramatic impact in this arena. Even the most modest SO will have a website that advertises its competency and capability. In return, any prospective OO can simply access a search engine to discover a plethora of prospective SO. So dominant is this becoming that many SO will invest considerable resources on 'Search Engine Optimization' to ensure that they feature highly in any such investigation by an OO.

There are organizations that have identified the commercial opportunities presented by needful parties. These are the project environment equivalent to a dating agency and will 'scan the milieu' on behalf of the prospective SO and, for a fee, will pass on any opportunity so discovered.

Under EU anti-corruption legislation, any prospective Owner Organization (OO) spending public money must advertise their intention to all prospective Supplier Organizations (SO) in Europe and invite their bids. This is done by putting a notice in the Official Journal of the European Union (OJEU). Such 'OJEU notices' provide a valuable resource to SO.

An important element of a marketer's network is 'Approved Suppliers' lists. Many large organizations maintain lists of SO who can demonstrate good service and they will be automatically invited to bid for any new opportunity. These lists are more common when the requirement is less bespoke or infrequent, however many prospective SO actively seek approval to be included in them.

Defining What the Owner Organization Wants

A very real difficulty at the start of a project is that the Owner Organization (OO) may not be wholly clear what it wants. Further, if the OO is at the early stages of its lifecycle, especially if it is prior to endorsement of the business case, it may be uncertain that its project will go ahead at all.

In such instances it may need the assistance of a prospective Supplier Organization (SO) to decide and articulate exactly what is required. Often, the cost estimates within an OO business case are derived from quotations from prospective SO.

Such instances present both an opportunity and a threat for the prospective SO. An early opportunity to influence the definition of the work can put it in a very strong position. Firstly, it is able to establish close working relationships with the personnel within the OO. People buy from people and a familiar SO will have an advantage over one that is unknown. Secondly, the opportunity to influence the stated requirement enables the prospective SO to shape it towards a solution that it can meet but which its competitors cannot. (Happy is the SO salesperson who is asked by the OO to help write the specification for the subsequent 'Invitation to Tender'.) In extremis, the SO may be able to persuade the OO to deal with it on an exclusive basis and not contact alternative SO.

The threat in such an instance is that the assistance provided to the Owner Organization (OO) may incur a considerable cost and there is no guarantee that the OO will place an order with the SO. The OO may choose not to proceed with the project or alternatively at the eleventh hour decide to favour another SO.

'He who pays the piper calls the tune' and so, although the SO will strive to exert influence, it is the OO that will actually decide whether and how the project proceeds. In doing so a number of details need to be addressed. Consider the following.

DEGREE OF DEFINITION

There are two ways in which an Owner Organization (OO) can define its need.

The first could be described as a 'duty specification'. Here the OO is not describing what the product is, but the effect that it will ultimately achieve, i.e. the duty it needs to service. An OO buying a pump may just specify the delivery pressure and flow rate, for example.

The second instance could be described as 'detailed specification' and is a precise description of what is to be supplied. In the example of the pump, this will involve specifying pipe diameters, motor capacity, electrical wiring details, paint type and colour, etc.

There are pros and cons with each.

For the Owner Organization (OO), the 'duty specification' is cheap to produce, and insulates it from any errors made in a 'detailed specification'. However, it does sacrifice significant control over what exactly it eventually gets. Also, comparing competing bids against a 'duty specification' can be tricky.

For the Supplier Organization (SO), responding to a 'duty specification' can involve minimal cost and risk since it offers a greater opportunity to deliver a known product (though if no known product exists then the cost and risks of responding may be significant).

PROCUREMENT CHAIN

Should the Owner Organization (OO) engage just one Supplier Organization (SO) on a 'turnkey' basis, or should it deal directly with each of the low tier suppliers, or should it have a hybrid that combines elements of both?

The pros and cons of this important decision were addressed in Chapter 9.

REIMBURSEMENT TYPE

Chapter 10 addressed the various options for determining the amount of consideration the Supplier Organization (SO) will receive, and the very different SO behaviour that each encourages.

It is a matter the Owner Organization (OO) must consider carefully.

PROCESS OF SUPPLIER ORGANIZATION SELECTION

The Owner Organization (OO) must make a decision about how it will select the favoured Supplier Organization (SO).

It may adopt an open and extensive competitive bidding process that engages as many SO as possible, from whom the cheapest compliant bid will be selected. By this the OO enjoys the benefit of a low price that will result from the competition, but there are drawbacks to this approach.

In selecting the lowest priced bid, the OO is seeking to identify the SO offering the best value, i.e. the best product for the minimum price. However, by favouring just the cheapest bid it may well select the SO that is most prepared to accept extreme risks, provide the minimum quality, treat its suppliers badly and hence is the SO most vulnerable to bankruptcy and bringing chaos to the project of the OO.

The opposite of an open and competitive bid is a 'single tender action', or a 'negotiated contract'. By this there is no competition; the Owner Organization (OO) deals exclusively with just one Supplier Organization (SO) in the development of the project. A contract is established by direct negotiation with the SO for the supply of its services.

Again there are pros and cons.

For the OO a negotiated contract avoids the time and cost of a protracted bidding process and the need to engage with, and assess, many competing suppliers. However, it is difficult for the OO to demonstrate subsequently that the decision was neutral and that the SO was not favoured for any inappropriate reasons. For large and public organizations demonstrating the latter can be a major requirement.

For the favoured Supplier Organization (SO), and each of the competing Supplier Organizations (SO), the cost of following a competitive bidding process is considerable. Ultimately these costs must be met by current and future OO, as overheads within the price offered. To mitigate these, many SO will be prepared to return to the OO part of any savings achieved by the 'negotiated contract'. Also, faced with competing bids, to win the contract the

SO need only just undercut its competitors, which may have the effect of taking the price higher than would have been offered within a negotiated contract.

In practice there are a number of different formal and semi-formal selection processes that can be adopted. For instance there may be a competitive bid only amongst specially selected and invited SO.

Defining What the Supplier Organization Can Offer

Outside of the project environment, Supplier Organizations (SO) supplying 'off-the-shelf' products avoid much of the technical risk of the product not being fit for purpose since the product is already established, and the marketer mostly focuses on identifying customers for that product.

This is not the reality for a SO within the project environment that is offering bespoke products. Here the likelihood of supplying something that does not work or is not fit for purpose is considerable.

This risk is best mitigated pre-contract, by steering the requirement of the Owner Organization (OO) to fit as closely as possible to an established product or service of the Supplier Organization (SO). In contrast, most likely, the OO will be steering the requirement to fit its 'unique endeavour' and away from a standard product.

The fact that a SO is prepared to operate within a project environment demonstrates that it is prepared to bear a degree of this technical risk, however, the amount is a judgement it must make. Each SO is able to offer an envelope of capability shaped around familiar, even standard, products and processes. This envelope can be stretched away from the familiar to embrace the bespoke but the further the stretch, the higher the risk of failure.

PRODUCT DEVELOPMENT

Any bespoke deliverable will require a degree of product development.

Some Supplier Organizations (SO) will anticipate the requirements of potential Owner Organizations (OO) and engage in proactive R&D activities. Others may choose to do it only in response to a specific enquiry. Each approach has inherent risks. The former may not secure any customers; the latter may not lead to an order.

However, if significant development is required, it is unlikely the OO will allow many SO to bid because of the cost of responding to similar queries from a number of parties. Also, the more bespoke the requirement the less likely the product can be fully defined at the outset. This will lead the OO away from Firm Price contracts towards Cost Plus which may be deemed an advantage to the SO.

The implication of this last point is that the Owner Organization (OO) may be prepared to share some of the development risk and even assist in the product development. This may be necessary if the risk of either technical failure or pre-contract termination is too much for the Supplier Organization (SO) to bear alone. Such arrangements can be of enormous attraction to SO, especially if it involves the SO developing capability and experience that will be attractive to other OO.

USE OF SUBCONTRACTORS

Often, an extension to the range of goods and services that can be offered by a Supplier Organization (SO) can be achieved simply, and at low risk, by augmenting it with products or services supplied by others. By this, risk is transferred to the subcontractor and away from the SO in question.

Very many SO secure huge advantage just from close relationships with an Owner Organization (OO), and simply supply goods and services that they procure in their entirety from elsewhere.

There are, of course, drawbacks. Firstly, if and when the OO realize that they can deal directly with the subcontractor then the business opportunity for the SO disappears (and often the relationship). Secondly, the SO retains full obligation for the goods and services it supplies and so bears the risk of any failure on the part of the subcontractor. If they do not have the technical or administrative capability to properly supervise the subcontractor then it is difficult for the SO to manage or mitigate this risk.

An alternative course of action is to engage a third party, not as a subcontractor but as a partner.

AGGREGATIONS OF SUPPLIER ORGANIZATIONS

In many instances, Supplier Organizations (SO) that do not have all the skills and facilities to satisfy a contract choose to form an aggregation of companies that collectively do have the capability. Thus a joint venture or consortium, described in Chapter 9, is formed.

This allows the SO to greatly increase its potential market without the risks of engaging major subcontractors, though it will inherit some liability for the performance of the other syndicate members, and its ability to mitigate this is limited.

COMMERCIAL CONSIDERATIONS OF THE SUPPLIER ORGANIZATION

In addition to the technical aspects, it is appropriate for the prospective Supplier Organization (SO) to consider the commercial basis upon which it will engage with the Owner Organization (OO).

More often than not it is the OO that is in the dominant position and will own the decision as to what commercial terms will be offered, but the SO owns the decision as to whether it will accept them.

Although it is tempting to leave decisions about commercial terms to closer to the negotiation of a contract, it is not in the best interests of the SO to pursue work, at great expense, solely on technical considerations only having to later reject a contract on the basis of unacceptable terms.

An early investigation is warranted.

Corporate Strategy of Supplier Organization and Fringe Benefits

We have established that the objective of the Supplier Organization (SO) is to make money by delivering contracts at a profit.

A straightforward interpretation of this will always have the SO pursuing the most profitable work. This is a good philosophy to adopt but there are other considerations.

As we have discussed, unlike Owner Organization (OO) project teams, SO are almost always permanent organizations. They seek to make money today, but also money tomorrow, on future contracts, so it can be appropriate to sacrifice short-term profit for the prospect of a larger long-term profit. Consider the following:

- An OO may be prepared to work in partnership with a SO to develop new products or techniques that may subsequently provide the SO with significant sales opportunities.

- Although an individual contract may not offer much by way of profit, it may provide an opportunity for the SO to become an 'approved supplier' to an OO, which will entitle it to bid for future, perhaps more lucrative, contracts offered by the OO.

- An OO may be based in another country and an individual contract may provide an opportunity for the SO to establish a presence and reputation in that country.

Ultimately, commercial organizations must speculate to accumulate and undoubtedly there are instances when each of the examples offered above would justify a small (or even negative) profit margin. This would be of particular relevance if securing access to new products or markets in question was part of the overall commercial strategy of the SO.

However, very great care is warranted here. The promise of 'jam tomorrow' has been responsible for very many significant losses on behalf of suppliers and any SO sacrificing short-term profit for the promise of a future, unquantifiable benefit is advised to proceed with great caution.

The Start of a Relationship

Marketing is just the start of what, hopefully, will be a long and mutually beneficial relationship between an Owner and Supplier Organization and this is aided by a strong personal relationship between those involved.

Much attention within books on project management is devoted to the discipline of stakeholder management; the influencing of those parties who affect or are affected by the project. The amount of such attention stands testament to just how important it is to get such relationships right.

The same principles apply here and, for the Supplier Organization (SO), there is no more important stakeholder than the Owner Organization (OO).

A good relationship increases the chances of securing the contract; increases the chance of that contract being on more favourable terms to the SO; makes the subsequent life of the project manager within the SO so much easier; and increases the likelihood of favourable extensions to the contract.

Many cultures, particularly non-western cultures, place great store in the value of such personal relationships, and prospective SO in these circumstances are often surprised at the amount of time and energy that they must invest in establishing such relationships long before a potential order materializes.

It is helpful if such relationships are at various levels. Consider the following:

- During contract execution the prime point of contact between the parties will be between their project managers. This relationship is necessarily formal and is sometimes not the best forum to discuss delicate and contentious issues. The ability for senior managers of the parties to engage with each other, preferably informally, to explore these issues is a very valuable facility.

- Having a few people intimate with the OO allows a broader perspective on subsequent decisions such as the 'Bid/No Bid' decision.

- The departure of a key team member is less traumatic if the relationship is multi-layered.

The 'Bid/No Bid' Decision Gate

The conclusion of the Marketing phase is the 'Bid/No Bid' Decision Gate, when a prospective Supplier Organization (SO) must decide whether to invest resources in compiling and submitting a formal offer for a prospective contract.

This presupposes that there is a formal SO selection process requiring formal bids since, in the case of a 'single tender action', there is no such obvious point. However the sense of the gate applies in all circumstances. In practice, any marketer considering a potential project is always alert to the question 'is it worth carrying on?'. Early termination is often the appropriate response, long before any 'invitation to bid' is offered.

The gate decision is based upon a comparison of future cost and benefit.

The benefit is the combination of the likelihood of securing the subsequent contract and the price (consideration) to be gained from its execution. Whereas the costs are those future costs to bid for, and subsequently execute, the work (those costs incurred up to this point in time can be dismissed as 'sunk costs').

The techniques for estimating of costs will be dealt with in the next chapter, but the likely price and the likelihood of winning the bidding competition are subjective judgements that must be made by the marketer.

As discussed in Chapter 4, this first Decision Gate within a lifecycle is the most important, and for the SO it is wholly reliant upon the marketer and their judgement of how much influence they can exert over the perspective OO relative to that of competing SO, as well as what others are likely to bid for the work.

Reference

Cova, B., Ghauri, P. and Salle, R., 2002. *Project Marketing, Beyond Competitive Bidding*. Chichester: Wiley.

Chapter 13

Selling in a Project Environment

Whereas marketing involves 'putting the right product in front of the right customer at the right time', selling is concerned with persuading that customer to buy that product on terms most favourable to the seller.

The discipline relies heavily on the interpersonal and influencing skills of the salesperson. These soft skills overlap with the project management discipline of 'stakeholder management' but they are not unique to the project environment.

Where selling activity within a project environment does differ from that in a non-project environment, is in its timing. For standard products, such as the much referenced washing machines, selling generally takes place after the product has been created. However, when creating bespoke products, by definition, the selling activity takes place before the product is created. The Selling phase of the Supplier Organization's (SO) project lifecycle must therefore anticipate the Create phase and this requires the salesperson to be intimate with two core project management disciples; namely estimating and risk mitigation.

Formal and Informal Selling Processes

In all but exceptional cases,[1] the choice as to how the Supplier Organization (SO) will be selected lies with the Owner Organization (OO) and the SO is obliged to follow it. There are many alternative approaches ranging from a closed and informal 'negotiated contract' to an open and formal 'competitive bidding'. Competitive bidding is generally favoured for high value contracts or when the OO is a public body and the protocol devised will be structured around the following features:

- Formal notifications such as 'Invitations to Bid' (ITB), 'Invitations to Tender' (ITT) or a 'Request For Quotation' (RFQ).

---

1   For example some EU legislation imposes constraints on publicly funded projects.

- A defined format for these documents.

- A mechanism to ensure all prospective SO receive the same information, i.e. specifications and replies to any queries from other prospective SO.

- Restrictions on the extent and nature of contact between each prospective SO and the OO.

- Explanation of how the various competing bids will be judged.

If the selected process is a 'negotiated contract' there will be less formality, and the influences which the Supplier Organization's (SO) sales team can bring to bear can be more imaginative and creative.

However, regardless of the formality of the process, ultimately, selling involves one party making an offer, which the other party then chooses to accept or reject, either outright or by making a counter-offer.

Accordingly, the following are relevant for all selling scenarios but for illustrative purposes we shall assume a formal process is adopted and that the contract in question is of a Firm Price type, since these impose the greatest discipline on the parties.

The Nature of Estimates

For the Supplier Organization (SO) to return a profit, its consideration must exceed its costs. Therefore, before offering a price (assuming Firm Price arrangement) it is essential that the SO understands what those costs are, but, since they have not yet been incurred, the SO must rely on an estimate.

When considering estimates, a useful premise to start from is that all estimates are wrong; it's just a matter of how wrong they are.

PRECISION AND ACCURACY OF ESTIMATES AND THE DEGREE OF CONFIDENCE

Often we talk of the need for an 'accurate estimate', but what do we mean by that?

Imagine an estimated cost of £3,678,887. For this estimate to be subsequently regarded as 'accurate', how close does the actual cost need to be to it? £3,678,887 exactly? Between £3.6m and £3.7m? Between £3m and £4m?

When exploring the concept of 'accuracy' we are immediately drawn into the need to express estimates, not as a single point, but as a range, such as the £3.6 to £3.7m mentioned above, and subsequently regarding it as being 'accurate' only if the true figure is contained therein.

The use of a range has a downside since it can encourage us to increase the accuracy of our estimates (likelihood of true figure being within the range) simply by increasing the width of our range. This can be overcome by imposing limits for the width, a process which also enhances the usefulness of the estimates.

Perhaps the simplest way is to adopt confidence limits. By this, for each estimate two numbers are quoted, a minimum and a maximum, such that the originator is, say, 90 per cent confident that the true answer is in this range. The breadth of this span is referred to as the 'precision' of the estimate.

Although the estimate will be regarded as being accurate if the real value is within this range, this cannot be known until after the fact.

By contrast, the precision is known from the start and it reveals the variability of the parameter in the eyes of the estimator, and hence indicates their confidence. In a practical sense, the precision of the estimate becomes more significant than the accuracy and serves, for instance, to differentiate from an estimate derived from a mere wild, uniformed guess and those derived from a six-month in-depth analysis.

A similar indication is given by the 'three point estimating' technique. By this, three estimates are created initially; a most likely, an optimistic and a pessimistic. Mathematical techniques such as PERT can convert them to a single estimate, but the span between the optimistic and the pessimistic estimates indicates the degree of confidence.

Practitioners can improve their estimating simply by adopting the use of such ranges. Assessing confidence can be tricky, and requires some practice but 'precision' offers a measure of the quality of the estimate and enhances the communication between estimator and user of the estimate.

A third technique that indicates confidence in estimates uses probability distributions. Figure 13.1 is a histogram indicating the durations of a commute to work over the last six months. The y-axis shows the percentage of times the trip duration was within the 10-minute period indicated on the x-axis. All other things being equal, we can use this graph to estimate the length of, say, next Tuesday's trip. The duration with the highest frequency is the single most likely estimate (the mode) but the average (the mean) is a more representative estimate.[2] Further, we could understand how much variability there was by how peaky or flat the curve is, and hence our confidence in adopting any single estimate.

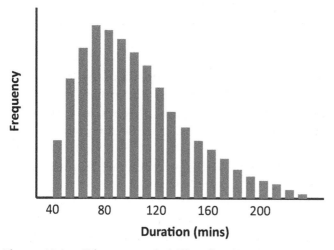

Figure 13.1   Discrete probability distribution

Alternatively we could use the data to plot a slightly different graph by plotting the frequency of trips of each duration, or less, i.e. the sum of the frequency of all readings to the left of the duration in question (see Figure 13.2). This results in a 'summation curve' which will have a characteristic S-shape. The y-axis (on the right-hand side) is calibrated in percent of the total number of readings.

We can understand the likelihood of next Tuesday's trip lasting less than any particular duration by reference to this curve. For instance, the probability

---

2   Discrete probability distributions for time or cost of a project are rarely symmetrical. It is almost always the case that it is more likely to cost more, or last longer, than the 'most likely' figure, than less, i.e. the mean is very likely to be greater than the mode. This results in a distorted distribution curve with a longer tail to the right of the mode. It is for this reason that the single estimate derived by the three-point estimating technique is usually greater than the mean and a more representative figure of the overall distribution.

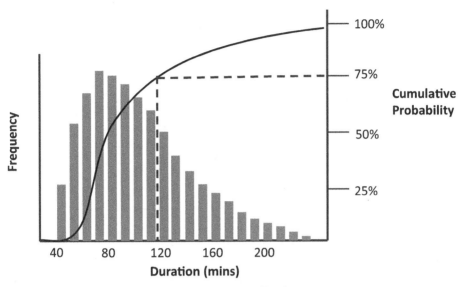

Figure 13.2   Cumulative probability distribution

of the trip lasting no more than 120 minutes is 75 per cent. This approach facilitates the notation P_{50}, P_{75}, P_{90}, etc. to signify values which we are 50 per cent, 75 per cent, 90 per cent, etc. confident will not be exceeded. These two graphs are probability distributions. The first is a discrete probability distribution and the second a cumulative probability distribution, and they are an extremely useful way of describing an estimate and the confidence inherent within it.

Unfortunately, generating the data required to plot them is not straightforward. The ideal situation is the one described above whereby the data is derived from historical records of many previous incidents. Another approach involves adopting the 'three-point estimating' technique to generate three estimates which are then subjected to a powerful mathematical algorithm such as Monte Carlo Analysis, which will express the estimate as probability distributions. Traditionally, such resources have been beyond the means of most organizations, however now, any modern laptop can happily run proprietary software that allows estimates to be expressed as distributions, presenting an opportunity that too few of us take up.

CLASSES OF ESTIMATES

A convenient way of describing the precision of an estimate is by expressing the range's minimum and maximum as percentages either side of a single figure.

These percentages are often standardized resulting in 'classes of estimate'. Common examples include the following, and each is used for different purposes.

Order of magnitude at +100%/-50%

Budgetary at +50%/-25%

Definitive at +10%/-5%

COST OF ESTIMATING AND BIDDING

In an ideal world all estimates would be produced with great (and justifiable) confidence. This would be evident from their high degree of precision. Unfortunately, precise estimates are expensive to produce and there is a balance to be struck between the benefits of precise estimates (in reducing risk) and the cost involved in creating them.

Data connecting the cost and precision of estimating is hard to come by. Some readers may be familiar with the 'rule of thumb' whereby the cost of compiling an estimate of project cost to within 5–10 per cent of the true figure, will cost 5–10 per cent of the project cost. Anecdotally, the author has heard clients estimate the cost of preparing such an estimate to vary from less than 1 per cent, to over 40 per cent.

The reality is that the cost of securing an estimate to a given precision can vary enormously, largely depending on the level of uncertainty about how controlled the environment is and how bespoke the goods or services in question are. (The '40 per cent' figure above was from an OO of highly complex and safety critical underground transport projects, whilst the '1 per cent' was from a SO producing similar products within a factory.)

The total cost of the Supplier Organization's (SO) bidding activity, which must be carried by each successful bid, relates not just to the cost of preparing the bid (estimate) in question, but also the success rate of bids. Consider a SO compiling 10 bids, each of £1million value, and the bidding cost for each is 5 per cent of that figure. A bid success rate of 80 per cent will involve each successful bid carrying an overhead of £62.5k. If the success rate is as low as 20 per cent then each must carry an overhead of £250k.

Avoidance of preparing unsuccessful bids is achieved by the quality of the 'Bid/No bid' decision and is of vital importance to a SO. In turn the quality of this decision is determined by the quality of the estimates at that point, which, of course, is related to the money spent on creating the estimate.

This is the 'inescapable conundrum' of projects, described in Chapter 4 that provides the rationale for Decision Gates. Regardless of whether discussing the project lifecycle of an OO or SO the use of a gated process to reduce unnecessary costs can be enhanced by requiring different classes of estimate to be available for each Decision Gate; each gate with a progressively more precise (and expensive) estimate.

However, regardless of how robust any gated process is, any way one looks at it, producing better estimates for less money is a major objective of any shrewd SO and this has implications for how it administers to its portfolio of projects, as shall be discussed below.

Estimating Techniques

The techniques for estimating described in the project management lexicon are as applicable to a Supplier Organization (SO) as they are to an Owner Organization (OO), with only a few minor reflections as to the appropriateness of each, as discussed below. Two core approaches exist; a 'top-down' or a 'bottom-up' approach.

TOP-DOWN ESTIMATING

A top-down approach estimates the cost of a project[3] by considering it as a single whole entity and comparing it to another similar whole entity, whose cost is known. For instance, the cost of repairing the damage to a city caused by a hurricane can be estimated by adopting the known cost of repairing a similar city after a previous similar natural disaster. The technique has the advantages of being quick and cheap and easy to use and does not rely on an extensive knowledge of the detail of the work scope. For these reasons it is generally associated with estimates made early in the project lifecycle.

The main concern with its use by a Supplier Organization (SO) is that, by definition, each project is unique and so no exact comparison can ever be made.

---

3   Or other entity such as Work Package.

Accordingly, the method is viewed as being appropriate only when the 'degree of uniqueness' of the work is low and relevant historical data is plentiful.

For some SO, especially those with products towards the bottom of the continuum in Figure 1.1, these criteria are met and this approach is satisfactory for justifying bids. For those SO involved in more bespoke work, it is more likely that the approach will be used only to inform the 'Bid/No bid' Decision Gate.

PARAMETRIC ESTIMATING

The 'top-down' approach is enhanced within the 'Parametric Estimating' technique. For many projects there is an aspect of the work or product, i.e. a parameter, whose value varies faithfully with the total cost of the work. For instance the cost of resurfacing a road varies faithfully with its length.

If there is sufficient historical data, from similar previous projects, to allow the relationship between cost and the parameter (length in this example) to be known, and the value for the parameter for the new project is known, then the cost of the new project can be estimated by applying this known relationship.

In practice, the relationship between the parameter and the costs does not have to be linear, and more than one parameter can be included in the analysis. Depending upon the nature of the work in question, and the size of the database, the results can be surprisingly accurate.

It can provide an excellent opportunity to a Supplier Organization (SO) to produce good estimates cheaply and quickly because there is often just such a similarity, i.e. a common parameter, between each of their projects.

BOTTOM-UP ESTIMATING

If the work at hand is highly bespoke, and a considerable precision of estimate is required, it will become necessary to embrace the 'bottom-up' approach.

Here, the work to be estimated is not considered as a single entity. With the aid of a Work or Product Breakdown Structure (PBS, WBS),[4] the whole is decomposed into a number of discrete elements such as Work Packages or sub-

---

4   The use of Product Breakdown Structures and Work Breakdown Structures (WBS) will be addressed comprehensively in Chapter 14.

assemblies. Estimates of cost are made for each element and then aggregated into an estimate for the whole.

A principal reason for the superior precision is that it allows more historical data to be brought to bear.

The unique aspect of a project often derives from it being a unique collection of Work Packages, rather than consisting of unique Work Packages. Individual Work Packages are often similar to, or sometimes identical to, those within previous projects. In such instances very precise estimates can be reached for the individual packages and hence, potentially, for the aggregated whole.

The word 'potentially' is included as a caveat here since bottom-up approaches are sometimes wildly inaccurate. This is because they are reliant upon a comprehensive understanding of the scope, i.e. an accurate work breakdown structure. If large elements of scope are omitted then the accuracy of the final estimate will be compromised.

The approach is also far more involved and complicated than the top-down approach since each Work Package needs to be analysed, one at a time. This renders the technique expensive and protracted, which is the main drawback to its use.

Practical Considerations to Improve Estimating

Major commercial advantage can be secured by those Supplier Organizations (SO) that can reduce the cost, and increase the precision, of estimating. Three considerations are worthy of note.

THE BID/NO BID DECISION

The quality of this decision is vital and a Supplier Organization (SO) that improves it can save itself a small fortune by not creating detailed, but ultimately unnecessary, estimates.

ACKNOWLEDGE THE DEGREE OF UNCERTAINTY WITHIN ESTIMATES

Expressing the likely cost as a single point estimate and comparing this to a marginally higher firm selling price offers very little insight into the likelihood of securing a profit as opposed to incurring a loss.

By contrast, comparing a firm price to an estimate of the cost expressed as a range (within defined confidence limits), or as a probability distribution (discrete or cumulative) or as a simple approximation of a distribution (using a most likely, pessimistic and optimistic estimate) conveys an enormously valuable insight into the perceived degree of uncertainty.

Inevitably this will provoke questions and discussions which will moderate expectations and hence improve decisions.

HISTORICAL DATA

The ability to estimate well is largely determined by the availability of relevant historical data. This data is, of course, the archived results of previous work undertaken by the Supplier Organization (SO). Too many SO fail to recognize the value of this data, and do not put procedures and mechanisms in place to ensure that accurate records are maintained.

Further, the format in which the data is archived should render it useful for future use. Of particular relevance here is the opportunities presented by top-down techniques. These techniques are an order of magnitude cheaper to use than the bottom-up approach and the investigation and development of parametric based databases can lead to algorithms that dramatically improve the precision of the estimates. In this respect these methods approach the holy grail of estimating by providing excellent estimates quickly and cheaply.

The usefulness of historical data for use within a bottom-up approach can be enhanced by a 'template breakdown structure' for the PBS and WBS that can be adopted by all of the projects of a Supplier Organization (SO). This will lead to a data base that identifies the cost of the same Work Package (or sub-product) across all the previous projects. This will help to identify those Work Packages that are identical, or very similar, in every project and hence can be estimated cheaply and with considerable precision. Estimating of cost of Work Packages that are not identical may still be aided by such an approach by providing a database that facilitates a parametric approach to be adopted.

THE HUMAN DIMENSION

Be it the perspective of an individual, or the group dynamics of a team under pressure, the 'human dimension' is a major source of serious errors in estimates.

We are all complex and delicate creatures whose reasoning and decision-making is far more intricate and subconscious than most of us realize, especially when put in stressful situations. Reference books are full of examples of how terrible decisions can be made in such circumstances. In this respect the conclusions of Janis (1982) and his work on Groupthink should be compulsory reading for anyone involved in a project team. When estimating, there needs to be a real bias towards objectivity and realism and away from subjectivity and optimism.

Pre-Contract Risk Mitigation

As discussed in Chapter 4, the early phases of a project provide the best opportunity for exerting influence and such opportunity reduces along the line of a pronounced curve (Figure 4.2). For the Supplier Organization (SO) this smooth curve is subject to a major step change since, once a contract is signed, there is very little, or no, opportunity for a SO to make alterations. Therefore, risk mitigation must be addressed pre-contract, i.e. prior to submitting an offer.

The following are key areas in this respect.

DEFINITION OF SCOPE

The fundamental importance of an explicit definition of scope, to the fortunes of the Supplier Organization (SO), has been exposed frequently throughout this book, and ensuring it is addressed pre-contract is a prime responsibility of the salesperson within the SO.

The need to eliminate any opportunity for ambiguity provides a very powerful argument as to why contracts should always be written agreements; may include references to all OO–SO correspondence relating to scope definition; and descriptions of any work, services, goods, access, etc. that the OO will supply to the SO on a 'free-issue basis'.

DISCRETE RISKS

When considering the cost (or duration or performance) of a project, there are some events which will impact upon the result, but the likelihood of them occurring is less than 100 per cent. For instance a vital machine may break down, key resources may resign, the work site might experience severe weather. Each of these is a discrete risk and they pose a difficulty to Supplier Organizations (SO) since they influence costs and hence confidence in estimates.

In addressing these, the SO will find some benefit in the risk management techniques to be found within the project management lexicon.

These include the use of a 'Probability Impact Grid' to assess and rank individual risks by consideration of the likelihood of them occurring (the probability), and the effect it will have on the execution of the project cost, duration or performance (the impact).

Practitioners are then invited to mitigate the risks by adopting one or more of the following strategies.

Avoidance

By this, the Supplier Organization (SO) restructures the work such that the risk will have no bearing on the project. For instance, by travelling to the airport by train, the risk of our car breaking down is avoided.

An imaginative SO may be able to significantly reduce its overall exposure by 'designing out' certain risks.

In extremis, a SO can avoid a risk by refusing to accept the contract in question; a strategy not available post-contract.

Within this category we can also consider *force majeure* risks. This class of risk relates to 'acts of God'. Flood, earthquakes, war, famine are examples and it is usual for a contract to have a clause whereby should the risk occur neither the SO nor the OO are liable to the other party for the consequences.

Transfer

This involves engaging a third party with skill and expertise such that, firstly, the likelihood or impact of the risk is reduced and then, secondly, they will bear some of the consequences of that impact. It is for precisely this reason of 'transfer of risk' that most Owner Organizations (OO) engage Supplier Organizations (SO).

For the SO, 'transfer' can take three forms.

- They can engage other SO as subcontractors, to take responsibility for the element of work associated with the risk.

- They can create a syndicate, such as a consortium or joint venture, with other SO whereby specific risks are borne by these other members.

- Ownership of the risk can be transferred back to the Owner Organization (OO). Simplistically, this can involve simply defining the area of the risk as being within the ownership of the OO but some OO and SO take a partnering approach to risk management whereby the risk analysis is carried out jointly and ownership of individual risks apportioned to each party.

Reduction

This involves the reduction of either the probability or impact, or both, of a risk.

For example the probability of our car breaking down can be reduced (but not eliminated) by having the vehicle serviced beforehand.

The impact of our car having a puncture can be reduced by carrying a spare wheel and the necessary tools in our car.

Such mitigation measures usually result in a negative impact on cost, duration or performance of the project but this will be seen as an acceptable price for the risk mitigation so afforded.

Accept

As discussed in Chapter 1, projects are risky ventures and ultimately all parties involved in them, be they an Owner Organization (OO) or a Supplier Organization (SO), will be obliged to accept certain risks.

USE OF CONTINGENCY

Contingency can be regarded as an amount of money (or time, etc.) that needs to be reserved so as to render an unacceptable risk, acceptable.

Although classed under 'risk management', it doesn't really involve managing the risk, only the consequences of it. Since prevention is better than cure, it should not be considered as a first choice mitigation strategy, but it is a practical response that can be used to good effect.

Determining the magnitude of the contingency is often haphazard. It is sometimes expressed as a percentage of the total, based upon previous experience. For example a Supplier Organization (SO) may take the view that 'on the basis of our experience, we need to retain a contingency of 4 per cent for projects of this type'.

Alternatively, it may be derived on the basis of a cumulative probability distribution (see Figure 13.2). Consider an Owner Organization (OO) envisaging a project. Its business may use the P_{50} estimate of cost, but what contingency would be required so as to obtain a cost estimate that had only a 10 per cent likelihood of being exceed? The amount of contingency required would be the difference between the P_{90} and P_{50} estimates of cost and these can be read directly from the cumulative probability graph.

CASH FLOW AND SECURITY OF PAYMENT

A vital aspect of risk mitigation for the Supplier Organization (SO) relates to the receipt of payment; its timing and its security. Imagine a prospective SO has estimated the magnitude and timing of likely costs for a piece of work to be sold on a Firm Price basis.

Figure 13.3 depicts the situation where the Owner Organization (OO) offers to pay the SO for the work on completion. Although there is a healthy surplus of revenue over cost (profit) this is a dangerous situation for the SO since throughout the project it is 'cash flow negative' because it has spent more than it has received. This represents both a cost and a risk.

The cost is incurred because, during this period, the SO has had to borrow money to fund the work (in which case it will incur interest charges) or, alternatively, fund the work from its own reserves (in which case it will incur an opportunity cost).

The risk derives from the exposure of the Supplier Organization (SO) to a default by the Owner Organization (OO). Although the SO may perform to the letter of the contract, owing to bankruptcy or fraudulent intent, the OO may fail to pay the bill. This is a disaster for the SO.

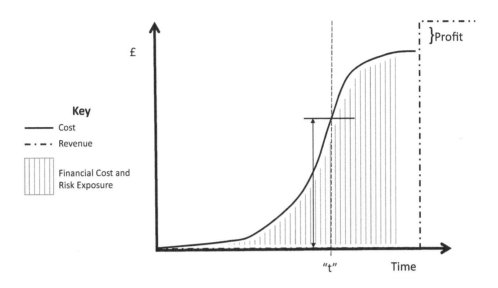

Figure 13.3   Negative cash flow

Should, for instance, the OO pass into bankruptcy at point 't' on Figure 13.3 it can be seen that the SO has spent a considerable sum and now may receive no payment. Although client default is a risk for all sellers, two aspects of the project environment enhance the risk.

Firstly, from the perspective of the Owner Organization (OO), a project relies on the future realization of benefit, after the expense of creating the asset and so financial solvency is always a concern. Does the OO have the capital to fund the project in the event of excessive costs or delayed benefits?

Secondly, a key aspect of projects is the temporariness of the structures involved. Many organizations will see no future business with a supplier beyond the project, and in some instances organizations are only created for the duration of a project. In both these cases security of payment for the SO can be a low priority of the OO.

The Supplier Organization (SO) can insulate itself from the risk of such a default by receiving payment at the outset. Such a situation is depicted in Figure 13.4. In this example, throughout the period, the SO has received more than it has spent; it is cash flow positive. This shaded area also represents surplus funds being available to the SO for other revenue-generating opportunities.

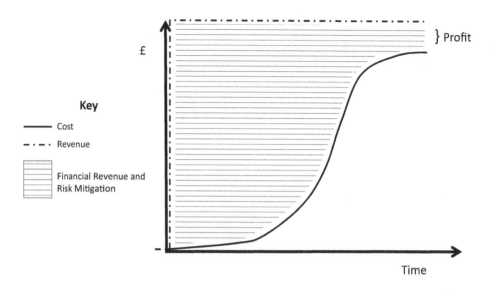

Figure 13.4   Positive cash flow

Although this insulates the SO from risk of OO default it does so at the expense of the OO who is now wholly exposed to a SO default.

Whilst there are occasions when either of these positions is appropriate, usually, a compromise is adopted involving 'staged payments', with both the Owner Organization (OO) and Supplier Organization (SO) alternating between being cash flow positive and cash flow negative (see Figure 13.5). Such staged payments are usually triggered by completion of a milestone identified within the contract. In any case, the SO position is enhanced by increasing and bringing forward receipts, and by reducing or delaying costs.

Timing of payments is not the only protection available to a SO to protect it from OO default. The 'legally binding' nature of a contract ensures that the SO has recourse to law to recover the situation. (Though bringing a case to court is expensive, offers no guarantee of success and, whilst this may offer the SO some protection from OO misdeed, it is unlikely to be of help in the event of OO bankruptcy).

The protection offered by the law is diminished if the Supplier Organization (SO) and the Owner Organization (OO) are not both under the same legal system, i.e. within the same country.

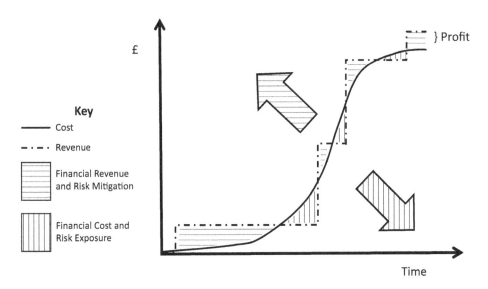

Figure 13.5   Stage payments

In such instances payment may be secured via a 'documentary credit' such as a 'Letter of Credit', issued by a trusted third party, typically a bank, which will agree to pay the SO on completion of the work, and hence underwrite the risk of OO default. By this, the SO is not reliant on the behaviour of the OO, but it does impose other difficulties such as proof of SO performance. Consequently, payment is usually triggered on receipt of some certificate, e.g. a Bill of Lading, produced by the shipping company when the goods have been handed into its care by the SO. The OO position can then be secured by the SO producing a bond (again, typically issued by the SO bank) which, if the goods are subsequently shown to be unacceptable, can be 'called', allowing the OO to recover some of the expenditure.

Unsurprisingly, contracts between Owner Organizations (OO) and Supplier Organizations (SO) that are located in different countries often include an elaborate system of bonds and letters of credit which must be agreed pre-contract (along with who will pay the issuing bank, since it is they who bear the risk and they require compensation).

Other options for mitigation of default risk are sometimes adopted that are based on the 'real politik' of the situation. For instance, the author was once made aware of a supplier of bespoke machinery who ensured that the PLC in each product supplied had a 'Doomsday' programme that incapacitated the entire machine and could only be reversed by the SO personnel. It was timed to activate around the time the final payment should have been received from the OO. Whereas the legality is in doubt its efficacy as an aid to credit management was not.

'Make or Accept/Reject Offer?' Decision Gate

The Selling phase ends with an agreed contract between the Owner Organization (OO) and the Supplier Organization (SO), or a termination of the prospective SO project. The prelude to this involves a process of negotiation that becomes entwined with aspects of contract law.

In a general sense, two parties negotiate over an issue when they have some interests in common and some interests that are divergent. A successful negotiation results in an agreement that maximizes those interests in common and diminishes those that are divergent.

Prior to the face-to-face bartering, the two parties should each draw up two lists; the first 'things that we can offer that are low cost to us and high value to the other party' and the second 'things that they can offer us that are high value to us but low cost to them'.

The subsequent bartering phase consists of one party bundling up a collection from the first list, which they are prepared to exchange for a bundle from the second list. The other party can then accept or make a counter-offer, with modified bundles selected from their lists.

In the particular situation when a negotiation is leading to the establishment of a contract between an OO and SO, there are some additional considerations. Firstly, in a formal bidding scenario many of the items to be exchanged, e.g. the technical performance of the product, are already strictly predefined and the negotiation revolves around just a few aspects such as price and delivery date. In less formal scenarios there can be very many aspects to negotiate. Secondly, the bartering has strict legal implications. Under UK law, a contract is formed when one party makes an offer and the other party accepts it unconditionally. Replying with a counter-offer is deemed a rejection of the offer.

In a very simplistic sense, we would have the Supplier Organization (SO) making an offer and the Owner Organization (OO) unconditionally accepting it, and hence forming the contract. In practice it is likely to be more complex, for instance the OO may explain 'yours is our preferred bid but we are only prepared to accept it if you agree to a 2 per cent discount on price'. This is actually a counter-offer on behalf of the OO, and the SO is now in the position of having to accept or reject.

Accordingly, although, it is the Supplier Organization (SO) that, traditionally, makes the offer and the Owner Organization (OO) who accepts or rejects, within the context of a negotiation, it can be either party making the offer and either party accepting or rejecting.

Also once an offer is made, to a large degree, the offerer loses control of the process[5] and its fate is then in the hands of the other party who must accept or reject it. The final act of the SO pre-contract, is either making an offer, or accepting one. Alternatively it may simply reject an offer and terminate further negotiations.

Accordingly, the gate decision that brings this phase to a close is a decision either to Make or Accept/Reject an Offer.

A Good Sale?

It is helpful to reflect on what constitutes a good sale, and hence a good performance from the Supplier Organization's (SO) salesperson.

A good sale is one that secures a contract that leads to a very satisfied OO and a handsome profit for the SO.

A terrible sale is one that secures a contract that leads to a very dissatisfied OO and a crushing loss for the SO.

The difficulty is that at the point of closing the deal, without the knowledge of the actual final cost and performance data, it is almost impossible to differentiate. This is a real dilemma and ensures that it is very difficult to assess the performance of salespeople without relying on wholly subjective criteria.

A good salesperson is one who maximizes subsequent potential for profit. This can be judged against the degree to which it aids further execution of the contract. Such aspects include the following:

---

5   There is an opportunity to withdraw an offer by the offerer, before the expiry of any validity period, but it is limited and different legal systems have different approaches. It is, for instance, an area of inconsistency between English and Scottish law.

- The degree to which what was sold aligns with what the OO actually wants and needs.

- The degree to which the scope reflects work that the SO can do comfortably, i.e. it does not commit to impossible deadlines.

- The clarity with which the scope, and the duties of both the SO and OO, are defined.

- The degree of appropriate risk mitigation conducted pre-contract, e.g. securing appropriate payment mechanisms.

- The quality of the relationship with the OO and the degree of influence that can be exerted by the SO.

- The size of the potential profit margin.

Though much of the attention is focused on the latter, care is required here. Profit is the difference between revenue and costs and, in the context of a Firm Price contract, whereas the price is defined, the actual costs can only be estimated. Accordingly, predicted profit is enhanced by reducing the estimated costs. If a salesperson both 'owns' the cost estimate and is incentivized on the number of contracts won, then they are exposed to a significant conflict of interest. Ill-thought-out incentive schemes can wreak havoc in such instances by encouraging salespeople to commit the organization to contracts that ultimately will incur a loss.

Good salespeople secure additional profit by driving up the sales price and it is upon this that any incentives should be focused.

The Handover

In many Supplier Organizations (SO), the execution of their project fragment is under the management of a different person to the one who sold it; the project manager (PM) and salesperson respectively. Responsibility for the work is transferred from the one party to the other immediately post-contract.

This handover represents the start of the responsibility of the PM and, often, it is the first time the PM looks at the work in any detail, and thus the first time the work of the salesperson comes under serious scrutiny. Similarly, the work of the salesperson is now ending and they are anxious to move onto the next sale. Unfortunately, often, it is only at this point that many of these criteria relating to a 'good sale' are discussed.

In an ideal world there is a smooth handover with the PM understanding, acknowledging, accepting, and even appreciating, the work of the salesperson.

In an imperfect world the salesperson is nowhere to be found and the incoming PM sits in increasing confusion and horror as they realize what they are obliged to deliver and at what cost. In such circumstances the attitude of the salesperson can be summed up as 'I shot it, you skin it', and from the PM the sense is that the incoming contract represents a grenade coming over a wall with everything in place apart from the pin.

Such a discontinuity is usually obvious to the Owner Organization (OO) and is damaging; it should be avoided.

An extreme, but unusual, way of achieving this is by ensuring the salesperson is then subsequently the PM.

Alternatively, many SO mitigate it by having the prospective PM accompany the salesperson during the final negotiations. There is, though, the risk that no agreement is secured in which case the SO may be reluctant to devote PM resources too early.

In the experience of the author, a very useful approach is to place authority for formally accepting the incoming contract with the prospective PM rather than the salesperson. The PM and the salesperson sharing the other's perspective pre-contract can be a very healthy thing!

The Project Manager as Salesperson

Marketers talk of 'farmers' and 'hunters'; those that cultivate existing clients and those who go out and seek new ones. The costs of pursuing the former are a fraction of the costs of the latter, and there is considerable benefit to Supplier Organizations (SO) in having a commercially astute PM encouraged to seek out extensions to the value of their existing contracts. Indeed, such business can represent between 56 per cent and 73 per cent of SO turnover (Naybour, 2012).

References

Janis, I., 1982. *Groupthink*. Boston: Houghton Mifflin Company.

Naybour, P., 2012. *Selling and Doing Good Business: An Engineer's Guide to Business Development*. [online] Available at: http://blog.parallelprojecttraining.com [accessed 11 April 2014].

Chapter 14

Project Planning for Supplier Organizations

Planning is synonymous with project management; a fact evidenced by our familiarity with a myriad of sayings attesting to its benefits.

As previously stated, nothing is cheaper and quicker than getting it right first time during the implementation of a project, but getting it right first time requires time and energy to be devoted to it beforehand; that is to say, devoted to prior planning.

The need for extensive project planning is a direct consequence of the intrinsic uncertainties associated with projects and their environments, and it is the breadth and depth of the planning needed to manage a project that sets it apart from the management required of non-project work.

Compare again, the manufacture of washing machines (a routine operation) and the construction of an Olympic stadium (a project). At the commencement of the manufacture of a washing machine, the necessary manufacturing and test equipment; the specialist and experienced personnel; the tried and tested procedures and methods, are all to hand. At the commencement of the stadium project there exists only a plot of land. In the former scenario the question as to 'how' the machine was to be created had already been answered. This stands in stark contrast to the second scenario where a great deal of thinking is required, not only about the nature of the product but also about how it will be created and tested.

For this reason, an organization moving its products up the continuum described in Figure 1.1 (for instance, by embracing the supply of bespoke rather than standard products) will need a step-change in the breadth and depth of its planning, and a new appreciation of how important the Project Management Plan (PMP) is to successful project execution.

The planning techniques described in the lexicon of project management relate directly to Supplier Organizations (SO) as much as Owner Organizations (OO) and so no attempt is made here to explore individual planning techniques in depth. The following offers an overview of the subject, written from the perspective of a SO.

Why Plan?

The simple truth is that careful planning dramatically improves the chances of project success, but how exactly does the planning process help? In reality, planning assists subsequent implementation in a great many ways but they can be summarized under four headings (see Figure 14.1).

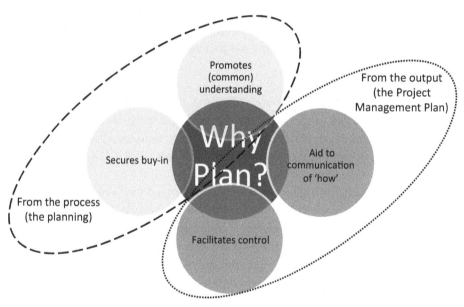

Figure 14.1   Why plan?

PLANNING PROMOTES (A COMMON) UNDERSTANDING

Why do theatre troupes rehearse? They do it to increase the likelihood that their performances will be 'alright on the night'.

It is the same for projects. By planning the project team 'rehearse' the project by talking through, or otherwise modelling the project, perhaps by creating drawings, schedules, budgets, procedures and the like, and one of the reasons why they do this is to increase their understanding of what is to be achieved, and how best it is to be done.

This dramatically reduces the uncertainty and hence the likelihood of destructive changes being required later in the project.

Further, if this is done in a collegiate sense, with the whole team engaged, then the deep understanding so developed is a common understanding and this is even more valuable, particularly in the context of subsequent team dynamics, collaboration and co-ordination.

For a Supplier Organization (SO) moving along the 'Organizational Continuum' of Figure 2.4, collaborative planning sessions will be essential for identifying and understanding what changes to the usual ways of working will be required by the project.

PROMOTES BUY-IN

An important part of the answer to the question 'How do I motivate my team?' is 'involve them in the planning'.

It is unclear why it is the case, but it most certainly is the case, that the earlier we are involved in a project the more interest, commitment and buy-in we have for it.

Look back over your career and think of all the projects you have been involved in and consider which are most dear to you. Chances are they are instances when you were involved early in the lifecycle and were able to shape and influence how the project was approached.

Team members are more likely to 'own' the content of the PMP, and accept the implicit challenges inherent within the time and cost estimates, when they have had an opportunity to influence their creation. Imposing a PMP on a team that had no involvement in its creation is a far less favourable situation.

Again, this is hugely relevant for any Supplier Organization (SO) embracing the project environment. Enhanced buy-in reinforces the identity of the project team (as opposed to the functional divisions), encouraging the 'cross-function integration' required of project work, and diminishing the 'silo mentality' of Functional Organizations.

FACILITATES CONTROL

Imagine receiving a project progress report stating that at week 34, two-thirds of the deliverable is complete and that expenditure was a mere £78 million. Is this good news?

The progress report clearly states what had been achieved, the elapsed time and the amount of money spent but, on its own, the information is almost completely worthless.

For it to be of use we need to have some statement of what we had expected to have achieved by this point in time, and for this amount of money. This need for a comparator is met by the plan and it is an indispensable element of control.

To put it more starkly, if a project has no appropriate plan it is out of control, by definition.

The PMP must document anticipated progress in a format, and using units, that subsequently can be replicated by measured quantities of the actual work. This provides the comparison on which control decisions are made.

AID TO COMMUNICATION OF 'HOW'

The PMP is a written, and approved, document that explains to anyone with an interest, how the project is to be delivered. This conveys many benefits.

First and foremost, the detailed PMP is proof that planning has taken place. This provides vital reassurance to senior management and, since the actual act of writing something down requires individuals to structure, clarify and validate their thoughts, its creation improves the thinking process.

Secondly, the PMP document provides a reference point, to any relevant stakeholder, for any aspect of project execution they have an interest in. These may include the demand that it will make on internal resources, the demand it will make for cash, the timing of key events, the risk exposure it imposes, and many other important details. It also represents a significant contribution to the wealth of documented expertise within the organization. As will be discussed in Chapter 18, a well-managed archive of such documents can be a serious boon to those addressing subsequent and similar endeavours.

Thirdly, the PMP is the primary mechanism by which the project manager exerts influence over the project team. For team members it is an instruction manual, or rule book, which ensures mutual co-ordination and alignment by communicating in a clear and unambiguous way what is expected of each of them and what they can expect of the Project Manager. Certainly, the team members will have had an input into the process of creating it, but nonetheless, the final approved version is owned by the Project Manager and reflects their expectations. A well thought-out and clearly presented plan goes a very long way in promoting respect and confidence within the team, and the standing and authority of the project manager. It is a golden opportunity that can never be recreated. Conversely, recovery of reputation after a chaotic, unplanned start is very difficult.

FINAL OBSERVATION REGARDING PLANNING

Readers are encouraged to note the shading used in Figure 14.1. In response to the question 'Why plan?' four points have been offered but two of these refer to the physical output (the PMP) whereas two of them actually refer to the process of creating the PMP. The creative act is as important (in some respects more important) than the documented output. Many of the benefits are intangible and address the soft side of project management, but this does not mean that they are unimportant; far from it, in fact.

Project Management Plan Contents

Many thousands of students of project management have been taught a certain poem by Rudyard Kipling as a mnemonic to aid the recollection of a PMP's content. A far less high-brow mnemonic involves a sketch of the backsides of five naked rugby players sitting on a rugby post crossbar, but they both serve to advise us of the six question words: Who, What, Why, Where, When and How (conveniently abbreviated to 'W^{5}H'). Collectively they provide an excellent structure for a wide range of activities (journalist articles, police investigations, research) that includes project planning. All PMPs should answer these six question words.

Many would further suggest that 'how' is an even simpler summary since it is a question that contains the others (a sense reinforced by the rugby sketch described above).

THE STRUCTURE OF A PROJECT MANAGEMENT PLAN

Since all projects are unique there will be differences in the extent and detail of each PMP. Consequently, for very small projects it may be just one document, but for most projects the PMP is best thought of as an umbrella document that contains a number of elements, or individual plans.

However, although there is variation in detail, all PMP can usefully share the same broad structure and although the W⁵H approach offers a good overall guide and checklist, if we refer to the purpose for which the PMP is created, it is possible to adopt a more convenient structure.

It is suggested that each PMP should consist of three sections:

- Project Background.

- Baseline Estimates.

- Subsidiary Management Plans.

Each of these are addressed under their own headings below.

PROJECT BACKGROUND

Projects are delivered by teams and a main characteristic of an effective team is that they have a clear understanding of the objectives of the team (most projects that fail, fail not because of a failure of delivery, but a failure in understanding and communicating the requirements). It is therefore appropriate to have this section of the PMP that offers a condensed version of the project rationale that will serve to orientate the team, provide context to their decision-making and enable them to offer good advice and ideas.

The essential reason 'why' a Supplier Organization (SO) engages in a project is the receipt of the consideration detailed in the contract with the Owner Organization (OO),[1] but it is sometimes necessary to add to this. As discussed in Chapter 12, a particular contract may have been accepted, not on the basis of the inherent profit, but on some other strategic advantage, such as

---

1   For an OO the 'why' is addressed within the Business Case and the 'Project Background' section of their PMP is informed by this.

providing an entrée into a particular market. This needs to be communicated to the team and it can be done here.

It is also appropriate to orientate the Supplier Organization (SO) project team towards the objectives of the Owner Organization (OO). Although nothing written here will supersede the contents of the contract, the SO can help the OO only if the SO are aware of what the OO is trying to achieve. Such an understanding may indicate how and where the SO can be of further assistance, with extensions to contract, for example.

This section of the PMP also allows for continuity between those managing the project through the preceding phases (Marketing and Selling), and those managing it during subsequent phases. Inevitably there will have been some assumptions made during these earlier phases relating to such aspects as resources to be used, existing designs to be used, profit margin expected, major risks, constraints, dependencies on other projects, and the like. These will not feature in the contract but are important to the team executing the work.

It can also be appropriate to indicate here the priority of a project. If it is part of a portfolio of projects that share resources, it is almost inevitable there will be some form of conflict. Many such disputes between different teams can be avoided if, at the outset, senior management indicate the relative priority of the projects.

BASELINE ESTIMATES

During the lifecycle of the project, many estimates will be made of time and cost but the 'baseline estimates' are those that are agreed and signed off at the end of the planning process. By this they become 'locked' and can only be changed by formal change control protocol.[2]

A fundamental purpose of baselines is to provide the comparator against which progress and performance can be assessed, and hence control decisions made. However, in the first instance they are essential for arranging and co-ordinating the activities of the team members by indicating when work will occur and for what cost.

As suggested earlier, the exact makeup of a PMP is largely within the gift of the PM but, regardless of the size, shape or nature of the project, the three

---

2   This 'locking' of the estimate is sometimes referred to as 'baselining'.

core baseline estimates of scope, time and cost, need to be addressed within any satisfactory PMP.

These three aspects cannot be planned in isolation. They depend upon and influence each other in complex ways so need to be evolved in a structured and formal way. There is a coarse sequence whereby the scope is planned before the duration, which is planned before the cost though, inevitably, there will be a degree of iteration involved. For instance, if on calculating the cost of a project, the projected total is well beyond an externally imposed budget then, most likely, the solution will lie in changes to the scope, and hence an iterative loop is created.

Creation of these baselines is demanding upon the team but the reduction of uncertainty and promotion of understanding it achieves is colossal.

Inevitably, these baselines will become targets which may deviate from the parameters within the contract. For instance, the senior management of a Supplier Organization (SO) would be unhappy if a PM simply adopted the contract price as the limit of the cost baseline. Profit (their ultimate objective) is dependent upon the costs being less than the price and so the target, for control purposes, will be a lesser amount. This is addressed further in Chapter 16.

Scope baseline

This describes the content of the project. Depending upon the context, 'scope' can refer to the sum of the products to be delivered, or the work to be done by the project team, or both. For the purpose of the PMP we shall consider it referring to the work to be done by the team.

It is the most important of the three baselines since the other two are based upon it and errors in scope estimation will lead directly to errors in the baselines for duration and cost.[3] Unless and until the totality of scope can be ring-fenced, estimates for duration and cost will be meaningless.

Many projects come in late or over-budget and very often this is blamed upon poor control of the execution phase. However, closer inspection often reveals adequate control but baseline estimates for duration and cost which

---

3   It is the case for project control as it is for planning. 'Scope creep' (doing something that was not intended) impacts upon duration and cost and, without a scope baseline, 'scope creep' cannot be recognized and hence project cost and duration cannot be controlled.

were grossly optimistic. In turn, these estimates were poor because insufficient time and energy had been invested in fully defining the scope in the first instance, such that the scope upon which they were based was understated. Very many organizations become obsessed with the planning of duration and cost, largely encouraged by the availability of specialist computer-based tools, without first having established a robust scope baseline. As a consequence their efforts are often futile.

The format adopted for the scope baseline is a Work Breakdown Structure (WBS)[4], sometimes supported by a WBS Dictionary.[5] A WBS decomposes the work into discrete parcels of work, defined by a verb and a noun, known as Work Packages (Figure 8.1). These 'manageable chunks' of work are then passed onto team members or alternatively other Supplier Organizations (SO), who become the Work Package Owner. These Work Packages become the common currency of the project that link all the different perspectives of the project such as expenditure, responsibility (Figure 8.2), scheduling, and the like, and are instrumental in making the project manageable. This is often aided by each Work Package having a unique number, the format of which is based upon the structure of the WBS.

In identifying the Work Packages, the totality of the work scope required to meet the contract's requirement, is defined. The imperative is that everything that needs to be done on the project fits into one of these packages, and there is nothing in any of those packages which is not necessary; there is a place for everything and everything is in its place.

When compelled to compile a WBS, and its attendant dictionary, for the first time, practitioners are often surprised at just how extensive the array of Work Packages is, and how mundane many of them are. Readers should be under no illusion as to whether this is anything but a good thing, since the reality of projects (as well as for our working life) is that we spend most of our time and money doing mundane tasks. How much of your time do you spend doing things that only you can do by dint of your expertise and how much addressing tasks such as travelling to meetings, booking a meeting room, filling in a timesheet? It is the same for a project. The technically challenging aspects usually account for a small amount of time and far more is spent on organizing

---

4   For projects with very large physical deliverables, such as machinery, many practitioners choose to draw up a PBS (Product Breakdown Structure) that decomposes the deliverable into discrete parts, as a prelude to creating the WBS.
5   A Work Breakdown Structure Dictionary is a textual document that supports the WBS by containing additional information about individual Work Packages.

deliveries, holding meetings, disposing of surplus material, compiling QC documentation, demobilizing site facilities, and the like. Creation of a WBS helps recognize these essential but mundane tasks as well as commonly overlooked work like the project management effort and the creation (and removal) of temporary works.

The beneficial effect of this is best evidenced by the step-change in the quality of estimates for time and cost made after the exercise is complete.

Although the design of the structure of the WBS (for example, whether the decomposition is based on sub-product, location, phase, etc.) is usually at the discretion of the PM, there are instances, especially for SO projects, where it is appropriate to impose a predesigned structure. Such 'WBS Templates' can be part of a project management method described in Chapter 4 that is imposed on similar projects within a portfolio. A particular benefit of this relates to management of historical data used for estimating purposes, as discussed in Chapter 13.

Time Baseline

Having identified the work to be done, its duration can be estimated and the project schedule, the time baseline, created. The process can become complex but follows these essential steps.

In the first instance, Work Packages are converted into activities. In an ideal world there would be a 1:1 relationship but in practice some rationalization or further decomposition of Work Packages is necessary.

Secondly, the logical sequence inherent within any project that determines the sequence of the activities must be understood and documented (a roof cannot be built until the walls are complete, which in turn cannot be built until the foundations are poured, for example). The result is a Precedence Diagram (also known as an Activity on Node diagram, or simply a 'network') showing the activities as boxes (nodes) connected by arrows, indicating the precedence. This exercise is not straightforward and demands a thorough understanding of the project.

Thirdly, a duration must be estimated for each activity.

Fourthly, this information allows analysis to be carried out – critical path analysis – to create a provisional schedule which identifies the shortest period of time the work can be completed within; the sequence of activities that determine this period; and also the amount of float each activity has within that schedule (the amount the activity can be delayed or extended before it impacts upon the rest of the schedule). This analysis can become quite involved and for this reason most practitioners choose to take advantage of one of the myriad of specialist software packages designed for project scheduling.

In reality, this provisional schedule is almost useless in predicting completion dates. This is because there is an unspoken assumption that all resources required will be available as and when required. Of course, this is not the case for real organizations where the availability of resources is severely limited. Accordingly, any meaningful schedule needs to be based on the interplay between the project's demand and the organization's provision of resources. This is such a crucial topic for every Supplier Organization (SO) that it is the subject of a dedicated chapter (Chapter 15).

Should the projected end date be beyond the requirements of the contract (or indeed any other internal SO target) then the scope and time plans will need to be iterated.

Cost Baseline

Projects consume resources and it is the quantity of these resources so consumed that is referred to as the cost of the project. For convenience the units used are usually financial (pounds, dollars, euros) since most resources can be expressed as a financial cost.

Some commentators, i.e. the APM in the UK, refer to two different types of resources, reusable and replenishable.

Replenishable resources are sand, wood, concrete, fuel, paper; things that can be used once and afterwards need to be replaced. They are the 'bought out items' that incur a one-off fixed cost. Once a WBS is in place an idea of what is to be bought can be drawn up, and once a schedule is available the timing of the purchase, and hence incurring of cost, can be estimated.

Reusable resources are people and machinery, things that can work hard today but then work hard again tomorrow, and they incur costs on the basis of a rate such at £ per hr, $ per day, euros per month. Accordingly, their total cost cannot be estimated before establishing the duration of their engagement (hence the importance of the planning scope before time, before cost).

The connection to the schedule allows the anticipated accumulation of cost[6] to be calculated against time. A graph of cumulative cost against time is the result. By this, rather than simply expressing the cost as a total figure, it can be expressed as a profile. As discussed earlier, the shape of this profile has important implications for the management of aspects such as risk and cash flow.

Other Baselines

'Baselines' are a statement of expected performance that can be used as the basis of co-ordination and control, and it can be appropriate to establish a baseline for other aspects of the project. Consider the following:

- Payment – SO must submit invoices and expedite payment in a timely manner.

- Quality – A statement of what is to be expected in terms of performance of the final deliverable and indeed interim deliverables that are available at the end of each Work Package or phase.

- Risk – Many project teams maintain a 'Risk Register'. This is a structured list of the risks that the project is exposed to and ancillary data such as response strategies and owners. The label 'baseline' is appropriate since it can be used as a comparator to show how risk is being managed, and reduced, during the lifecycle of the project. It is unlike the previous baselines in that it is not an early statement of expectation since the expectation is that at the end of the project all risks will have been eliminated.

- Assumptions – Similar to a risk register, a list of assumptions can be used to facilitate control by indicating how the number of assumptions reduces during the life of the project. As such it offers some tangible evidence of a reduction in uncertainty.

SUBSIDIARY MANAGEMENT PLANS

A subsidiary management plan describes how the project team is to manage a specific facet of a project. They are processes and procedures and as well as identifying techniques to be used, they may also establish such things as who is responsible for what. The W^5H approach is highly relevant to their content.

---

6   'Cost' is a complex entity and care is required here. Chapter 17 refers.

Conveniently, they can be titled '_____ Management Plan' whereby the facet of the project that it addresses is inserted as the first word. There can be a subsidiary management plan for any facets deemed worthy but the following are typical:

Requirements	Scope	Schedule	Cost
Quality	Risk	Configuration	Communication
Change	Procurement	Health and Safety	Environment

Some of these, such as cost, can be the subject of both a baseline and a subsidiary management plan but the two documents are very different in purpose and content. The cost baseline will be the documented estimate of cost, whereas the latter will instruct the project team about the ways things are to be done; assisting individual team members and ensuring a common and known approach. For instance, the Cost Management Plan may contain definitions of the different types of cost (accruals, committed costs actual costs); tolerances for different classifications of estimate; protocols for financial management (e.g. profit will only be taken once 50 per cent of the contract value has been delivered); templates for formal documents (spreadsheets or other financial reporting tools to be used).

The number and type of such subsidiary plans depends not just upon the project itself but the context in which it is delivered. For example, a Supplier Organization (SO) delivering a portfolio of similar projects may require the same facet of each project to be managed in an identical way. In such instances each project simply adopts the 'house standard'[7] as the relevant subsidiary management plan. For example, the SO may have an 'approved supplier' list and established 'call-off' contracts that impose constraints on how individual project teams (and their project manager) are to behave in relation to procurement. These are adopted by each project as their own Procurement Management Plan.

Another common example relates to quality management, especially if the SO in question is accredited to a formal standard such as the ISO 9000 series. In such instances the organization's accredited quality manual becomes the Quality Management Plan for each of their projects.

A caveat is appropriate here. Since each project is unique, and for the SO the minimum requirement is ultimately dictated by the contract, there may

---

7   Such 'house standards' will be key elements of the project management method adopted by the SO.

be instances where the 'house standard' is not sufficient or appropriate. Accordingly, when an SO embarks on a new project the project manager (or salesperson) will review the 'house standards' against the contract requirement before either adopting them, or else drafting a new plan specific to their project.

Planning and the Project Management Plan Through the Project

Planning is a time-consuming activity and any Supplier Organization (SO) will be reluctant to start it before it has received a clear commitment from the relevant Owner Organization (OO) in the form of a contract. However, in very many instances the SO must engage in a significant planning effort pre-contract, for reasons of risk mitigation.

As discussed earlier, the Decision Gates of 'Bid/No Bid' and 'Make or Accept/Reject Offer' are vitally important here and these decisions are informed by an estimate of the likely cost and duration of the work.

If these estimates can be reached with sufficient accuracy using 'top-down' estimating techniques then significant amounts of the cost of planning can be deferred (or, in the case of unsuccessful bids, avoided). However, at some point it will become necessary to have very precise estimates (e.g. a 'Definitive Estimate' with 90 per cent confidence limits at +10 per cent/-5 per cent) and for bespoke items this level of accuracy, most often, can only be achieved with the detailed 'bottom-up' techniques associated with the WBS and precedence diagrams discussed above.

Accordingly, within the SO lifecycle, detailed planning may well first be done to facilitate estimating and reduce the risk of underbidding a contract, rather than as a prelude to project execution.

Even if this is the case, it is most likely that much more detailed planning will occur post-contract (not least to secure the soft benefits of the planning process described earlier). There is merit in the SO imposing a common planning approach such that plans started by the marketing team can be evolved through the entire SO lifecycle, rather than starting from scratch at the commencement of each phase.

Such an approach would be an intrinsic part of any project management method adopted by the SO.

Chapter 15

Management of Resources

In Part 1 we explored how, in a project environment, the demand for resources was erratic; but that the size of an organization's resource pool is largely static; and that this has an impact upon the culture and structure of the organization.

In Part 2 we explored how these impacts were disproportionately felt by Supplier Organizations (SO), rather than Owner Organizations (OO).

Also in Part 2, we discussed how the commercial imperative of a SO was to make a profit and, since its resources are its primary source of both costs and its revenue, resource management is vital to its success. Further, in Chapter 14 it was acknowledged that the availability of resources was a major determinant of the duration and scheduling of project work, and hence the ability of the SO to satisfy its contractual time commitments.

Any way it is looked at, it is imperative that Supplier Organizations (SO) are able to manage their resources.

RESOURCE DEMAND VERSUS RESOURCE AVAILABILITY

As alluded to earlier, the challenge of resource management derives from two facts. Firstly, demand for resources is not stable. Figure 4.2 shows how the rate of expenditure varied during the life of a project but, since all money spent on projects (either directly or via suppliers) is spent on resources, the curve also shows the aggregated demand made for resources. If we look at each individual type of resource demanded by a project, then the picture is even more volatile. Secondly, the size of resource pools is not easy to change. How long would it take to recruit a new full-time employee? How long would it take to lay-off a full-time employee?

These parameters of demand for, and supply of, resources can each be represented pictorially as a type of graph known as a histogram (see Figure 15.1).

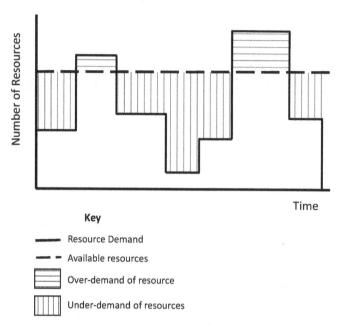

Key

——— Resource Demand

– – – Available resources

▭ Over-demand of resource

▥ Under-demand of resources

Figure 15.1   Typical demand for, and availability of, resources

The resource demand profile is created during the planning of the project. In Chapter 14 we discussed how, when establishing the time baseline, a provisional schedule was created on the basis of the sequencing and duration of project activities. This can be augmented by specifying the demand made by each activity, for each resource, within each time period. Aggregating the demand across all project activities gives the total project demand for each resource. Although this sounds quite complex, the myriad of software packages available for scheduling projects make this task relatively straightforward.

Resource availability is a feature of the organization; the amount of its resources and their working times. Again, scheduling software can assist the process of creating a graph that can reflect shift patterns, holiday periods and the like. It is sometimes known as a 'resource calendar'.

The interplay between the two graphs shows that in some instances the project is demanding more resources than are available, and at others there are more resources available than demanded.

The first point to make is that the situation so depicted in the figure cannot actually occur in practice since it is impossible to use resources that are not available. Changes must be made to eliminate times of over-demand.

The simplest way of doing this is to secure more resources, but even ignoring the practical difficulties of recruitment, it does not provide an ideal solution. Figure 15.2 applies.

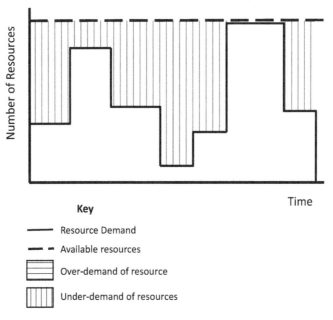

Key

——— Resource Demand

— — Available resources

▭ Over-demand of resource

▯ Under-demand of resources

Figure 15.2   Over-supply of resources

On a positive note, the schedule can now be achieved because at no point are more resources being demanded than are available. However, a significant price has been paid since the area of the graph showing the under-utilization is now very considerable. From a purely commercial and simplistic point of view this is unattractive because it represents resources that are being paid for, but not used: it represents inefficiency.

Inefficiency also derives from making changes in the size of the resource demand, though this is not easy to represent diagrammatically. Starting and stopping resources working on an activity requires mobilizing and demobilizing resources, which is problematic and risky. In a simple world the area under the resource demand graph would be a single rectangle, but this is rarely achievable.

An alternative, but again simplistic, approach maintains a minimal number of resources and reschedules activities to suit. This will delay the project, which may well be unacceptable. It also presupposes that activities are 'elastic' whereby they can be addressed by any number of resources and the time just varies accordingly. This may hold for some tasks (picking a fruit harvest) but it will not for others (moving a heavy table needs at least four people).

From a resource management point of view, the challenge is to manipulate the two curves so that a satisfactory solution is obtained. The conundrum is rendered complex for a number of reasons not least of which is that different projects have different priorities for completion time, final cost and the quality or performance of the product. There are a number of responses that are available and the selection is largely based upon which of these aspects are the most important.

Consider the following.

Resource Management Techniques[1]

Name	Description
Rescheduling within float (When used: Always)	In Chapter 14 we discussed the concept of float. There are two types (Free and Total) but each relates to the degree with which an activity can be delayed or extended without affecting the rest of the project schedule.
	By moving activities within their floats it is sometimes possible to reach a solution that lies within the constraints of time, resources (money) and scope. This approach should be used before those described below.
	It can also be used to improve the profile of the resource demand graph so as to minimize mobilizing and demobilizing of resources.
Smoothing (When used: Time and scope constrained projects)	If the primary constraint on the project is time such that the end date cannot be relaxed, and all the scheduled activities are essential, then it is appropriate to compromise cost to preserve time and this involves securing more resources. For the

---

1   Although presented in the context of management of resource, since time and cost are inextricably linked, they can be thought of as time or cost management techniques, depending upon the context.

reasons described above it is most likely that these resources will be temporary, i.e. 'contractors'.

Sanctioning 'overtime' is an example of 'smoothing'.

Levelling
(When used: Cost and scope constrained projects)

If the primary constraint on the project is cost, such that more resources cannot be afforded, or alternatively that no more resources are available, and all the scheduled activities are essential, then it is appropriate to compromise time. By this, the amount of available resources is held at a fixed level and activities are delayed until such a time as resources are available.

Inevitably this will delay completion of the project.

De-scoping
(When used: Cost and time constrained projects)

If more resources cannot be secured, for instance through a lack of money, and the completion date cannot be delayed, it may be appropriate to de-scope the project. This will involve reducing the requirement such that some Work Packages and activities are no longer necessary. Does that new house you are building really need a swimming pool?

Relaxing of specification
(When used: Cost and time constrained projects)

This is similar to the above but rather than reducing the breadth of the requirement, the grade or specification may be relaxed.

Perhaps a hot tub instead of the swimming pool?

Activity splitting
(When used: Cost, time and scope constrained projects)

In some instances it is appropriate to divide an activity that is not on the critical path and which is consuming a scarce resource, into two or more tranches. During the stand-down period in-between, the resources can be diverted to other, critical, activities.

There will be an inefficiency deriving from the added mobilization and demobilization of the resource but this may not be significant in the context of the whole project.

Revision to logic
(When used: Cost, time and scope constrained projects)

In some instances it is possible to alter the logical sequence of activities to improve the utilization of resources. Whereas a decorator would prefer to paint walls before fitting the carpet, with care it can be done the other way around if it provides a better solution in the context of the whole project. This technique sometimes involves temporary works. A construction project may elect to build a temporary bridge so that the old bridge can be removed before the new bridge is ready. There will be a cost penalty incurred but this may be acceptable in the context of the overall project.

Reallocation of resources (When used: Cost, time and scope constrained projects)

Activities such as picking the fruit harvest are sometimes described as 'fixed effort' and the duration of such activities are elastic and can vary depending upon the number of resources allocated to them. In reaching an original estimate of duration (that allowed the provisional schedule to be put together) an assumption will have been made as to how many resources should be allocated to it. Once the total resource demand for the provisional schedule can be compared to the resource availability, it may be appropriate to revise the number of resources allocated to selected activities. This will extend or reduce the duration of those activities that may secure a good solution for the overall project.

Revision to method (When used: Various)

In some instances it may be possible to simply change the method adopted and in doing so provide an acceptable solution. If two of you want the company car for different trips on the same day then one of you could simply go by train.

There may be consequences for cost or even duration of an individual activity, but, crucially, it will alter the resource demand which may provide a better solution in the context of the whole project.

Fast-tracking (When used: Cost, time and scope constrained projects but where there is tolerance of risk)

'Fast-tracking' relates to a technique that is a special case of 'revision to logic' described above. It relaxes the logic constraints whereby a successor activity can start before the predecessor is complete. An example would be where manufacture of a component was commenced before design was fully complete. It compromises risk to reduce time.

Crashing
(When used: Time
and scope constrained
projects)

'Crashing' is a special example of the 'smoothing' technique described above. It is more often referred to as a 'schedule compression' technique for the whole project but it has relevance when trying to resolve resource conflicts. It compromises money for time and involves selecting an activity and flooding it with resources to reduce the activity duration. When applying it to compression of the whole project is necessary to:

1. only select activities on the critical path;
2. select that activity which will give the maximum compression for the minimum cost; and
3. recognize that at some point the compressed activity will be so short that the critical path will flow through another part of the schedule and at that point the 'crashing' efforts need to be directed at another activity.

In the context of resolving resource conflicts, the activities requiring compression may not be on the critical path.

Training
(When used: Various)

When faced with a project that makes demand upon a range of different types of resource (see below) it is helpful to have multi-skilled resources that embrace many different disciplines. A domestic appliances repair service may choose to train its service personnel in electrics, plumbing and mechanics rather than sending three separate experts on each call-out. There are drawbacks to this technique. Extensive and expensive training is required and doubtless the highly trained individual would command higher remuneration.

Application of these techniques will require a revision to other aspects of the plan; the scope, the schedule, the budget. Many iterative steps will be taken before the provisional schedule (used to derive the first resource demand estimates and discussed in Chapter 14) is replaced with a final schedule, that is resource loaded and compliant with resource availability, which can be adopted as the time baseline and provide the basis of the cost baseline.

Practical Difficulties of Resource Management

On the face of it, this extensive range of solutions is very attractive and comforting, however, in practice resource management is very difficult. The following addresses some of the reasons for this.

ERRORS IN ESTIMATED RESOURCE DEMAND

The graph of resource demand shown in Figure 15.1 was established by a complex sequence. Consider the following.

The estimate of the project's scope will have errors (often very considerable errors). Subsequently modelling of this work into a sequence of activities tied by the logic of predecessors and successors will have simplifications, and hence errors associated with it. Subsequent estimates of the duration of those activities will have errors. The estimate of the resources required by each of those activities will also contain errors. If each of these four steps introduces only a +/- precision of 10 per cent, the eventual output will have a precision of 60–146 per cent.

Further, this presupposes all the factors are under the influence of the project team. The schedule of a Supplier Organization (SO) is often reliant upon its client, for instance by making facilities and sites available at specific times. Similarly, it is often reliant upon the performance of its sub-suppliers to produce goods at specific times. Further, some activities are reliant upon good weather. Each has the capacity to wreak havoc with the plans of the SO but none are under its control.

ERRORS IN ESTIMATED RESOURCE AVAILABILITY

Estimates of the availability of resources are also subject to errors.

Firstly, resources are not available for revenue-earning work at all times. Resources such as machinery require regular maintenance but also suffer unexpected breakdowns. Human resources need rest and recuperation periods that include holidays, but are also subject to unexpected interruptions to service associated with sickness and personal issues.

Also, people are obliged to service indirect work requirements that are not attributable to fee earning work. Training and staff meetings are obvious examples here but the aggregated effect of minor interruptions, such as answering a colleague's question, is significant.

Many organizations cater for these issues by establishing empirical 'availability factors' that indicate how much of their total time they are available for fee-earning work.

Another difficulty relates to the capacity of individuals. The simplistic mathematical approach assumes that one resource is as capable as the next, but in real life some resources are more experienced and energetic than others and complete work much faster.

MULTI-RESOURCE PROJECTS

The above techniques can be applied to just one resource at a time. This is a problem because most projects have activities that engage a variety of different types of resources, indeed some individual activities use more than one type of resource. This adds complexity because the situation depicted in Figure 15.1 must be repeated for each of the resources engaged, with each having a differing level of supply and each subject to a different aggregate of demand.

Adoption of techniques such as 'smoothing' or levelling' will optimize the situation for the resource type in question, but inevitably will make the situation worse for the others.

THE EFFECT OF PORTFOLIOS

The situation is complicated yet further if the project in question is part of a portfolio of projects that are each feeding off the same resource pools.

In such instances, contagion occurs whereby a delayed project over-demands resources and deprives another project of those same resources, extending the delay to the second project.

In such instances 'portfolio management' becomes of critical importance. Portfolio management is defined as follows (APM, 2006):

> The selection and management of all of an organization's projects, programmes, and related operational activities taking into account resource constraints.

This definition is noteworthy for its focus on resources since, when delivering a project within a portfolio, any meaningful resource management must be carried out at a portfolio level rather than just at an individual project level.

Further, by referring to a 'selection of projects … [on the basis of] resource constraints', it indicates how the objectives of a Supplier Organization (SO) relate more to the management of its resources rather than any particular project. For the SO contemplating whether to accept a contract, the question 'Is this the best project for my limited resources?' is more relevant than simply examining the net profit of any individual project. The starting point for the deliberations of a SO is its resource pool and its most gainful use.

USE OF SOFTWARE

Scheduling and resource management involves much manipulation of data and the reliance on software for the bulk of this work is not surprising. Many readers will be familiar with their use to create the schedules, critical paths and resource demand histograms discussed earlier and also to superimpose resource availability to create charts such as that depicted in Figure 15.1.

Far fewer readers, however, will have had positive experiences of using software to automatically reschedule their project's activities on the basis of resource availability constraints.

There are many reasons why appropriate software is unable to offer a panacea to all resource management challenges.

High on the list of these is the old adage about 'garbage in, garbage out' and as discussed above there are plenty of opportunities for errors in the base estimates to quickly render resource plans obsolete.

Secondly, the portfolio context will require that many projects are analysed simultaneously. Whilst there is software that will do this, it does require consistency in how resource demands are presented for all projects across the portfolio.

Thirdly, how a solution is derived is not straightforward. For example, 'critical path analysis' is an established technique (or algorithm), and if followed the same answer is reached regardless of who is carrying out the analysis. This is not the case for resource management since, as demonstrated above, many different techniques can be employed and there may well be many potential solutions. In response, the software adopts a series of heuristics, or rules, that facilitate a solution. Very often these rules are not easily understood and the radically altered schedule that results is no longer recognized, or trusted.

Practical Solutions for Resource Management

ACKNOWLEDGE THE PRECISION OF FORECASTS

It may appear defeatist, but Supplier Organizations (SO) must acknowledge just how difficult it is to effectively manage resources across a portfolio of projects. Despite the importance of the topic, and in particular its effect on the profits, practitioners should have a realistic view of the degree of precision that can be brought to bear on estimates of demand and availability. It is very unlikely that the degree of control possible when managing routine operations will be achieved when managing projects. This is not evidence of any lack of ability or professionalism on behalf of the project team; it is a feature of the project management environment.

PRIORITIZE EFFECTIVENESS OVER EFFICIENCY

Chapter 3 offered the relative prioritization of effectiveness over efficiency as a key difference between a project and routine operations environment. This distinction becomes clearer when looking at resource utility.

Referring again to Figure 15.1, efficiency is promoted by reducing the margin between the availability of, and demand for, resources. However, this restricts the ability of the project manager (PM) to manage, since without surplus resources they cannot respond to emerging problems or overly optimistic estimates. This increases the likelihood that actual demand will exceed the availability (and hence compromise the schedule). It reduces their ability to manage risk, and hence their effectiveness.

The constantly repeated short cycle activities associated with routine operations generates a flat, stable and very predictable aggregated resource demand. This enables a resource availability to be established that exceeds the former by only a small margin, indicating an efficient use of resources.

The uncertainty, erratic resource demand and high levels of risk within the project environment demands a generous margin between resource demand and availability.

Although this generous margin will be seen as inefficiency, in practice it is necessary and a Supplier Organization (SO) must be very wary of seeking to improve efficiency simply by restricting the availability of resources.

Of course, the above is not to say that management of risk is not important to those SO involved in routine operations, and it is not to say that efficient use of resources is not important to those delivering projects. Clearly each is important to both but, in a practical sense, the first instinct of a PM is about managing risk and the inherent uncertainties of a project.

IMPROVE PLANNING OF WORK AND SCHEDULE

Establishment of the resource demand is at the end of a planning sequence that contains many steps, and therefore many compounded errors. Accordingly an effective way of improving the accuracy of the final estimate is to improve the accuracy of these earlier steps.

Of particular relevance here is scope. An accurate and comprehensive Work Breakdown Structure is the very foundation of subsequent planning, including scheduling and resource management. It is worthy of the investment of considerable time and energy.

Estimating of parameters such as activity duration and resource demand for individual activities is another major source of errors. In this respect the careful management and archiving of actual data from previous projects is crucial.

OPTIMIZE THE SCHEDULE ONLY FOR THE MOST EXPENSIVE RESOURCES

In a multi-resource project, attempts to optimize one resource, almost inevitably, results in a detrimental situation for another resource. Also, the more resources for which optimization is attempted, the more complex and fragmented the overall schedule will become.

Practitioners should seek to optimize the schedule for the most expensive resource first and then consider only the two or three next most expensive resources. Beyond this, the added complexity will erode the advantages to be gained. A consequence of this is that resource utilization for the cheaper resources will be very inefficient.

MANAGE AT A PORTFOLIO LEVEL

As suggested, for Supplier Organizations (SO) engaged in more than one project, meaningful resource management must be undertaken at a portfolio, rather than a project, level.

To secure visibility across the portfolio, each of the projects must submit their plans, and specifically their resource demands, in a common format that is amenable to aggregation.

Further, there must be a central facility which collects and collates these and a role in the organization (a portfolio manager) that is empowered to interrogate and instruct those responsible for individual projects, and subsequently make decisions about prioritization between those projects.

CONSIDER THE SOFT SKILLS

Projects are managed by and for people and whilst a consideration of technical procedures and algorithms is appropriate, it must never be forgotten that the whole exercise is ultimately about influencing people's behaviour. With resource management, as with all other aspects of project management, there must be consideration of the human dimension and appropriate soft skills.

Of vital importance here is openness and honesty on behalf of everyone involved, and also an acceptance that the overall needs of the organization take precedence over individual projects (the latter is something that does not come easy to a tenacious and dedicated PM). Particular care is required with estimates. Too many Supplier Organizations (SO) are plagued with personnel trying to outwit colleagues by inflating or deflating their own and others' estimates, to precipitate a favourable situation. It serves only to compromise portfolio planning and control.

There needs to be respect for the scheduling needs of others, for instance by not consuming float for our own purposes and thus unnecessarily rendering activities as critical.

Those with executive responsibility for the SO must be prepared to make difficult decisions, especially about prioritization even though, inevitably, this will be to the detriment of individual projects, teams and clients.

Critical Chain Method

In recent years a new technique for managing resources within a project and a portfolio has emerged, known as the 'critical chain' technique (Goldratt, 1997).

It is based upon the Theory of Constraints, which asserts that the overall rate at which a system such as factory or project team can perform is determined by a single constraint. In the case of a factory this constraint will be a bottleneck in the production line but for a project it is a single scarce resource. Subsequent management is focused at this constraint.

As applied to project management, the approach has two elements.

One element addresses the soft aspects of behaviour and takes a view on how estimates are put together and, subsequently, how the individual resources schedule their own workloads.

The second element relates to the scheduling algorithms. The critical path is modified to create a 'critical chain'; a sequence of activities that takes account of the appropriate resource demands. This sequence is more practically relevant to determining the overall project duration. During execution it is protected by the inclusion of resource 'buffers' in the non-critical chains.

Published case studies indicate a dramatic improvement in overall project durations and also inventory levels. However, the technique is still reliant upon the understanding of scope, logical sequencing of activities, critical path analysis and activity resource demand estimating referred to above.

References

Association for Project Management (APM), 2006. *APM Body of Knowledge*, 5th edn. High Wycombe: APMKnowledge.

Goldratt, E.M., 1997. *Critical Chain*. Massachusetts: The North River Press.

Chapter 16

Project Control

Anyone who has been involved in project management will be very familiar with the need to plan before doing the work.

The sequence is entirely appropriate since, for all the reasons offered in Chapter 14, the act of planning dramatically increases the chance of the successful implementation. Also, since the ability to influence the project diminishes over time, the project manager (PM) has more of an opportunity to influence the project during the earlier activity of planning than the later act of implementation.

However this is not to say influence cannot be exerted over the project during its implementation, it can, but it is associated primarily with control; of ensuring the project proceeds in accordance with the plan.

Control Theory

In 1943, during the Second World War, the average accuracy of bombs dropped from the air was 1,200 feet. By 1991, during the war in Iraq, for a certain category of bombs this figure had reduced to 10 feet (Correll, 2010).

The category in question is, of course, 'Precision Guided Munitions'; bombs which are able to control their direction during their flight.

OPEN LOOP CONTROL (FEED FORWARD CONTROL)

The bombs of the Second World War were subject to 'Open Loop Control' (also known as Feed Forward Control). See Figure 16.1.

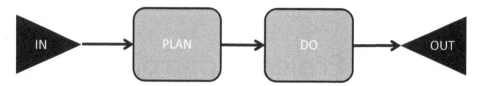

Figure 16.1   Open Loop Control (Feed Forward Control)

In many respects this is a misnomer since there is no control post-launch. By this, at the commencement of the operation, an assessment of the conditions is made. A plan is conceived and enacted without further intervention.

For our bomber crews, the conditions (altitude, wind speed, aircraft speed, air pressure) were assessed. A plan conceived ('taking aim'), whereby a heading and altitude was adopted by the aircraft, and the bomb released at a certain point. However, from hereon in no intervention was attempted (or indeed possible).

The approach has the advantage of simplicity, but the disadvantage is that it cannot respond to any subsequent change in the conditions. In some instances this disadvantage is not significant.

Imagine a commercial bakery making bread. The dough mix, the ambient conditions, the temperature of the oven, are well-known and consistent. In such an instance it can be known with some confidence that putting the bread in the oven for a planned period of time will result in a perfect loaf. Of course the planned period (equivalent to our bombers' 'aim') is 'known' from many previous repetitions of this routine operation and, since all the other variables are controlled, the result will always be the same; a perfect loaf.

The bakery is, of course, an example of a routine operation and 'Open Loop' control is deemed entirely satisfactory in many such situations.

However, for many other situations, the environment is more complex.

If the environment is characterized by considerable uncertainty in relation to the variables which affect the result, and little experience of the outcome of previous attempts then, the Open Loop approach will give unpredictable results.

CLOSED LOOP CONTROL (FEEDBACK CONTROL)

The dramatic increase in the accuracy of the Iraq war was achieved because they were subject to 'Closed Loop Control' (also known as Feedback Control). See Figure 16.2.

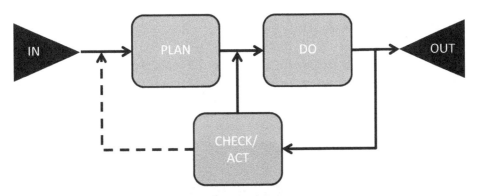

Figure 16.2   Closed Loop Control (Feedback Control)

By this, again an assessment of the conditions is made and a plan conceived but, crucially, this is not the end of the matter since, during its descent, the guided weapon has a capacity to analyse its exact position; compare this with where it should be; and, if necessary, make adjustments to its moveable fins, such that its flight is brought back onto the correct path. Even more sophisticated devices allow the target point to be altered during the descent (for instance when targeting a moving vehicle).

There is, of course, a huge price to be paid for such a facility, in terms of complexity and resource consumption. Converting a 'dumb bomb' to a guided weapon requires the addition of many features:

- An ability to identify where it should be at any point in the descent.

- An ability to identify its exact position throughout the descent.

- An ability to compare between the two, resulting in a revised instruction.

- An ability to actually change the direction of travel.

However, the Closed Loop Control conveys enormous advantages. Firstly, it allows the projectile to deal with variable and unpredictable conditions in the environment (wind speed in this example) and secondly, it reduces the need to be absolutely precise over the initial planning (the 'aiming').

The attraction of this approach to the control of projects is enormous.

PLAN–DO–CHECK–ACT

An approach that is frequently applied to the management of projects, that includes the four required features of Closed Loop Control System, is the Plan–Do–Check–Act cycle.[1] See Figure 16.3.

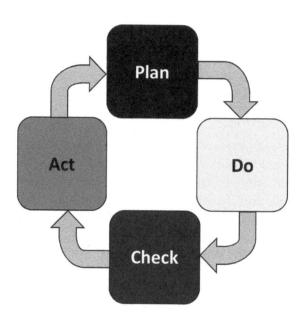

Figure 16.3   Plan–Do–Check–Act cycle

By this, firstly we 'Plan' our work on the basis of our best estimates. This identifies the expected performance (the first feature listed above).

---

1   To many, this four-part cycle is known as the 'Deming Cycle' or the 'Deming Wheel' on the understanding that it was originated by W. Edwards Deming. However, in his book *Out of the Crisis*, Deming (1982) himself attributed the original design to W.A. Shewhart.

Others, such as Ronald D. Moen and Clifford L. Norman (2010) differentiate between 'Deming's Wheel' and the PDCA cycle, attributing the latter to a reworking of Deming's work by a group of Japanese executives after receiving a presentation by Deming in the 1950s.

We then 'work the plan', that is to say we actually 'Do' the work.

At some appropriate point in time, after we have started to 'Do' the work but long before we have completed it, we pause and examine what we have achieved (the second feature). We then 'Check' this with what we would have expected the outcome to be at this point, on the basis of our earlier plan (the third feature).

This comparison gives an insight upon which we can 'Act'. If the outcome is as expected we may choose to continue enacting the plan. Alternatively, if the outcome is not as expected then we may choose to either alter the plan, or else how we are carrying it out (the fourth feature).

Whatever we choose, we continue around the loop. This is an iterative process and one that takes us gradually closer and closer to the eventual goal. Its attraction is its dynamism and ability to respond to imperfect initial plans, imperfect execution or indeed other external, unexpected influences such as risks becoming events. Its similarity to our guided munitions is obvious; uncertain winds may blow during the journey but the system will respond and, in any case, take us to the chosen final destination.

Variations on a Theme

As with many great ideas and models, there are always attempts to improve it which results in a myriad of similar, but different versions, and so it is the case for the Plan–Do–Check–Act cycle.

Some variations maintain the four-step cycle and simply substitute some of the words, for very similar meaning words, which some feel better express the steps involved.

Other evolutions introduce new steps and interactions. For instance, readers familiar with the *Guide to the Project Management Body of Knowledge*, produced by the Project Management Institute (PMI) (2013), will recognize this cycle as being the basis of the five-element process approach to their management of projects.

Alternatively, readers familiar with the 'Six Sigma' approach to quality management will recognize this cycle as being the basis of the Define Measure Analyse Improve Control approach to process improvement initiatives.

Application of the Cycle

It should be recognized here that the sequence can be applied to just about any task, big or small. It can be applied to the idle task of throwing pebbles at a tin (each time the aim is improved on the basis of previous throws); it can be applied to the management of a day-long meeting ('it is now time for lunch and how many of the agenda items have been addressed?'); and it can be applied to a city's transport strategy ('construction of the new bridge has not relieved traffic congestion to the degree hoped for, what other bridges or infrastructure should be constructed?').

In each of these instances the time taken to progress around the cycle is very different. For pebbles it is matter of seconds, for our transport policy it will take very many years.

In addition to time, it is appropriate to consider the cost of completing the cycle. Pebbles have a negligible cost but the construction cost of a bridge is colossal.

Clearly we cannot take the 'pebble tossing' approach to a transport policy by simply building dozens of bridges in the hope that eventually we will build one that is appropriate. Accordingly, the ability to control should not be used as a substitute for careful planning. As discussed earlier, there is nothing quicker and cheaper than getting it right first time.

'WATERFALL' VERSUS 'AGILE'

The recent evolution of 'Agile' techniques provides an interesting perspective on the application of the Plan–Do–Check–Act cycle to the control of a project's product.

The classic approach to project management (adopted within this book) is based upon lifecycle models that have linear phases. They are sometimes referred to as 'Waterfall Models' and a quick reference to Figures 5.3 and 7.1 will show why.

Inherent within this approach is an acknowledgement that late changes to the deliverable are ruinously expensive. This is perfectly understandable if we consider a construction project such as that for an Olympic stadium, and trying to instigate the location change discussed in Chapter 4. In response, considerable energy and resources are invested early on to ensure the requirement is fully understood and the conceived solution robust.

In recent years, however, very many projects have involved the creation of computer software and these projects have certain key characteristics that differentiate them from more traditional projects. These key differences relate to the requirement and the cost of change.

- Computer science is evolving fast and within this environment the ability of a client to fully specify their final requirement at the outset is questionable.

- Software is relatively cheap to produce and subsequently easy and cheap to change. For example, it does not involve the expensive concrete and logistics of construction projects.

In response to this scenario, 'Agile' techniques were evolved on the basis of the 'Manifesto for Agile Software Development' that was conceived by a group of software developers known as the 'Agile Alliance' at Snowbird, Utah, in February 2001.

These techniques relax the need for precisely understanding final requirements at the outset in favour of rapid, time limited, prototyping followed by a formal review of the prototype against the latest understanding of the requirement. By this, late changes are welcomed and not resisted.

Within 'Agile' techniques the focus is predominantly on the 'Check' and 'Act' elements of the cycle, whereas for the 'Waterfall' approach, the focus is on the 'Plan' element, and thus reducing the need for subsequent changes during the 'Check' and 'Act' elements.

The superiority of one approach against the other is the subject of ongoing debate but the cost of making late changes would seem to be a significant factor and as such 'Agile' would be restricted to projects that produce products that are quickly and easily changed. This can apply to the creation of computer software or else the phase products, such as a design, produced during the earlier phases of a traditional 'Waterfall' lifecycle.

Different Levels of Project Control

PROJECT SUCCESS

When applying the concept of control to projects, we are concerned with the ongoing management of efforts such that we achieve our objectives. It is therefore a perquisite that we are able to define those objectives.

In the context of our guided munitions, this is quite straightforward since success is measured by just one parameter; the final location of the projectile relative to the target.

In the context of the project environment the situation is far more complex. Firstly, in Chapter 1 we discussed how projects have 'complex outcomes' and the implication of this is that the concept of 'project success' is not quite as straightforward as it may appear. Secondly, as we have established, not all project objectives are shared by both the Owner Organization (OO) and Supplier Organization (SO).

PROJECT SUCCESS FOR THE OWNER ORGANIZATION

To explore the concept of 'success' it is helpful to adopt a diagram commonly used in the world of systems engineering, known as a V-model. In essence it is

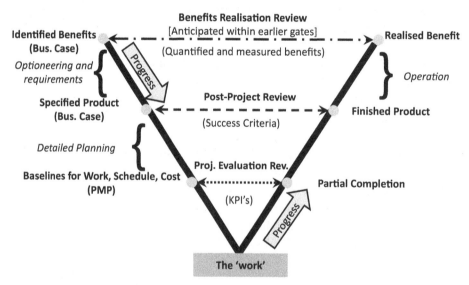

Figure 16.4   V-model of Owner Organization project lifecycle

a depiction of the project lifecycle. Consider taking the lifecycle model offered in Figure 5.3, putting your foot in the middle and your hands at either end and pulling it up into a V-shape (see Figure 16.4).

The project progresses down the first leg and then up the second. At the start of a project an Owner Organization (OO) conceives of some benefit to be had. A power company, for instance, needs electricity to sell.

Moving on from there, it becomes appropriate to specify a project product whose operation will realize that benefit. Typically this would identify constraints on the cost and duration required to build the product, as well as the technical constraints. In the short term, these criteria (often known as 'success criteria') can be used to judge competing potential solutions. The benefit of electricity can be generated by coal-fired, nuclear, wind-powered stations, etc. and in our example an early decision must be made as to which of these 'options' should be adopted; a selection process referred to as 'optioneering'.

The quantified benefit, the 'success criteria' and favoured option will be identified in the Business Case.

Detailed planning can now occur and baselines for the work scope, duration and cost will be included in the PMP.

The actual work of creating the deliverable can commence and, at some point, a partially completed deliverable will be available.

Later, the deliverable will be completed at which point the final cost, duration and technical capability of the deliverable will be known.

After this, the new asset can be put into operation and the benefit realized.

The V-model allows us to consider the multi-faceted nature of project success.

WAS THE PROJECT WORTHWHILE? (BENEFITS REALIZATION REVIEW)

In the final analysis, for the Owner Organization (OO), the only important measure of success is the degree to which net benefits (benefits less cost over the Extended Project Lifecycle) were realized as compared to those anticipated in the business case. However, this can only be known at the very end and so it is of no relevance to the control of the project at hand since, at this point, there is nothing left of the project to control (it is only possible to influence future events, not those in the past). This lack of relevance to the individual project is one of the reasons why such retrospective analysis of benefits (known as a Benefits Realization Review) is rarely carried out.

The analysis is, however, of fundamental interest to the Owner Organization (OO). It has relevance to the control of a larger entity that the project may be part of, that is trying to achieve some specific benefit (such as a programme or overarching strategy), for example in answering questions such as 'Has sufficient benefit been realized or do we need another project?'.

It has an enormous value to the OO in the sense of 'lessons learned' and ongoing capability improvement since the review contains the whole extended lifecycle, including project selection and justification, and so is the only truly holistic and comprehensive review of the project.

Within the OO, responsibility for benefit realization lies with the sponsor and this review primarily addresses their performance.

It is this fundamental analysis of success, and hence judgement as to whether the project was worthwhile, that is anticipated within the Decision Gates discussed in Chapter 4.

Was the Project Delivered Satisfactorily? (Post-Project Review)

Within an Owner Organization (OO), the project manager (PM) and the team are responsible only for the delivery of the product and will be disbanded at the point of handover.

For practical reasons it is necessary to assess how well the PM and team have performed prior to their departure and such assessment can only be made on the basis of information available at the time. Whereas, in most instances, assessment of the benefit can be made only after many years of operation post-handover, at the point of handover, the actual cost, time taken to create the new asset, and its technical capability are all known. These can be compared to the success criteria laid down earlier. The formal assessment of whether these criteria have been met is made at a Post-Project Review.

As discussed in Chapter 1, satisfaction of the success criteria is not the same thing as the realization of benefit. Many projects create products that are late, over budget and fail to fully meet technical requirements and yet go on to realize far more benefit than expected. The reverse also can be true.

This comparison of actual performance against the original success criteria is a vital control point for a project since it is when closure of the project is applied for (a 'Check' element). There is an option (an 'Act' element) to decline the request and instruct further work to be carried out.

Although this degree of control can be applied here, any major corrective actions so late in the project, most likely, will be extremely expensive.

Reviews at this stage also have considerable value in the sense of 'lessons learned', though not quite as comprehensive as a Benefits Realization Review.

Is It Likely That the Success Criteria Will be Met? (Project Evaluation Reviews)

The significant advantage of exercising early control is tempered by the significant disadvantage that final cost, time and performance data is not known. We are therefore faced with having to anticipate the likelihood of subsequently meeting the success criteria, on the basis of parameters that can be measured before the fact.

The parameters in question are known as Key Performance Indicators (KPIs) and are assessed at the periodic Project Evaluation Reviews that are typically held every week, month, or quarter during the project. It is these reviews (and the periodic progress reports they require) that comprise the most obvious control activity within the project.

Inevitably, KPIs relate to achievement of work (lines of code written, square metres of runway surfaced, etc.), incurred cost and elapsed time As well as being easy to measure, anticipated values for the KPIs must be included within the PMP. This facilitates easy comparison between the actual and planned values, upon which the likelihood of success (of meeting the success criteria) is indicated and, hence, the basis for control decisions.

The need for regular comparisons through the lifecycle imposes constraints on how the baselines are to be expressed, for instance the cost baseline must be expressed as a graph of expenditure over time rather than just a final total figure.

Chapter 17 further addresses the management and presentation of this information. But, before leaving the topic of KPIs it is worth reflecting on their less obvious implications and, in particular, their influence on behaviour. Publishing performance as measured against specific parameters, most likely, will encourage team members to improve their score, so measured.[2] Whereas this can be taken advantage of (pay-by-results incentive schemes) they can often result in inappropriate behaviour. Factories and building sites were in the habit of putting up large signs at their entrance declaring slogans such as '562 accident-free days'. Whereas the intention was to promote careful and safe behaviour, it was later discovered that it simply stopped people reporting any accidents, thus stifling the very improvements sought. KPIs need to be carefully selected and managed.

PROJECT SUCCESS FOR THE SUPPLIER ORGANIZATION

Whereas much of the above analysis has relevance to a Supplier Organization (SO) as well as an Owner Organization (OO), their situations are different, not least because the reason why SO engage in projects is fundamentally different to that of the OO. The latter seek operational benefits, the former a profit from the supply contract. Accordingly, a different V-model is required, based upon the SO lifecycle model. Figure 16.5 applies.

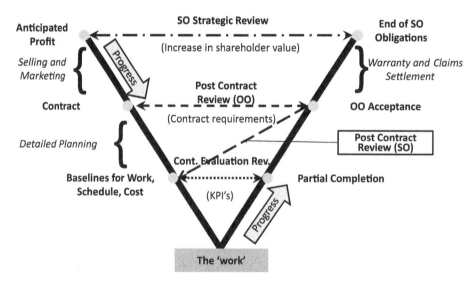

Figure 16.5   V-model of Supplier Organization project lifecycle

---

2   This can be considered as an example of the 'Hawthorne Effect' (Buchanan and Huczynski, 2004).

Supplier Organizations (SO) are concerned with making money, now and into the future. This is most easily evidenced by an increase in shareholder value.

In pursuit of this they engage firstly in marketing; identifying customers and products that may result in profitable work.

The following selling activity seeks to establish attractive contracts. Chapter 12 discussed instances where the SO may identify strategic benefits associated with a contract, such as breaking into a new market, but these are rare; attractiveness is primarily based upon potential profit.

A contract will define the level of performance that the SO must meet relating to time and technical performance of the deliverable and the price to be paid,[3] but not the cost of the work.

After the contract is established, the PMP will be completed and contain baselines for scope, time and cost. The targets implicit within these baselines will be a statement of the performance expected by the SO management team and inevitably will be more onerous than the limits imposed by the contract.

Subsequently the work is undertaken and partial completion achieved.

At some point the Supplier Organization (SO) will assert that the work is complete and will invite the Owner Organization (OO) to offer formal acceptance.

Chapter 18 will address in detail what work will be required after this point. It includes aspects such as the settlement of any claims and servicing of the warranty period.

As with the OO lifecycle, various control points can be identified using the V-model of the SO lifecycle. However, as discussed below, the situation is different for the SO

Was the Project Worthwhile? (Supplier Organization's Strategic Review)

As with the Owner Organization (OO), the ultimate measure of whether the project was worthwhile is whether it achieved the net rewards that were originally identified.

---

3   For convenience we will consider a Firm Price contract.

If this reward is solely concerned with the profit associated with the individual contract then the difference between the total revenues and total costs must exceed that originally envisaged by the marketer. The principal difficulty here is that the total costs will include the costs of any claims for which they are liable, including warranty claims; and the total revenues will include any claims to which they are entitled. These will not be known until after the resolution of any disputes and the expiry of legal obligations of the Supplier Organization (SO).

The situation is more complex if the rewards are associated with a strategic initiative, such as the contract in question leading to further work since, again, the timescale can be significant, extending well beyond OO acceptance.

As with the equivalent point in the OO's model, although this is the ultimate test of project success, it is too late for the control of the project at hand, but it does have relevance to the SO.

It has relevance to the control of any greater initiative of which the project is part. For instance, on the basis of their experience with a project, a SO may choose to abandon a market sector.

The main value of this review is in the sense of 'lessons learned'. As with the equivalent review within the Owner Organization's (OO) lifecycle, this review encompasses the whole 'cradle to grave' activities of the Supplier Organization (SO) that include selection as well as execution of projects. However, unlike the OO, there is no equivalent role of the sponsor who retains overall responsibility over this whole lifecycle. Within the SO, responsibility for the day to day management is passed from marketers, to sales team, to the implementation team and one can therefore expect many lively discussions about quite who was responsible for the success or otherwise of the endeavour.

As was the case for the OO, it is the result of this final comparison (of rewards less costs) that is anticipated by the SO within its Decision Gates.

Has the Contract Been Completed Satisfactorily? (Post-Contract Review)

The point of formal acceptance of the project product will involve comparing what is offered, against what the contract required. From a control perspective it is more relevant to the Owner Organization (OO) than the Supplier Organization (SO), not least since the decision is largely within the gift of the

OO and not the SO.[4] In respect of the technical performance of the product, the OO will simply withhold acceptance until a satisfactory product is offered. (Such withholding will trigger an 'Act' element within the SO control cycle.)

Acceptance of the product by the Owner Organization (OO) is a major milestone for the Supplier Organization (SO) primarily because it represents the expiry of much uncertainty and risk associated with the product, and hence cost and duration. However, in terms of a control point for the SO project, it is far less significant that the equivalent point within the V-model of the OO project.

The contract[3] specifies price and not cost, and so, whereas it may provide a realistic comparator for the duration and product capability aspects of the SO performance, it does not provide a comparator for cost performance. In this respect it is not equivalent to the 'success criteria' of an OO project. To 'Check' the SO cost performance at this point, the actual cost must be compared to another measure of anticipated cost.

The cost estimate of the salesperson at the point of agreeing the contract may be of some relevance here, but in reality this will be superseded as the target performance, and hence control comparator, by the baselines of the PMP. This is so for a number of reasons.

Firstly, the estimates in the PMP are far more precise than the pre-contract estimates and so are far more realistic targets.[5]

Secondly, the estimates in the PMP would have sufficient resolution to show the anticipated cost at this point, as opposed to just an indicated final cost. For the reasons discussed above the final cost will not be known at this point.

Thirdly there is a connection between cost and revenue. We can fully expect that during a project, the OO will instruct changes that will increase both the consideration to be paid and the cost incurred by the SO. Accordingly the cost baseline used for control purposes must reflect these. In an ideal world all such changes will be reflected immediately in a formal variation to the incoming contract but in practice, often costs are incurred before such formalisation, also,

---

4   As discussed in Chapter 7, through the life of a contract the SO has progressively less influence over the gate decisions than the OO. For example, once the contract is signed the opportunity for the SO to terminate the contract is negligible.

5   If the estimated cost within the baselines of the PMP is less than that within the pre-contract sales estimate it is inconceivable that SO management would not insist on the former being adopted as the target cost.

some changes will be contentious. The PMP baseline for cost is relatively easily updated and will therefore be a better instrument for advising the appropriate cost for purposes of comparison and control.[6]

A consequence of these is that the target cost adopted as the comparator for control of the SO project, post contract, may result in a negative profit. Such a situation may occur if, during the creation of the baselines, an error is revealed in the pre-contract estimates resulting in it being an over-optimistic figure. It is appropriate for the SO to 'take the hit' at this point since imposing an unrealistic target upon the delivery team will be counterproductive.

Is It Likely That the Profit Will Be Secured? (Contract Evaluation Reviews)

In the same way that an Owner Organization (OO) will hold regular Project Evaluation Reviews, the Supplier Organization (SO) will hold regular Contract Evaluation Reviews. In both instances KPIs will be used to exert control over the endeavour by comparing actual performance against that anticipated within the baselines of the PMP.

For a SO that is to receive staged payments, it is also important to control the receipt of these payments, in which case a Payment Baseline is required.

STRATEGIC VERSUS TACTICAL CONTROL

In Chapter 4 the concepts of both strategic and tactical control were introduced. In the case of both the Owner Organization (OO) and the Supplier Organization (SO), the V-models help us differentiate between these two levels of control.

Strategic control is associated with the question 'Are we delivering the right project?' and is answered at the higher level of the V-model, within Decision Gates, for instance. Within the OO this level of control is associated with the role of the sponsor. As suggested above, the situation is not as clear cut for an SO since there is no equivalent role of Sponsor.[7]

---

6   Although it is easy to refer to just cost, the real goal of the SO is profit and so there is a pressing need to manage and control revenue, both in terms of expediting payments to which the SO is already entitled, and also maximising the amount of entitlement. The latter will involve the SO's PM acting as a marketer and salesperson seeking out new opportunities within the context of the existing OO and project. Such activity is akin to the 'farmer' aspect of selling as opposed to the more conventional 'hunter' aspect, as addressed in Chapter 13.

7   To some extent this is because this strategic level of control is not as easy to exert within an SO because, once a contract is signed, the SO has no option to withdraw.

Tactical control is associated with the question 'Are we delivering the project right?' and is addressed at the lower of the V-model, primarily within the evaluation reviews. Within both the OO and SO this level of control is associated with the role of the project manager.

Controlled and Output Variables

The fuel efficiency of a car is not improved by restricting the fuel supply to the engine, in the same way that the cost efficiency of a project is not improved by simply restricting the supply of funds.

The variable that is used to measure the output is not the same variable that is altered to effect control.

In the context of the guided weapons discussed above, the 'output variable', that was used to measure the result, was the location of the projectile at the end of the flight. However the 'controlled variable' that was changed so as to alter the projectile's position was the angle of the incidence of the projectile's vanes.

Although the likely success of projects is assessed by references to parameters such as cost and time, these are not the parameters that are amenable to control.

OUTPUT VARIABLES

In Chapter 1 we established that a key feature that characterizes projects is that they have complex outcomes.

This is particularly evident within the interplay between benefits and products that the V-models within Figure 16.4 depicts.

Even if we restrict our analysis to the product of the Owner Organization's (OO) project, we see that it is not straightforward to measure success by reference to just one output variable since the success criteria, typically, relate to cost, time and technical performance. These are related insofar as attempts to expedite progress will, most likely, lead to an increase in costs or reduction in technical performance; attempts to increase performance result in delays and additional costs. It is for this reason it is imperative that, within the success criteria, the Sponsor indicates the relevant priority between these parameters such that appropriate control decisions are possible.

As discussed in part 3, it is vital that this prioritization of the OO migrates across the contractual boundary with the Supplier Organization (SO) such that the SO is motivated and incentivised to pursue these priorities when exercising control over the project.

As already acknowledged, there is considerable scope for conflict here since the SO's imperative of increasing profit, by the reduction of cost and increase of revenue, is not immediately compatible with the priorities of the OO.

The OO must respond by, when drawing up the agreement with the SO, seeking to connect their imperatives with those of the SO.

The selection of appropriate reimbursement methods discussed in Chapter 10 has enormous relevance here but other 'Carrots and sticks' abound.

For instance, most crudely, within Firm Price contracts the payment is only contingent upon the SO providing a product that is technically compliant. Further, performance to schedule can be encouraged by the imposition of liquidated and ascertained damages.

Although these' sticks' have their place, it would seem that 'carrots' are preferable. Anecdotal evidence suggests that the offers of bonuses contingent upon some specified performance criterion are far more persuasive.

CONTROLLED VARIABLES

Parameters that are amenable to control within the Supplier Organization (SO) relate to their resources, predominantly people. They can decide what work is to be done, how and by whom, but in practice, their options can be very limited. For example, the scope of the work and the manner in which it is to be carried out are often are often very much restricted within the contract.

There is often more latitude for determining when work is to be done, but, as discussed in the previous chapter, if the resources are limited in number, and are obliged to carry out many tasks, the control over when the work is to be done is often limited to just deciding the sequence (priority) of work.

As discussed in Chapters 2 and 15, within a matrix environment, most likely there will be a number of projects competing for such priority and as such decisions about prioritisation become very complex and contentious.

In these circumstances a PM's authority to control events can be very modest and many of them, especially those in Supplier Organizations (SO) located towards the left of the continuum in Figure 2.4, will expend most of their energies just seeking to persuade or cajole others, especially Functional Managers, to reprioritise work within their departments.

References

The Agile Alliance, 2001. *Manifesto for Agile Software Development.* [online] Available at: http://agilemanifesto.org [accessed 17 June 2014].

Buchanan, D. and Huczynski, A., 2004. *Organizational Behaviour: An Introductory Text*, 5th edn. Harlow: Prentice Hall.

Correll, J.T., 2010. The Emergence of Smart Bombs. *Air Force Magazine: Online Journal of the Air Force Association.* [online] Available at: http://www.airforce mag.com/MagazineArchive/Pages/2010/March%202010/0310bombs.aspx [accessed 16 April 2014].

Deming, W. Edwards, 1982. *Out of the Crisis.* Massachusetts: Massachusetts Institute of Technology.

Moen, Ronald D. and Norman, Clifford L., 2010. *Circling Back, Clearing Up The Myths about the Deming Cycle and Seeing How It Keeps Evolving.* [online] Available at: http://apiweb.org/circling-back.pdf [accessed 16 June 2014].

Project Management Institute, 2013. *A Guide to the Project Management Body of Knowledge (PMBOK® Guide)*, 5th edn. Pennsylvania: Project Management Institute Inc.

Chapter 17

Management of Information

A very common complaint amongst those involved in the management of projects relates to (what, before emails arrived, was referred to as) 'paperwork'.

Complaints usually relate to either the sheer magnitude of reports, forms, correspondence and other formal documents that need to be processed, or alternatively, the insufficiency of the various systems that exist within their organizations to manage them.

The reality is that projects generate and devour enormous amounts of information and data and most practitioners spend a significant portion of their time simply servicing the administrative demands of their project; completing, filing and subsequently retrieving (or looking for) key information.[1] Whilst we all dream of some clever IT solution that will free us from this burden, it seems unlikely that this will ever happen.

In some ways, the adoption of IT over paper-based systems has acted to disguise some issues.

The author has happy memories of, as a young man, starting a new project with an empty cupboard then filling it with 20 or so lever arch files, having written on each 'Correspondence file # x', 'Documents file # y', etc. This was the project information system. It was there in preparation for the coming deluge of paperwork and its existence, and the care with which it was maintained, was very obvious to all.

Without physical paper, computer-based systems are less obvious. It saves office space but can disguise some very poorly maintained and untidy collections of documents.

---

1   It is said that project managers spend upwards of 90 per cent of their time simply communicating with others (Heldman, 2009).

But, regardless of the format, the information management system is vitally important to appropriate management of the project.

Why So Much Information?

All commercial organizations are obliged to undertake some information management. Payroll, purchase ledger, health and safety records, training certificates and the like apply to all, but, in moving from the non-project environment to the project, the Supplier Organization (SO) will face a step-change increase in the amount and range of information that they must manage. Consider the following:

- As discussed in Chapter 6, SO offer an expertise and capability within a specialist, and often rare, niche. In this respect their intellectual property (and very often their single most valuable asset) is their archive of drawings, calculations, cost data, risk registers. These detail their experience of previous, similar projects, and hence their eligibility for future work.

- Since each product is bespoke, standard technical documents become inappropriate. Each deliverable requires its own defining documents. This specialist need is addressed by the topic of Configuration Management.

- Bespoke products usually have unique commercial arrangements. Individual contracts must be established with each client and the inevitable prelude to this is extensive correspondence.

- Controlling the creation of bespoke products incurs a huge demand for documentation such as the bespoke plans and subsequent reports discussed in Chapter 14.

- Often, the project deliverables are documents. An architect, for instance, just produces drawings, calculations and specifications. Even if the principal output is a physical deliverable, like machinery, the SO will be obliged to produce documents such as operating and maintenance manuals and quality control records.

- Supply control. As discussed in Chapter 8, SO often sit within a procurement chain and as such the complexity of supplying bespoke products up the chain is mirrored by the complexity of managing suppliers of bespoke products, lower in the chain.

- The control of the SO portfolio by interfacing between different projects, for instance in relation to resource management, makes further information demands. An important aspect of this relates to the need for continuous improvement and documenting lessons learned.

The expense, in terms of man-hours, associated with servicing this system can be considerable and is often overlooked when estimating the cost of the project.

Planning the Information Management System

As with all aspects of project management, the earlier in the lifecycle an activity occurs, the more influence can be exerted. We have discussed this by reference to the importance of planning and this applies to the management of information.

In Figure 4.2 we explored how the number of people involved in a project increased rapidly during the mid-part of a project. We may expect the amount of the information generated and required to be consistent with the number of possible communication links between the team members. Within a team of n people, this is given by the formal $0.5(n^2-n)$; it increases with the square of the number of people and represents a far steeper and dramatic curve. Also, the most important documents (business cases, contracts, plans) are created at the start of a project. The combination of these two factors point to the importance of considering very early in the project, how information will be managed.

Many inexperienced practitioners start projects without plans for managing information, expecting to evolve systems as they proceed. Unfortunately, the rate of increase indicated above can seem like a tsunami when it arrives, quickly overwhelming any rudimentary systems. Practitioners are therefore faced with having to design and implement a system at the very time the need for it (to control the burgeoning project) becomes critical.

The more experienced avoid this. Many Supplier Organizations (SO) do so by establishing an enterprise-wide facility, and having procedures for the management of information as part of the project management 'method' they choose to adopt.[2] Such an approach has very many advantages.

Firstly, it provides economies of scale, for instance by relieving each PM of having to invest the time and energy to 'reinvent the wheel' for every incoming project.

Secondly, a consistent approach ensures the other members of the project team will be familiar with the approach and already know where to find or store information. This has particular benefits to the management of portfolios such that personnel being switched between roles and projects can quickly access the necessary information.[3]

Thirdly, it becomes easier to implement 'lessons learned' from previous projects especially within the disproportionately important early documents, such as contracts.

Increasingly, the design of project information systems is being taken over by proprietary software. A simple search of the Internet will reveal a myriad of products that purport to address the entire requirement for information management within a project environment, from scheduling to document control. The selection of the most appropriate will lie with each individual SO and no attempt is made here to discuss the various merits of individual products. Instead, we shall focus on understanding the detail of the requirements and how it supports effective project management.

Types of Information to be Managed

CONFIGURATION MANAGEMENT

'Configuration Management' is an expression that readers will have come across but few will be comfortable with defining.

Configuration Management is best viewed as being all that is said and done to control the physical and performance characteristics of the project deliverable throughout the extended lifecycle; from the point of conception,

---

2   Care is required here since some projects will have their own contractual requirements that may not be adequately serviced by the existing facility.

3   This also helps to manage the risks associated with the unexpected departure of key project staff.

through specification, design, construction, operation and disposal. The most familiar manifestation of the Configuration Management is likely to be a document control system.

In simple terms, for us to ultimately get what we want from a project, at the outset we need to be able to describe what it is that we want. In relation to the project deliverable, this requires that, prior to its creation, we must be able to describe what it is (will be) in a document such as a drawing or specification. Such a document is the core of Configuration Management, but the need for some enhancements become obvious.

Firstly, as the project evolves and more is known about the product, the document in question that describes it will change from a need statement, to a specification, to a drawing, to an 'as-built' record of the asset. Consequently, we see the need for a suite of connected documents with one directly influencing and shaping another; a specification influencing a drawing, for instance. Easy and accurate referencing between these documents is vital so, inevitably, a system of numbering is evolved such that each document has a unique reference number.

Secondly, as established in Chapter 11, changes are an unwelcome but inevitable aspect of projects and there is a need for this to be reflected in documents. Chaos is guaranteed if different team members are working to different editions of the same drawing. This is avoided by each having a 'version number' (sometimes known as a revision or issue number) and the authorization and release of revised versions being carefully managed. (In turn, version numbers provide the facility to actually instruct change.)

These two aspects are the basis of the document control system which makes up the majority of the Configuration Management System (CMS).[4]

Straightforward though these principles may be, it would be a mistake to assume that the practice of configuration management is straightforward, especially if the project is large, the product complex or the team members geographically dispersed.

Consider making something as complex as an aeroplane consisting of many thousands of sub-assemblies that must fit and perform together, and each

---

4   Some practitioners also include the processes and documents required to manage change as being part of the Configuration Management System (CMS).

made by different parties spread across the globe and arranged into a complex procurement chain. Simply designing a suite of documents that describe the product and each sub-assembly is an enormous challenge.[5]

In such projects the number of documents becomes colossal. This in turn requires additional roles dedicated to administering to the CMS such as Configuration Control Boards, Configuration Item Owners and Configuration Librarians.

We can also see the need for an Owner Organization (OO) to impose one CMS consistently across its whole project. This has implications for the Supplier Organization (SO) since its system must align and interface with that of the OO.[6] The practicalities of this are often perverse and may, for instance, involve a document or drawing having more than one reference number (one for the CMS of the OO, another for that of the SO).

Inevitably, the CMS will overlap with many other aspects of the SO project. For instance the contract must identify the deliverable either directly (in which case the contract becomes the principal specifying document) or else by reference to another document (in which case the unique reference and version of the document will be needed). If the version of these documents changes then this needs to be accommodated within variations to the contract.

Each SO engaged in project work will need a CMS that, at minimum, includes the following:

- The 'Configuration' – A list of those documents (including drawings) that collectively define the deliverable and its method of creation, each with a unique sequential reference number and document owner.

- Issue status – A record of the current version of each document including the date of approval (by owner and any other appropriate bodies), the date of issue, and the recipients.[7]

---

5   For instance, to avoid potential for any contradictions such suites should, ideally, ensure that a requirement (such as a dimension) is only stated once, in one document, which is then referenced by the others.
6   Or alternatively with a CMS imposed by a SO higher in the supply chain.
7   Some recipients will receive a 'Controlled Copy' in which case they will automatically receive any subsequent updated versions. Recipients of 'Uncontrolled Copies' do not atomically receive updated versions.

- Appropriate document formats – The documents will conform to a standard format, or else have a cover sheet appended that allows the pertinent data, including that above, to be displayed.

- Change control information – An audit trail is required indicating how each document has evolved in response to changes.

COMMERCIAL INFORMATION

Incoming Contract

As an absolute minimum, the information management system of the Supplier Organization (SO) must contain a copy of the agreed incoming contract, including all approved variations.

As often stated, this is the ultimate reference document that determines what the SO is to do and its rights to receive payment. It must be available to all relevant SO personnel and control their behaviour accordingly.

Client Correspondence

A similar level of care is required with correspondence. In the event of a dispute between the Owner Organization (OO) and Supplier Organization (SO) as to the obligations of either party, it can become necessary to look for additional information that clarifies a position. In these instances the communication between the SO and OO is vital. Letters, emails, minutes of meeting and notes of telephone calls must be religiously recorded.

Good housekeeping and administration are vital here and many readers will have experienced some harsh instruction earlier in their careers in the appropriate etiquette.

Clear, well written and suitably recorded correspondence will not only dramatically reduce the likelihood of a dispute, but will increase the chance of resolution in your favour since with contractual disputes it is the party with the best records that usually prevails.

Some of this correspondence will have such importance that its format will be defined within the contract, for example, Acceptance Certificates.

Outgoing Contracts and Supplier Correspondence

Most likely, the Supplier Organization (SO) will engage further SO as sub-contractors and the requirements discussed above for recording contracts, correspondence and approval certificates are replicated, with the SO taking the client role.

Other Commercial Obligations

The nature of an individual project may impose special considerations on a Supplier Organization (SO) in relation to management of information.

For instance, if the incoming contract is on a 'Cost Plus' basis, then evidence of incurred costs must be made available to the Owner Organization (OO) on an 'open book' basis. Alternatively, if the incoming contract requires material to be sourced from, say, a sustainable source, evidence of the supply chain must be presented.

INFORMATION AS DELIVERABLES

Because it is easier to visualize, this text has tended towards discussing project deliverables as being physical items such as machinery, but in very many instances the deliverable is simply a service which does not have such a tangible output.

For instance if an Owner Organization (OO) were to engage a structural engineer as a Supplier Organization (SO), to assess whether an existing building was capable of withstanding an extension, the deliverable is simply a justified opinion.

Further, even when there is a physical deliverable, it is often incumbent upon the SO to submit supporting information. For instance, SO engaged in 'design and build' type projects are well used to formally submitting drawings of their proposal which will be subject to the OO approval before construction can commence.

When the output of the SO work (or part thereof) is information, inevitably, the principal contractual deliverable is some form of document (physical or as a computer file) and it is appropriate to determine the format and outline content of this well in advance of the handover (preferably pre-contract). In this respect the importance of information management is further reinforced since now it is not just an adjunct to the main creative process of the project – it is the main creative process.

Examples of types of documents that can constitute deliverables can include the following:

- Specifications.

- Technical reports.

- Drawings.

- Despatch and delivery documentation, e.g. Bills of Lading.

- Quality control records.

- Conformance certificates.

- Warranty certificates.

- Operating and maintenance manuals.

- Software documentation.

PROJECT CONTROL

Chapter 16 discussed the mechanisms of project control at both a strategic and tactical level.

As discussed below, the process is heavily reliant on the presentation of appropriate information.

Strategic Management

Strategic control is associated with the question 'Are we delivering the right project?' and is formally exercised at the gate decisions along the project lifecycle (Figure 5.3 and 7.1).

Quite simply, the quality of the decisions made at these points will determine the success of the Supplier Organization (SO) and whilst there is inevitably a judgmental element to these key decisions that is based on subjectivity, it is better if the objective element, based upon quantitative data, is to the fore. This requires the preparation of reports and supporting documentation prior to the decisions.

For instance the 'Bid/No Bid' decision is contingent upon factors such as the likely cost of bidding, likely cost of the work, the likely price, the likelihood of winning a competitive bid, the existing and anticipated workload, the commercial strategy of the organization. To facilitate objective decisions, the information system must be capable of providing hard information on each of these.

Further, it is appropriate that these decisions are overt, ideally made within formal meetings and that the decisions are recorded (including signatures). There is anecdotal evidence that the act of recording why decisions are made is a major success factor for those involved in managing projects.

Tactical Management

Tactical control is associated with the question 'Are we delivering the project right?' and is formally exercised at the Contract Evaluation Reviews discussed in Chapter 16.

Within this, a comparison is required between what was expected to occur and what has actually happened. The latter requirement is met by measured performance whereas the former is met by the baselines within the PMP. The prime requirement of information management in this respect is demonstrating the comparison between the two.

As discussed in Chapter 14 the three principal baselines relate to scope, time and money. These three parameters are inseparably entwined and in an ideal world it would be possible to demonstrate project progress as a single holistic process. Although attempts have been made to devise such a method, i.e. Earned Value Management, the reality is that most reporting considers just one baseline at a time. Each has its own particular challenges.

Scope   As with planning, scope is the most significant of the baselines in the context of project control and, ultimately, project progress is measured by how much of the scope has been completed. Unsurprisingly, the 'per cent complete' parameter becomes the core of any progress report.

However, work can only be known to be complete when it has actually been completed and so to have a 'per cent complete' figure for a project of anything but 0 per cent or 100 per cent requires dividing the scope into fragments. Obviously the WBS and the division of the work scope into Work Packages is of key relevance here.

Simply counting the number of completed Work Packages gives a good indication of progress, though this can be enhanced by weighting the Work Packages with their value.

Consequently a very useful control report can be created by a table with a row for each Work Package and columns containing 'Planned' and 'Actual' dates for when the work package was/will be 'opened' (a 'Go' ticket issued by the PM to the Work Package Owner) and 'closed' (output accepted by the PM).[8]

Time   Progress in terms of the amount of work done (effort) and progress in terms of time are different.

Imagine a DIY project to install an external lamp (digging cable trenches, erecting mounting post, etc.). Almost all the work may be completed over a weekend before realizing that the bulb element was broken and then having to wait 10 days for the replacement. In terms of effort, 99.9 per cent of the work is complete (only five minutes' work remains to unpack and screw-in the new bulb) and yet in terms of time only two of the now anticipated 12-day schedule have passed.

Accordingly, when it comes to tracking progress against time, in addition to the simple calculation of 'per cent complete' described above, other methods are required that recognize the durations, logical dependencies and interactions of the various project activities. We are again reliant upon precedence diagrams, and the like.

As with the planning activity described in Chapter 14, the use of computers and scheduling software is ubiquitous here and they provide a very valuable opportunity for producing semi-automatic progress reports that compare the actual with the planned schedule. However, there are drawbacks to their use.

---

8   Further enhancement can be adopted when using a spreadsheet's logic to colour the cells to indicate status (for instance: Green – Work Package has started/finished before its planned date; Amber – Work Package has started/finished but after the planned date; Red – Work Package has not started/finished and it is after the planned date).

The first problem relates to just how much effort is required to service the software. Many project teams are tempted to create very detailed models of their project schedule with a very high degree of 'granularity'.[9] However, the degree of granularity determines the amount of actual completion data to be measured and analysed, leading many to conclude later that they have 'created a monster' that makes increasing demands on their time and resources to reflect every evolution and twist in the project.

The second relates to just what level of detail can be interpreted by stakeholders. Many is the project team that, at the end of each reporting period, takes the trouble to create very impressive and elaborate Gantt charts, running to numerous pages, with bars for both planned and actual progress, and which are entirely beyond the understanding of most of the report recipients.

There are actually very many formats, other than the Gantt chart, that can communicate progress against plan in a very simple and effective way and too many project teams show surprising lack of creativity in adopting them. Consider the following.

Figure 17.1 shows how a Gantt chart can be updated with actual progress reports, not by plotting additional bars but by staggering the 'time now line' in relation to the original bars. This is often referred to as a 'Progress Line'.

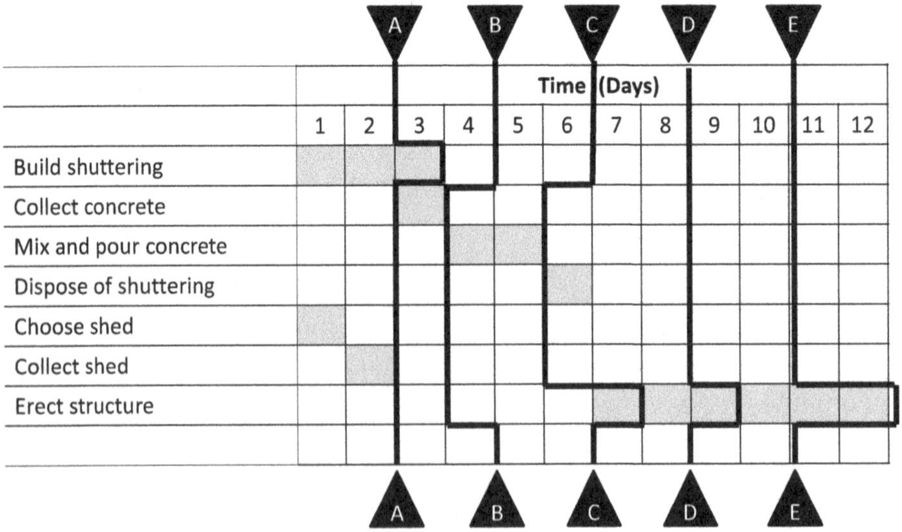

Figure 17.1   Reporting project progress with a 'Progress Line'

---

9   The size (and hence number) of the smallest fragment into which the project is decomposed.

New Progress Lines for each successive reporting period can be added to the same diagram and progress relative to the original plan, and to the previous report, is effectively communicated. The author has very positive experience of such an approach for reporting progress.

An alternative technique is the 'Milestone Slippage Chart' (see Figure 17.2). Within this technique, the project is represented by milestones, ideally located on the project's critical path. Each remaining milestone is plotted as a graph with co-ordinates of Actual Time (the current project period) and the Planned Time (the period in which the milestone is expected to be achieved). A trace

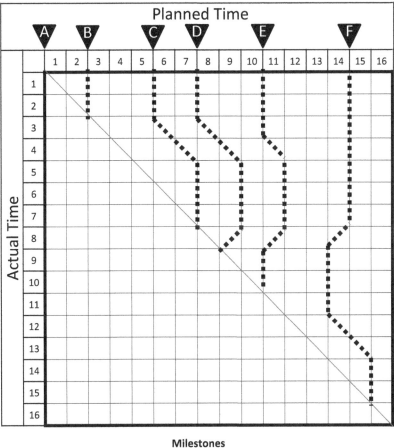

Milestones

A   Project Start   D   Contract with Lead Contractor Signed
B   Option Selected   E   Provisional Acceptance
C   Design Complete   F   Final Acceptance

Figure 17.2   Reporting project progress with a 'Milestone Slippage Chart'

stepping to the left indicates a milestone being brought forward, a step to the right indicates delay.

Milestones having a vertical trace that terminates at the diagonal line reveals a project team that both achieves its milestones and can anticipate this. Traces that are vertical until they meet the diagonal line and then slide down the diagonal reveal teams that cannot achieve milestones but cannot anticipate this (everything is on schedule up to the point when completion should be achieved, at which point they are delayed by a period each period). A slightly better scenario has the traces drifting parallel to the diagonal from early on; milestones are not being achieved but at least the team is able to anticipate this sometime in advance.

This striking and easy-to-interpret visual impact offers many advantages, especially when having to quickly understand the situation with a large number of different projects, for instance when reviewing a portfolio.

For projects where time is of the essence, an effective reporting technique involves a clock face and project phases as concentric rings (see Figure 17.3).

Within this the project period is fixed and the spiral trace of actual performance must stay inboard of the spiral indicating planned performance.

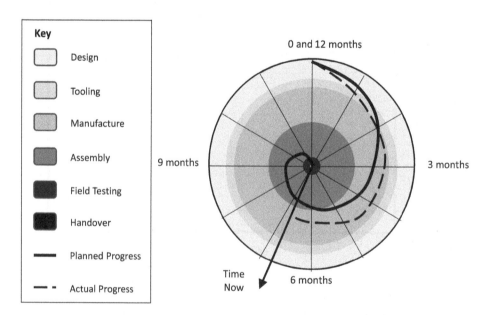

Figure 17.3   Reporting project progress with a 'Clock-Face Chart'

It is particularly effective for motivating a team towards a fixed completion date.

Cost   This is a measure of the consumption of resources and allows comparison to that which was expected.[10] It is a process fraught with complexity not least because there are very many different types of resources, for instance different types of internal human resources, and to avoid the need to consider them all separately there is a tendency (not always helpful) of converting them all to a common unit; money. Even ignoring exchange and inflation rates, expenditure is often a very unreliable indicator of project performance. Consider the following.

Firstly, expressing internal labour costs as money requires the evolution of a 'charge rate'. This is reached by the Supplier Organization (SO) after considering the overheads (fixed and variable) that must be overcome. Recovery of fixed overheads is necessarily based upon an estimated quantity of work to be completed in the period and if this proves to be grossly inaccurate, an 'under' or 'over recovery' of fixed overheads can give an unrealistic representation of the performance of the SO.

Secondly, when does a cost become an 'actual cost'? For externally purchased goods is it when the money is transferred from one party's bank to the other? Is it when the invoice is received? Is it when the contract is signed? There are often very many months delay between these dates and simply considering the former will inevitably give a gross underestimate of the true exposure. This lag is accommodated primarily by 'accruals'; the difference between the payment/ receipt of money and the legal obligation or right to pay/receive it. If we are using 'actual' cost as measure of performance then the timing is crucial, and at minimum there must be consistency throughout the organization as to what is exactly meant by 'actual costs', 'committed costs, 'accruals' and when they are recognized.[11]

---

10   Implicit within all these discussions of costs incurred by a SO, and their use in the strategic and tactical control of projects, is the assumption that costs can be attributed to each individual bespoke product. Those SO who currently only produce standard products and are looking to embrace the supply of bespoke products may find this requirement surprisingly onerous. This is because, currently, many will operate a cost collection system that uses only functional departments as cost centres and lack the facility to record costs against individual products. Converting such a system can represent a significant amount of work and may, for instance, include the need for employees to create timesheets. Cultural resistance can be expected as well as significant technical difficulties and additional complexity.

11   Many SO choose to have a 'Cost Management Plan', as a subsidiary management plan within the PMP that contains such definitions and conventions.

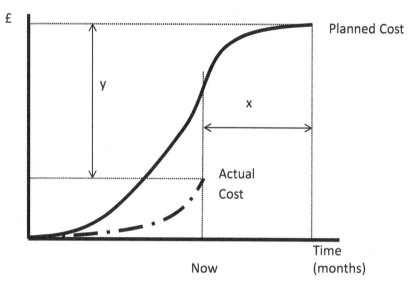

Figure 17.4   Planned versus actual expenditure

Thirdly, even if the above can be overcome, there is huge ambiguity as to what expenditure represents. Consider the graph in Figure 17.4. Is this good or bad news?

It could be that the project has just been completed, x months ahead of schedule and y under budget. Alternatively it could be that the project has achieved next to nothing and is now woefully over budget and behind schedule. Without a further parameter, a measure of how much of the total project scope has been achieved, the simple comparison of planned and actual expenditure is largely meaningless. This is the logic that underpins the 'Earned Value Management' technique and the parameter of Earned Value; a measure of what has actually been achieved (based upon 'per cent complete').

These complexities need to be managed before reports can be effective in supporting project control.

Reporting Frequency and Cost

The timing of the Decision Gates is determined by the lifecycle, but the frequency of the Contract Evaluation Reviews, and how often the PM is obliged to compile a progress report, is a matter to be decided and the outcome has a significant impact on costs.

If, for instance, a PM is obliged to compile, submit and discuss a report every month (20 working days) and it takes two days' effort to compile this, we can see, immediately, that they will be spending 10 per cent of their total time just reporting on progress. (In practice many reports take much longer and often the frequency is higher.)

It explains why the activity (along with other project management tasks such as planning and procurement) should be within the WBS to ensure that they are recognized in subsequent schedules and budgets.

ENTERPRISE-WIDE INFORMATION MANAGEMENT

As we have discussed, the Supplier Organization (SO) is an enterprise that is far more than any individual project and much information management is driven by concerns beyond its immediate needs. A distinction can be made between managing the current portfolio, and future activity.

Portfolio-wide Information

Supplier Organizations (SO) most often manage a number of projects simultaneously and the management of this portfolio requires information.

The most significant aspect is the management of common resource pools discussed in Chapter 15. The type of information required in this respect will be identical to that for managing the individual projects but there is a need to ensure all projects output the information in the same format so as to facilitate aggregation.

A further portfolio requirement relates to risk. In addition to understanding the total risk exposure of the portfolio, some risks are better managed at a portfolio, rather than a project, level. For instance, a specialist machine that reduces a technical risk may be too expensive for any individual project, but it may benefit many projects. In such instances it is appropriate for the portfolio to purchase the machine. The information system is required to identify and justify such opportunities.

Future Supplier Organization Commercial Activity

Supplier Organizations (SO) are permanent organizations and look to win future contracts. This gives rise to a need for the following information:

- Selling and marketing collateral – When marketing and selling, the SO needs to demonstrate competence by reference to previous, similar work. A formal Reference List complete with calculations, designs, trials and test reports, fault investigations, etc. can be of enormous worth, in offering such reassurance. Similarly, for bespoke equipment, it can be a relatively rare event to have access to a complete or partially complete product at some notable stage of its creation and PM are often asked by the selling and marketing personnel to factor into their project schedules time for extensive photography, and sometimes even for visits by prospective new clients.

- Planning and estimating – The need for SO to quickly and cheaply estimate costs and duration for future work was established in Chapter 13. This is achieved primarily by a carefully compiled archive of historic data from previous projects.

- Continuous improvement – SO must always strive to improve their performance on successive projects. Documentation of techniques, risk mitigation, vendor assessment reports, innovative technical solutions and the like all contribute to continuous improvement. Similarly, assessments of internal resources allows for training and organization improvements.

- Client records – As discussed in Chapter 18, the commercial opportunities for the SO do not end with the supply of the project deliverable. Supply of spares and servicing can provide a lucrative revenue stream. Accordingly, complete technical information for the product in the 'as-built' condition as well as names and contact details of the relevant personnel of the Owner Organization (OO) are needed.

Openness and Honesty

When considering the management of information there is a tendency to focus only on the hard aspects such as the apparatus and systems used and the reporting format and frequency adopted.

Ultimately, information management facilitates communication and the ability to communicate is essentially a soft skill.

Indeed the role of PM is first and foremost about communication and their inherent skills in this regard will largely determine their competence. Proficiency in presenting, listening, negotiating, writing, debating, arguing are all examples of such essential skills.

The soft element is also important at the organizational level. If an organization fails to evolve a culture that ensures openness and honesty then no formal information management system will save it from an eventual demise.

Reference

Heldman, K., 2009. *PMP® Project Management Professional Exam Study Guide*, 5th edn. Indianapolis: Sybex.

Chapter 18

Warranty Phase and Post-Project Considerations

We have defined a project as a 'temporary endeavour' and as such it must come to an end.

Whereas it is attractive to imagine this as a simple event involving a delighted and grateful customer, the popping of champagne corks and the triumphant exit of the project team, the reality is usually very different. For many reasons the end of the project is a difficult time for both the Supplier Organization (SO) and the Owner Organization (OO). Consider the following.

Firstly, it is only when a bespoke product is complete and operated for the first time that the success of the team's endeavours is revealed. This 'acid test' can be a heart-breaking experience especially if it reveals errors made early in the lifecycle. For the SO, an early customer acceptance and swift conclusion to a project is a symptom of an excellent earlier performance by the project's marketing, selling and delivery teams. By the same token, a difficult drawn-out and expensive project closure, with the OO and SO holding very different views about the acceptability of the product, is usually a symptom of a poorly planned and rushed earlier effort, very often in the pre-contract phases.

Secondly, there can be a curious reluctance to bring the project to an end. The project in question may offer very practical benefits to the participants (a favoured location or simply ongoing employment). Alternatively, the next phase may bring unwelcome factors (the OO representative will have to assume full responsibility for the deliverable). Such reluctance, often accompanied by nostalgia, can present difficulties such that some SO adopt measures, such as completion bonuses, to keep the focus on a swift conclusion.

Thirdly, the end of the project does not coincide with completion of the deliverable. As discussed below, there is much work to do after the OO has accepted the goods and such is its importance to the success of the project, and the SO, that it warrants this dedicated chapter.

Fourthly, consistent with the point above, establishing when, exactly, a project finishes is surprisingly difficult.

The End of the Supplier Organization's Project

Consider the following project of a Supplier Organization (SO), involving the design, manufacture, installation and commissioning of the turbine of a hydro station.

After the manufacture and acceptance at factory tests, the SO was paid 90 per cent of the project value. Ownership of, and responsibility for, the equipment transferred to the client and the equipment was shipped. On arrival in the destination country a delay to the construction work at site (client responsibility) led to the parts being stored for three years before installation. Commissioning was then delayed for a further two years, after which the client issued a preliminary acceptance certificate which referenced a list of 'snags' that required correcting before final acceptance could be issued. However, such was the client's need for power generation at this stage that access to the equipment was withheld. After three years' operation the SO was granted access to address the snags. Only then was final acceptance conveyed and the warranty period started. In parallel with these events the SO drafted a claim against the client for additional delays which was presented at the time of preliminary acceptance. The client wholly rejected the claim, leading to the SO taking legal action. The resulting court case that led to the final payment being made concluded three years after the expiry of the equipment's warranty period.

When did the SO's project finish?

Although it is convenient to consider the point of last payment, from a practical point of view this is not very helpful since this occurred many years after the team was disbanded, commencement of operation and expiry of warranty.

As discussed in Chapter 7, from a practical perspective, the point when the legal obligations of the Supplier Organization (SO) conclude can be considered to be the point when the warranty period expires. However, there are many instances when an earlier point must be identified that is associated with the end of the creation of the deliverable (and its acceptance by the OO). Such instances can be contractual, such as the need for a trigger point for liquidated and ascertained damages, or the commencement of the warranty period (defects liability period); or practical, such as when to hold the post-contract review.

Unfortunately, establishing this point is fraught and it is a response to this ambiguity that legal concepts such as 'practical completion 'or 'substantial completion' have evolved, but even here, their precise meanings are the subject of much debate.

The matter is easier to deal with when considering individual projects where the matter is (should be) addressed in relation to specific elements of the project scope. For instance, in the case described above, the definition of both a 'Preliminary Acceptance' and 'Final Acceptance' sought to address how the end of this particular SO project would be defined.

Within the SO generic lifecycle offered in Figure 7.1, the decision gate of 'Accept Deliverable?' establishes the divide between the 'Create' and 'Warranty' phases. As discussed in Chapter 7 this Decision Gate is, in effect, owned by the OO and the 'Create' phase will only conclude once they answer it in the affirmative. For the purposes of the lifecycle model, such acceptance will conclude the phase even if a caveat is involved, relating to a 'snagging list' (described below). Inevitably this decision gate is by no means such a clear-cut point as the Decision Gates of 'Bid/No Bid' and 'Make or Accept/Reject Offer'.

Although the following phase is entitled the 'Warranty' phase, this is largely a label of convenience since aspects of the defects liability is only one such element of the varied work, described below, that it contains. The work can be divided into two classifications; work that is required by the current project and work to benefit future projects of the SO.

Work Required by the Current Project

BALANCE OF SUPPLY

Customer acceptance at, say, factory tests, are rarely the end of Supplier Organization (SO) involvement. In many instances there is remaining work such as shipping, installation and on-site commissioning. Even if this is not the case, as discussed in Chapter 17, it is common for the scope of the SO contract to include the supply of significant amounts of documentation such as Operating and Maintenance Manuals, and these can represent Substantial amounts of work.

SNAGGING LISTS/PUNCH LISTS

There is often a feeling that projects never actually finish, they just reach the point where both parties are so fed up with it that they abandon it. Hopefully this takes place after the product works well enough for the client to use it, and the supplier has covered its costs.

This is offered not with a view to encouraging poor administration, but to illustrate that the act of 'acceptance' is rarely a one-off event. In reality the products are often granted initial acceptance on the basis of a number of caveats relating to minor faults and omissions that the Supplier Organization (SO) agrees to remedy. These are often referred to as a 'snagging list' or a 'punch list'. Only after these have been resolved will final acceptance be conveyed.

Inevitably therefore, a drawn-out period of gradual acceptance follows, as remedies to the individual items on the list are offered to the Owner Organization (OO), which it may choose to accept or decline. The law of 'diminishing returns' means that each party rarely gets to the point of complete and absolute satisfaction.

A word of warning is appropriate here since there is usually a clamour on behalf of the SO to achieve the initial acceptance as soon as possible (especially if the date triggers liquidated damages or a payment), even if this leads to accepting very long snagging lists. However, once initial acceptance has been conveyed, access to the product for the SO may well be reduced (for instance, the OO may put the product into commercial operation). In such instances the SO loses control of the timetable and location for the remedial work. As a consequence, it can become a very drawn-out and expensive experience.

DEMOBILIZATION

After the work, there is a need to dismantle the temporary facilities established by the Supplier Organization (SO) for the project. Whilst some of this is ongoing during the project, it is unlikely that it will be finalized until after acceptance has been conveyed. This can represent a significant amount of work, especially if the SO has been obliged to establish on-site facilities at a construction site.

In the same way that dinner isn't over until the dishes are washed, the project does not conclude until surplus material and facilities are properly disposed of or returned to storage.

Such activities can be time-consuming and expensive and, without suitable provision in the budgets and schedules, will lead to overspends and delays.

CLAIMS AND COUNTER-CLAIMS

As discussed in Chapter 11, it is common for there to be disputes between the Supplier Organization (SO) and the Owner Organization (OO) about changes and what additional compensation the SO is entitled to from the OO, and indeed whether the OO is entitled to compensation for a failing on behalf of the SO.

Whilst it is good practice to address these as early as possible, and indeed some contracts such as the NEC family require it, it is commonplace that much of the detailed discussions in relation to these matters occur after acceptance of the product.

The pursuit of, and defence against, claims and counter-claims can become a major exercise that involves legal representatives, considerable sums of money and a time period often in excess of the original project. It can also have a dramatic effect on the profit that the SO secures from the work.

In addition to reaching settlement with the OO, the SO may also be obliged to reach a settlement with its own suppliers who in turn may feel they are entitled to compensation.

Project accounts cannot be fully closed until these matters are resolved.

WARRANTY ISSUES

Whilst it is comforting to think that final acceptance[1] represents the end of the liability of the Supplier Organization (SO) for the technical performance of the product, this is rarely the case.

---

1   The precise point of commencement of the warranty period is defined within the contract in question.

With the best will in the world, it is unlikely that testing for the purposes of customer acceptance will reveal all imperfections within a product. Accordingly, it is commonplace for the contract between the SO and the Owner Organization (OO) to identify a period of time within which the rectification of any fault that emerges is to be resolved by the SO, at its cost. This is known as the 'Defects Liability Period' or, more often, the 'Warranty Period'.

As discussed in Chapter 4, discovery of an error late in the lifecycle that requires a change is a very expensive proposition. However, the costs of such faults discovered by the SO prior to despatch are as nothing as compared to the costs associated with faults discovered by the OO whilst in operation. Consider the following example.

In February 2013 a Rolls Royce Trent 900 engine on an Airbus A380 failed whilst in flight over Singapore. The plane landed safely and no one was hurt and subsequently the cause was found to be a faulty oil pipe. The price of the pipe was very modest and yet the incident costs Rolls Royce £56m and a 10 per cent dip in share price (Chan, 2011).

Such warranty issues are a major risk to SOs and underline the need for a diligent approach to the management of quality.

Work to Benefit Future Projects

Supplier Organizations (SO) seek to exist beyond the current project and secure increased shareholder value into the future. This requires them to seek further projects and to enhance their ability to execute them. The following activities seek to achieve just this.

SECURING COMMERCIAL OPPORTUNITIES

Spares and Servicing

As discussed in Chapter 12 and 13, the process of marketing and selling is very expensive.

Much of these costs can be avoided by developing existing customers, rather than seeking new ones. One way to do this is by nurturing the post-supply market of spares and servicing. This is especially relevant if the products supplied by the Supplier Organization (SO) are physical products such as machinery.

The opportunities here can be enormous. For instance only half of the revenues of companies like Rolls Royce and Xerox Corporation are from the supply of equipment (Deloitte Research, 2006). The rest is from the aftersales market.

Suppliers of bespoke equipment have the natural advantage over post-supply competitors since they alone have the detailed product knowledge, they retain the intellectual property in the product's design and they have existing relationships with the relevant contacts in the Owner Organization (OO).

The end of a supply contract is the start of an aftersales opportunity and SO should maximize the opportunities this provides, not least by establishing the information records discussed in Chapter 17.

Hosting of Potential Clients

Once a project has been completed, the 'in service' product is an invaluable aid to marketing and selling.

Sometimes a 'tame' Owner Organization (OO) is prepared to host potential new clients of the Supplier Organization (SO) and demonstrate a product in operation. The situation generally needs delicate prior negotiation, since they are often competitors of the OO.[2]

Such opportunities are an absolute boon to the selling team within a SO.

Product Improvement Through Access to 'In Service' Products

Similarly, access to an 'in service' product that it had previously supplied offers a very valuable opportunity to a Supplier Organization (SO) for product improvement.

Simply access to operational data provides an excellent resource to the product developers within the SO, but in some instances there are other opportunities. Occasionally, Owner Organizations (OO) are prepared to fund

---

2   In some instances such access is an element within the original supply contract. It can be a useful negotiating token for the OO.

research and investigation work by the SO that may further improve their own product. Not only can the SO benefit from enhancement of technical capability and know-how, it will be paid as well.

Future Supply

By their nature, products supplied by a Supplier Organization (SO) are an infrequent requirement, but, nonetheless many customers do offer repeat business and, as discussed in Chapter 12, maintaining a network of contacts is a vital activity for marketers.

IMPROVING FUTURE SUPPLIER ORGANIZATION PERFORMANCE

If we fail to learn from our mistakes then we will repeat them. From the perspective of the Supplier Organization (SO), at minimum this means that performance will not deteriorate, but in a competitive environment this is rarely satisfactory to ensure survival. To prevail in the long term, the SO must continuously improve its products and how they are delivered.

Two activities are of major significance here; 'lessons learned' exercises and the maintaining of an archive of project data.

Lessons Learned

At minimum, these sessions are carried out as part of the Post-Contract Reviews but they can occur at any appropriate time through the project lifecycle, for instance at the conclusion of phases or as an agenda item on all Contract Evaluation Reviews. They involve the project team reflecting and commenting upon the project and its management and deciding what went well, and what not so well. The output is best summarized in the format of answering the question, 'How would I approach a similar project next time?'.

Their potential value is such that the author once conceived of a marketing ploy for a management consultancy whereby they would provide, free of charge, a meeting facilitation service for 'lessons learned' sessions to anyone on their client list. For the client, the benefit of a neutral facilitator influencing these potentially contentious discussions was obvious, but there was also much in it for the consultancy. Quite simply, the opportunity to listen in on such meetings, even for a short period of time, would allow them to learn all they would ever need to know about the shortcomings of the client and hence what products, interventions and training they should be offered. As an exercise in marketing it would be hard to beat.

Although the benefits of such sessions are obvious, they are not something that organizations do well. There are a number of reasons. Consider the following:

- Since the costs and inconvenience accrue to the current project but the benefits to a future, hypothetical project, there is little incentive for the current project manager (PM) to undertake it.

- It is human nature to want to prevent the exposure of our work that, with the benefit of hindsight, can be seen to be erroneous. This is especially the case if there are opportunities for those with a political agenda to emphasize such errors.

- The timing of such reviews is very difficult to judge. Hold them too early and it may not be possible to properly assess whether success has been achieved, too late and much of the team will have departed, taking the knowledge and expertise with them.

- Accessing 'lessons learned' can be difficult. Without an effective and permanent archive structure, PMs of prospective projects may spend considerable time wading through historical documents trying to distil the salient points.

Archiving of Project Data and Records

This is often considered in the same breath as lessons learned but there are some differences.

Like 'lessons learned', archived project data aids future rather than current projects but rather than commenting upon the project in hand, the records are simply the final version of the Supplier Organization's (SO) management documents. Their uses are more specific and include the following:

- Estimating – The need for SO to quickly and cheaply estimate scope, costs and duration for future work was established in Chapter 13. This is achieved primarily by a carefully complied archive of historic data from previous projects.

- Risk management – The risk logs from previous similar projects provide an excellent source of relevant risks that must be considered.

- Subsidiary management plans – As discussed in Chapter 14, subsidiary management plans describe how a specific aspect of a project is to be managed and although all projects are different, successive projects may not be so different as to render such subsidiary plans as inappropriate for reuse.

References

Chan, S.P., 2011. *Rolls-Royce Settles with Qantas over A380 Engine Explosion.* [online] Available at: http://www.telegraph.co.uk/finance/newsbysector/industry/engineering/ 8590975/Rolls-Royce-settles-with-Qantas-over-A380-engine-explosion.html [accessed 24 April 2014].

Deloitte Research, 2006. *The Service Revolution in Global Manufacturing Industries.* [online] Available at: http://www.apec.org.au/docs/2011–11_training/ deloitte 2006.pdf [accessed 24 April 2014].

Afterword
Towards Excellence

In Chapter 1 we discussed what constituted a project by comparing it to a non-project. Many books that address this topic choose to label such non-project endeavours as 'business as usual activities'. This has always struck me as a strange turn of phrase.

The distinction is appropriate for those who, say, work in our washing machine factory of Chapter 1. For them non-projects are the norm and projects are a rare opportunity to undertake something different, but for those who undertake projects on a continuous basis, the distinction is unhelpful since their 'business as usual' is always a project.

For those Supplier Organizations (SO) that traverse substantially to the right of the Organizational Continuum offered in Figure A1.1 and whose

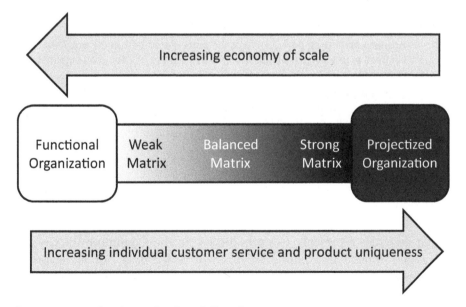

Figure A1.1   The Organizational Continuum

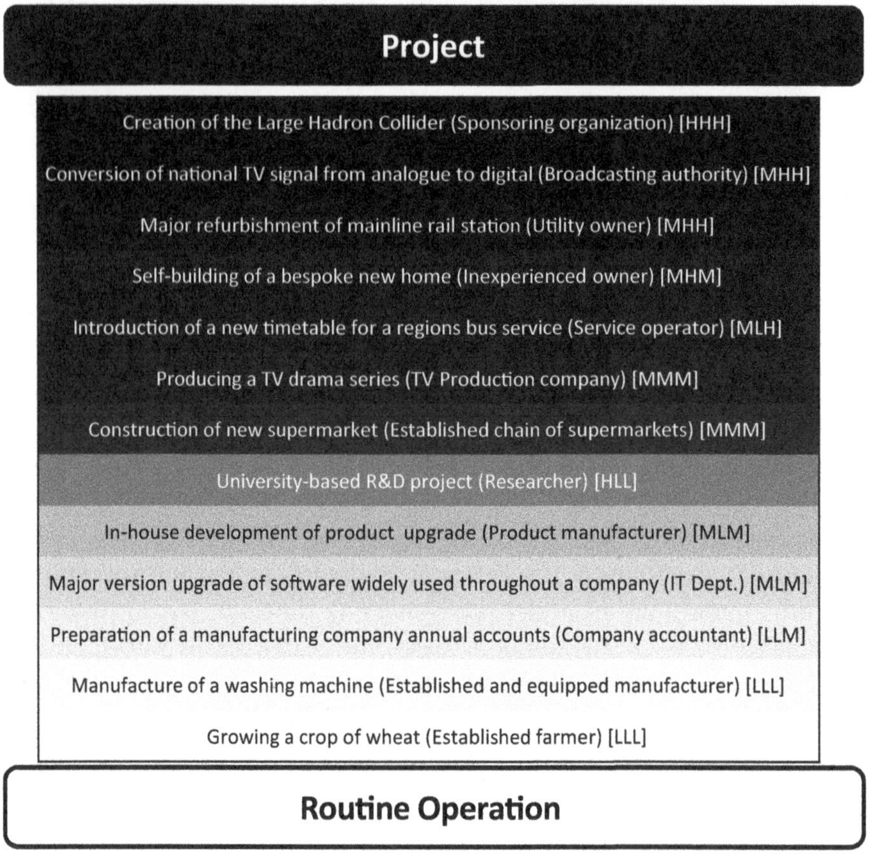

Project

Creation of the Large Hadron Collider (Sponsoring organization) [HHH]

Conversion of national TV signal from analogue to digital (Broadcasting authority) [MHH]

Major refurbishment of mainline rail station (Utility owner) [MHH]

Self-building of a bespoke new home (Inexperienced owner) [MHM]

Introduction of a new timetable for a regions bus service (Service operator) [MLH]

Producing a TV drama series (TV Production company) [MMM]

Construction of new supermarket (Established chain of supermarkets) [MMM]

University-based R&D project (Researcher) [HLL]

In-house development of product upgrade (Product manufacturer) [MLM]

Major version upgrade of software widely used throughout a company (IT Dept.) [MLM]

Preparation of a manufacturing company annual accounts (Company accountant) [LLM]

Manufacture of a washing machine (Established and equipped manufacturer) [LLL]

Growing a crop of wheat (Established farmer) [LLL]

Routine Operation

Figure A1.2   Continuum of Creative Endeavours

Notes: 1. Assessment is from perspective of the party stated within the brackets.
2. Characters in square brackets indicate assessment of endeavour against criteria of:

> Degree of uniqueness
> Degree of temporariness & transience
> Complexity of outcome

Assessment made as:

> H – High
> M – Medium
> L – Low

regular activities are firmly towards the top of the Continuum of Creative Endeavours offered in Figure A1.2 this will be the case. For them, project management is not an occasional distraction from the routine, it is their permanent modus operandi.

Accordingly, for them, an expert level of proficiency within project management is a prerequisite but in reaching for this level, as we move from novice to expert, a subtle change occurs.

Inevitably, when first embracing project management, proficiency is a collection of isolated pockets of learned behaviour, primarily associated with the topics discussed in Part 4 of this book. However at its more exalted levels, proficiency transcends this and becomes an innate and holistic pattern of behaviour; it becomes second nature.

Condensing complex organic systems, such as behaviour, into a brief description is not easy, but an insight can be gained by considering 'fractals'. A fractal is a pattern that repeats itself at every level of scale.

They provide an opportunity to reach a deeper understanding of some of the most beautiful and complex shapes, patterns and series that nature can offer, and how such infinitely complex shapes can be defined in the most simple of ways. River networks, mountain ranges, snowflakes, lightning bolts and coastlines are all examples of structures that conform to the concept of fractals.

Consider the cauliflower shown in Figure A1.3. Its shape is a fractal. At first glance the shape appears to be a loose spiral made up of small nodes. However,

Figure A1.3   A classic fractal

looking closer at just one of the nodes we see that this too is a spiral made up of smaller identical nodes. Study just one of these smaller nodes and we see that at this next level of scale too, the same pattern is repeated. In the case of true fractals this pattern repeats ad infinitum, regardless of scale, and whether you are using a telescope or a microscope the picture is always the same.

The attraction of such a concept here, lies in the fact that both projects and their management are fractals.

For the project itself, the Work Breakdown Structure (WBS), an example of which is offered in Figure A1.4 opposite, reveals the repeating pattern. Project managers use them to decompose the scope of their projects into Work Packages, which are handed over to a Work Package Owner. In essence each of these Work Packages is a sub-project and the Work Package Owner a 'sub-project manager'. They then decompose their sub-project into smaller packages, which in turn become sub-sub-projects. The pattern repeats.

Applying this to the Olympic stadium considered in Chapter 1, from the perspective of the overall Olympic project, the construction of the main stadium is just a Work Package; however from the perspective of the construction company responsible for it, it is a project in its own right. Similarly, the stadium's steel structure may be a Work Package from the perspective constructors of the stadium but the specialist company engaged to complete it will see themselves as the mangers of the steel structure 'project'.

The same repeating pattern cascades through the many levels of a procurement chain, or layers of an organizational structure, and, although the scale varies enormously, the predicament of anyone responsible for a fragment of a project work, be it an activity, a Work Package, a project, or indeed a programme of projects, is essentially the same.

Thus, we can say that although the range and scale of projects, or fragments thereof, is infinite, the nature of the challenge is always the same. It is a task that has an element of uniqueness, which will be addressed by a team that is both temporary and transient, which will have a complex outcome that both affects, and is affected by, its environment and other ongoing activities therein.

By the same token, there is a framework for project management which also is a fractal. The fractal in question is the four element 'Plan–Do–Check–Act' cycle described in Figure A1.5.

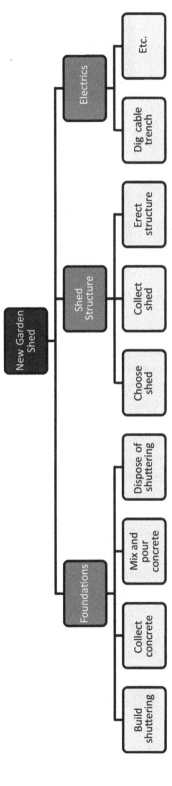

Figure A1.4   A Work Breakdown Structure

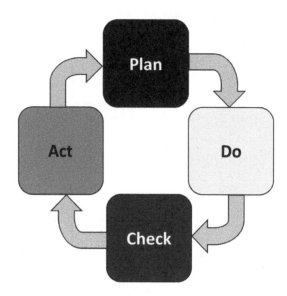

Figure A1.5   Plan–Do–Check–Act cycle

The cycle can be applied at the scale of the whole project. Indeed such is its relevance at this level we can easily see how it gives rise to the identification of project phases, for instance the 'Definition' phase of Figure A1.6 is concerned with planning and the 'Implementation' phase is associated with 'Doing'.

However, take any of the individual four elements, and the cycle is repeated within it. For instance the result of planning a project (and the deliverable of a planning phase) is the Project Management Plan (PMP). Creation of this requires a degree of preparation and planning (planning the planning), the actual doing of the work (creating the PMP) as well as assessing its acceptability (checking) before electing to revise it or issue it (acting).

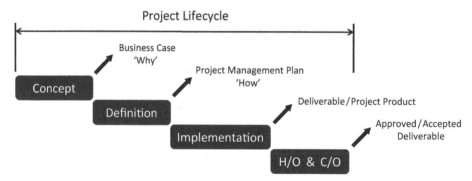

Figure A1.6   The project lifecycle

And so the cycle repeats at smaller and smaller scales. Eventually we come down to just one member of an enormous project workforce addressing just a minor task. In the morning they will 'Plan' what they are to do that day before 'Do[ing]' it. Towards the end of the day they may 'Check' whether they had achieved what was expected and 'Act' by either accelerating the pace of work or else bringing forward tomorrow's work.

The decomposition can be taken further, until the fragment of work in question is too small to be described, at which point we are left simply with the innate behaviour of the practitioner. The detail of the four-element cycle provides clues as to what that innate behaviour contains. Consider the following:

- A strong focus on asking searching questions at the outset, especially about why the project is being undertaken and hence the relative priorities of the objectives.

- A readiness to invest considerable efforts in establishing and maintaining strong relationships with stakeholders, especially team members, and contract partners.

- A heightened awareness of the latent risks and uncertainty that lie within any project and the pragmatic approach to estimates and plans that this demands.

- Recognition of the importance of planning, in both reducing uncertainty and binding together the project team.

- Such recognition will be evidenced by the willingness to devote considerable time and resources to a wide variety of planning activities.

- A diligent approach to the recording, use and storage of information.

- An ongoing awareness of how well the team is performing and a preparedness and ability to make changes when appropriate, but resist and prevent changes when not.

- A willingness to reflect after the event; to criticize and, if necessary accept the discomfort of being criticized, so that competence can grow in depth and breadth.

The mark of the true project management professional is that traits such as these have become instincts.

Index